INTERPRETING ISLAM

INTERPRETING ISLAM

Bandali Jawzi's
Islamic Intellectual History

Tamara Sonn

New York   Oxford
OXFORD UNIVERSITY PRESS
1996

Oxford University Press

Oxford   New York
Athens   Auckland   Bangkok   Bogota   Bombay
Buenos Aires   Calcutta   Cape Town   Dar es Salaam
Delhi   Florence   Hong Kong   Istanbul   Karachi
Kuala Lumpur   Madras   Madrid   Melbourne
Mexico City   Nairobi   Paris   Singapore
Taipei   Tokyo   Toronto

and associated companies in
Berlin   Ibadan

Copyright © 1996 by Oxford University Press, Inc.

Published by Oxford University Press, Inc.
198 Madison Avenue, New York, New York 10016

Oxford is a registered trademark of Oxford University Press

Library of Congress Cataloging-in-Publication Data
Sonn, Tamara
Interpreting Islam : Bandali Jawzi's Islamic intellectual history / Tamara Sonn.
p.   cm.
Includes bibliographical references (p.   ) and index.
Contents: pt. 1. Commentary — pt. 2. History of intellectual
movements in Islam / Bandali al-Jawzi.
ISBN 0-19-510051-4
1. Islam—History. I. Title.
BP55.4913   1996
297'.09—dc20   95-50616

1   3   5   7   9   8   6   4   2

Printed in the United States of America
on acid-free paper

In memory of Alia,
in fulfillment of a promise

Preface

Bandali Jawzi (1872–1942) belonged to a unique generation of Palestinian intellectuals, privileged to live in the days when Turkish domination finally came to an end and Arab Islamic consciousness was coming into full flower. The atmosphere was heady, confident, and full of optimism for the Arabs' impending independence and the return of Islamic culture to a leading position in science and the arts. Discussions in classrooms, mosques, coffeehouses, and salons centered around the causes of the weaknesses that had led to cultural decline and foreign domination, along with prescriptions for their remedy. Where had the traditional community gone wrong, and how could their errors be corrected? Jawzi's *History of Intellectual Movements in Islam* was a bold contribution to those analyses. It was revisionist history in an era when the intellectual atmosphere was receptive to revisionist history. In today's world, buffeted by a series of failed efforts to regain true independence and dignity, the Muslim community is more cynical. Gone is the general belief that the Arab Muslim world can revive its vitality and self-control just by reevaluating its past and shaking off the traditional tendency toward passivity and fatalism. Yet the conviction, widely popular at the moment, that the Muslim world is poised on the brink of a rebirth of its classical glory is still evident among those who claim simply, "Islam is the solution." Jawzi concluded that a socialist economic structure was necessary in order for Muslim society to recapture its egalitarian spirit and its empowerment of all levels of society, which he considered to be the source of its true strength. External, ritual practices were of negligible importance, he believed. These views are popular today only among a few remaining leftists, generally identifiable by their age group and socioeconomic background. The continuing importance of Jawzi's work, however, does not lie in its socialist conclusions regarding Islamic society (which were, in fact, frequently based on rather strained arguments), but rather in the interpretive methodology he employed to achieve them.

Bandali Jawzi came to his conclusions by reevaluating classical historical accounts of the Islamic caliphates. He was particularly interested in the treatment of rebel movements against the caliphates such as the Babakis, Ismaʿilis, and Qaramatis. To him it stood to reason that the accounts promulgated as authoritative, and thus bequeathed to successive generations, would be those approved by the imperial bureaucracies. They would, therefore, be uniformly negative concerning the reform movements, and, directly or indirectly, supportive of the image of the caliphate as Islamically legitimate. Yet given the condition of the Islamic world in the modern era, it is now clear that all was not well with the caliphates. Though Jawzi was a Christian, he accepted the Islamic assumption that had the caliphates been implementing the will of God, the source of true legitimacy in an Islamic context, God would not have allowed the Muslim world to sink into such degradation. Perhaps, Jawzi reasoned, those movements that periodically arose against the caliphates had had some merit after all. Perhaps they could be understood better as reform movements. Accordingly, he undertook to recreate the rationales for these movements. The groups he chose to chronicle were those which, he believed, rebelled precisely because the caliphates had reneged on their responsibility to maintain social justice. Piecing together various fragments he found more credible than those of the imperial historians, he created pictures of the subject groups as motivated, by and large, by quintessentially Islamic principles of social justice.

The assumptions upon which Jawzi based his critical method are clear. (1) Human intellectual production, whether it is called literary, historical, or religious, is the result of interpretation. (2) Interpretations are affected by a variety of factors, including the personal experiences of the interpreters. (3) Furthermore, there is a direct connection between the survival of certain interpretations—their promulgation as fact—and the political-economic concerns of those in a position to control official intellectual products. (4) Every generation must therefore reevaluate inherited "knowledge" in light of changed circumstances, paying particular attention to the vilified "others." (5) In the case of Islamic "knowledge," the Qurʾan provides clear guidance in this ongoing process of reevaluation. Its message of social justice based on human equality, all based on monotheism, is the criterion by which to judge whether or not something is truly Islamic.

The first four of these assumptions are characteristic of an interpretive method currently very much under discussion in postmodern Euroamerican academia, referred to by some as neohistoricism. Developed by such luminaries as Jacques Derrida and Michel Foucault, it became the basis of widespread reevaluation of traditional Eurocentric learning. Interestingly, one of the most noteworthy neohistoricists is Palestinian-

American Edward Said of Columbia University. Said's landmark *Orientalism* (1978) is an application of the methodology to European scholars' treatment of the Arab Muslim world wherein he demonstrates the Europeans' clear biases resulting from their colonial concerns. Fully fifty years before Said, however, Jawzi began his *History of Intellectual Movements in Islam* with an excoriation of European scholars' biased treatment of Muslims, pointing out that they were inevitably influenced by their imperialist ambitions and religious prejudices. He then applied the very same recognition of the relationship between knowledge and power, as Foucaultian scholars put it, to official Islamic scholarship. Clearly, Jawzi's analysis was not the result of postmodern hermeneutics (the study of interpretation). It is the fifth assumption—access to certainty through the Qur'an—that both distinguishes Jawzi's methodology from the neohistoricism of postmodernity and indicates its source in Islamic hermeneutics. Indeed, as I discuss in part I, Jawzi's era was also marked by increasing discourse among Islamic reformers of the need to exercise *ijtihad*. Ijtihad, a major interpretive method in Islamic jurisprudence, was becoming the means of choice for reevaluating Islamic traditionalism in light of changing circumstances, and was guided by the Qur'an's insistent calls for social justice. Jawzi simply took it upon himself to exercise ijtihad, and while his conclusions are no longer popular, his critical interpretive method has continued to grow in popularity, so much so that today it is difficult to find Islamic reformers who do not call for the exercise of ijtihad.

The growth and development of ijtihadism is what makes Jawzi's work still relevant to Islamic studies. The similarity between ijtihadism and key elements of neohistoricism is what makes it interesting to Euroamerican scholars. These are the two issues I detail in introducing Jawzi's *History of Intellectual Movements in Islam* to the English-speaking world. It is hoped that English-speaking students of Islam will find in this work not only a skillful and entertaining critique of Islamic history, but a basis of shared concern with the nature of intellectual production as well.

This project was started at the insistence of my mentor, Fazlur Rahman, whose intellectual courage continues to inspire me. Its development would not have been possible without the support of the American Council for Learned Societies, for which I am deeply grateful. St. John Fisher College generously provided me with a sabbatical leave, the Presidential Summer Research Grant, and expert clerical support in the person of Lin Mocejunas. Credit for any elegance in translation goes to Farhat Ziadeh, Muhammed Siddiq, Youssef Salman, Fadi Khoury, and Mazin al-Najjar, all of whom were extremely generous with their help in my effort to make medieval and early twentieth-century Arabic intelligible to late twentieth-century English readers. Responsibility for anything short of elegance is my own. I would also like to thank Nayereh Tohidi for making me aware of the existence of Shawki Abu Khalil's dissertation in Russian on Bandali Jawzi, and Ylena Shustef for translating passages of it so that I could understand it. The encouragement of my parents and the advice and support of my colleagues John Esposito, Yvonne Haddad, John Voll, and Richard Martin were essential in this, as in all my work. Ultimate credit for the completion of this project, however, belongs to John and Jordan Morreall, for whom I bother to do anything at all.

Tampa
August 1995   T. S.

A Note on Transliteration and Translation

Except in cases in which Arabic names and terms have been standardized in English (such as Hussein and Sunna), I have followed the modified *Encyclopedia of Islam* system used by the *International Journal of Middle Eastern Studies* for all Arabic terms and names, with the exception that long vowels have not been marked. In general, Arabic terms that have been incorporated into English usage (such as jihad) have not been italicized, and terms used in Arabic in the text have been italicized only the first time they are used. The translation presented is generally literal. However, a certain degree of license, particularly in cases of repetition and hyperbole, has been taken in order to provide for a fluid English text.

Contents

INTERPRETING ISLAM

Introduction

Biographical Sketch of Bandali Jawzi

Bandali Saliba Jawzi was born in Jerusalem in 1872 and was orphaned at an early age.[1] He studied for the Orthodox priesthood in Jerusalem and in a monastery near Tripoli before moving to Russia in 1891 to pursue an academic career in the land whose missionaries had educated him. In 1899 he received his M.A. from Kazan University, having written his thesis on the Mu'tazilis. According to a recent dissertation produced by Shawki Abu Khalil at the Institute of Oriental Studies in Azerbaijan, Jawzi eventually received a Ph.D. in law from Kazan University, where he also studied history and literature and taught Arabic and French. In 1920 he was appointed to the faculty of Oriental Studies at Baku University. He also earned a Ph.D. in Arabic philology and in 1925 he was appointed dean at the university.

Jawzi made several trips back to Jerusalem, as well as to Syria, Iraq, and Iran. He remained vitally concerned with the fate of his native Palestine. During his visits to Jerusalem, his brother's home became a popular center for literary and political discussions which were attended by members of leading Palestinian families. Abu Khalil mentions members of the Nashashibi, Khalidi, Husseini, and Sakakini families by name. Discussion seems to have centered around questions of political consciousness: the need to develop Palestinian solidarity on a new basis; overcoming sectarian, class, and gender gaps; and the importance of developing new leadership in light of the apparent inability of tradi-

tional leaders to deal effectively with continued European colonialism.
Jawzi also lectured widely on his trips home. His lectures were report-
edly well received, and were published in leading Arabic journals, such
as *al-Athar, al-Hilal, al-Kulliyat, al-Muqtataf,* and *al-Zahra*.

Bandali Jawzi died in Baku in 1942. Details surrounding his death
are not available. Palestinian scholar Constantine Zurayk reported in a
personal interview in 1984 that although he collaborated with Jawzi on
a translation of Noldeke's work on the Ghassanids, he lost track of
Jawzi after the Bolshevik Revolution. Surviving members of his family
in the Arab world had few details to add.

Bandali Jawzi's Works

Bandali Jawzi's *Min Ta'rikh al-Harakat al-Fikriyyah fi'l-Islam* (*The
History of Intellectual Movements in Islam*) was first published in Arabic in August of 1928, and was hailed as a model of scholarship.[2] It did
have detractors. Some disapproved of Jawzi's socialist orientation, for
in it he concluded that in order for Muslim society to implement its
egalitarian principles in the industrial age, it must adopt a socialist economic system. Arab nationalist Muhammad Kurd 'Ali (d. 1953), for
example, suspected Jawzi of trying to spread communism, and therefore
of misinterpreting the bases of Islam. Summarizing Jawzi's intellectual
history, he said, "The first of the principles at which Islam aimed . . .
was the spreading of the spirit of solidarity among its individual members and paying attention to the wretched classes of the Arabs in the
manner of socialism. This is the meaning which was dominant in Islamic society in every age. . . . and most of those who rebelled against
the states had socialist aims." Kurd 'Ali does not dispute this point.
But, he continues, unfortunately Jawzi "serves surreptitiously the Communist regime in the lands whose civilization has influenced him, and
he alleges things about Islam which have never entered the mind of any
Muslim until now."[3] In fact, Jawzi's surviving relatives in Ramallah
assure us that Jawzi was not a communist.[4] Furthermore, as will be
seen, Jawzi explicity rejected arguments by those who claimed that Islam is essentially socialist. Such criticisms notwithstanding, Jawzi's
work was quickly accepted into the body of Arab scholarship. It was
included, for example, in Darwish Miqdadi's standard text on Arab
history, *Ta'rikh al-Ummat al-'Arabiyya* (1931–39).[5]

Over the past twenty years renewed interest in Jawzi's work has been
demonstrated. In 1977 the Union of Palestinian Writers and Journalists,
in cooperation with the Oriental Institute of the Soviet Academy of Sciences, celebrated Jawzi's contributions to Arab scholarship. At that time
a commemorative collection of his articles on Arab social, intellectual,
and economic history was published, along with a new edition of *Min
Ta'rikh.*[6] In 1986 the Research Center for Arab Heritage in Tayiba,
Israel, organized a festival in honor of Bandali Jawzi. As noted, he was

also the subject of a doctoral dissertation produced at the Institute of Oriental Studies of the Academy of Sciences in Azerbaijan in 1992.

Yet despite Jawzi's enduring importance in the Arab world, he has been almost completely overlooked by Western scholars. One of the few Western scholars aware of his work is Maxime Rodinson, who mentioned Jawzi in a footnote in *Islam and Capitalism* (1973).[7] When questioned about Jawzi, Rodinson reported that he knew very little about him. He said he had been told by his teacher, Louis Massignon, that Jawzi was a Tatar from Kazan, but other than the fact that he had written *Min Taʾrikh*, Rodinson knew only that Jawzi was a professor of Arabic literature at Baku University. Then, Rodinson reports, in Paris he happened to meet an old communist Jew from Palestine, who was "vigorously anti-Zionist" and who had known Jawzi. This man told Rodinson that Jawzi was really an Arab from Bethlehem, which Rodinson considered doubtful. The old man had met Jawzi at an Arab nationalist congress, presumably either the Palestinian Congress of 1930 or the Islamic International Congress at Jerusalem in 1931, where the old man had been one of two Jews present to express solidarity with the Arabs. "But there was a linguistic problem," Rodinson related. "At this time the two Jews in question knew only Russian and Yiddish . . . and none of the Arab congressionals knew these languages except Bandali Jawzi, who knew Russian and offered himself as a translator." Rodinson added regarding Jawzi, "This is all I know."[8] I have found only two other references to Jawzi among Western scholars: German scholar Werner Ende referred to Jawzi in *Arabische Nation und islamische Geschichte: Die Umayyaden im Urteil arabischer Autoren des 20. Jahrhunderts* (1977),[9] and Ernest Dawn mentioned him in his 1988 article "The Formation of Pan-Arab Ideology in the Interwar Years" in the *International Journal of Middle East Studies* (1988).[10]

The Significance of Bandali Jawzi's Work

Jawzi's *Min Taʾrikh al-Harakat al-Fikriyyah fiʾl-Islam* is the first Marxist interpretation of the development of Islamic thought. As such it is an important component of our understanding of the turbulent yet productive period of intellectual activity in the Arab world in the last quarter of the nineteenth and first quarter of the twentieth century. This period is usually characterized as one of intense self-scrutiny as the extent of European domination began to dawn on Arab society. From the sixteenth century on, Europeans had made inroads into the Arab world. Not all came as spectacularly as Napoleon, who entered Alexandria, Egypt, in 1798 declaring he was punishing the local leaders for being wayward Muslims.[11] For the most part, European domination of the Arab Middle East was a gradual and complex process, carried out by merchants, missionaries, and only occasionally by armies backed up by official decrees. Indeed, the gradual and complex nature of the process made it that much more difficult to comprehend, much less combat. But by the end of the nineteenth century, Britain was clearly in control of Ottoman Egypt, and France was well ensconced in Syria and North Africa. Accordingly, the weakness of Arab society in the face of both Europeans and Ottomans became a topic of discussion among representatives of traditional elites throughout the Arab world. The tenor of their discussion was one of growing national consciousness, at once combative and self-critical. It was also quite optimistic: Arab society had become effete as a result of traditionalism, with its shallow commitment to personal dignity, social responsibility, and intellectual development. With a reaffirmation of those values, it seemed, Arabs would find the strength to throw off foreign domination and regain their leading position among the family of nations. Indeed, much of the discussion centered upon the shape this newly revived and independent Arab society would take.

This optimism was the first victim of the betrayal of the Arab people by France and Britain following World War I. Britain and the Arabs had worked together to defeat the German-Turkish alliance. In correspondence with Arab leaders preceding the outbreak of hostilities, Britain had agreed that, in return for Arab assistance, it would recognize Arab independence in all territories then ruled by Turkey.[12] At the end of the war, however, the British and French acted upon a secret agreement they had made prior to the war and awarded "mandate" control to France of the parts of traditional Syria that are now the states of Syria and Lebanon. Britain was given Iraq and the parts of traditional Syria known as Palestine (present-day Israel and the West Bank) and Transjordan (present-day Jordan), in addition to the control it had held in Egypt before the war. Furthermore, Britain designated Palestine as a homeland for world Jewry.[13]

Not surprisingly, there was palpable disenchantment among the Arabs, particularly university students, with the European system that had so ruthlessly exploited Arab enthusiasm and naivete. Prior to the war, democracy and progress, in the tradition of Enlightenment liberalism, were key themes in Arab thought.[14] After the war, many in the Arab world sought different models. Marxist ideology, which had recently been so effective in overthrowing the Romanov imperialists, provided a helpful tool in understanding recent events. Because imperialism is a result of capitalism, the reasoning went, European-style liberal capitalism was the culprit. But Arab disenchantment was not confined to European liberalism. The traditional Arab elites who had dealt with the European leaders lost credibility as well, especially when some of them accepted nominal kingships in the states created by the mandate powers.

These two reactions—anti-capitalism and anti-elitism—would help shape the socialist and populist political movements of the interwar years. Baʿthism and Nasserism became the most successful socialist movements in the Middle East, gaining control in three of the largest countries (Syria, Iraq, and Egypt) and earning credit for evicting the European overlords. The popularity of Bandali Jawzi's analysis of Islamic history reflected the broad popularity of this socialist trend in Arab thought. Ultimately, of course, further political and economic setbacks would lead to popular disenchantment with socialism, as well. Nevertheless, Marxian analysis remains a critical component of both modern and postmodern criticism, and Bandali Jawzi's *History of Intellectual Movements in Islam* is its first full-scale application to the development of Islamic thought.

Jawzi's work takes on even greater interest in the world of postmodern scholarship, particularly in the context of hermeneutics (the study of the ways people interpret texts; that is, interpretive methodologies). Jawzi's methodology is based on a recognition that all texts, including religious and historical documents, are the result of human interpretation, and that interpretations are inevitably influenced by the milieux in which they are produced. His history opens with a critique of certain European historians of "the orient," as Europeans used to call anything east of Moscow and southeast of Vienna. These "orientalists," according to Jawzi, were for the most part ignorant of the subjects about which they wrote. Furthermore, he wrote in his introduction, their ideas could only be explained by "religious or nationalist prejudice and political or imperialist goals." The body of his text is devoted to an examination of interpretations of Islamic principles for implementation in the various regions of the Islamic empire, especially to those of a series of rebellious movements within the Islamic empire, and to the judgments of historians regarding these opponents of the regime. Throughout his analysis, Jawzi identified those interpretations he believed were consistent with basic Islamic principles of social justice, distinguishing them from those which were motivated by more worldly concerns. In order to demonstrate that distinction, Jawzi took great pains to determine who was doing the reporting, and in what power structure(s) the reporters were involved.

Aside from the fact that Jawzi tended to emphasize economic concerns over other sociopolitical components of the historical milieux that influence intellectual production, his interpretive methodology is not specific to Marxism. In his creative efforts to distinguish authentically Islamic principles from the contingent conditions in which interpretations of them were produced, Jawzi shares a common methodological heritage with a trend in Islamic reform that has enjoyed significant popularity in the nineteenth and twentieth centuries. Based on *ijtihad,* the central hermeneutic of Islamic jurisprudence, this trend calls for critical reevaluation of Islamic intellectual heritage, in recognition of the fact that all interpretations are influenced by issues specific to the time and place in which they are produced.

What makes Jawzi's employment of this hermeneutic intriguing is its striking similarity to one only recently developed in the Euroamerican context. French historian Michel Foucault (d. 1984) inaugurated a trend in Euroamerican postmodernism, sometimes called neohistoricism, that focuses on the practical dynamics of discourse (language as it is used).[15] Language has all kinds of interesting characteristics, but it is primarily a tool. It is used for something, and that use is what interested Foucault. Agreeing with nineteenth-century German philosopher Friedrich Nietzsche (d. 1900) that human beings tend to recognize as true only those interpretations conducive to their quest for power, Foucault asked (implicitly, at least), would modernist Europe have ever bothered to devise its dichotomies—civilized versus uncivilized, for example, or sane versus insane—and to subjugate in their names had it not been for the power that subjugation promised? In other words, maybe those we have been taught to think of as uncivilized or insane, for example, are not necessarily so much uncivilized or insane as they are a threat to the status quo and to the power of those benefiting from the status quo. Such speculation led Foucault to question the validity of virtually all knowledge, but especially the kind that divided people into opposing groups.

Foucault uses the term "knowledge" to mean the body of accepted truths about things in any given context; he does not think of it as truth as such. In that sense, knowledge, he believes, is the vehicle of the process whereby institutions maintain their dominance. The meanings that we learn as we receive our language are meanings that are considered somehow conducive to the survival of the dominant power structure in which we learn our language.[16] Thus, the same set of terms can be construed in multiple ways, and generally are, but the interpretations that are accepted are those that are useful within the dominant power structure. For example, children in the 1950s in North America learned negative connotations for the terms "socialism" and "communism," while at the same time children in the Soviet Union learned negative connotations for the term "capitalism." Individuals are involved in the construction of those connotations, of course, but in the service of the dominant power structure. Those intellectuals who achieve success— who are accepted as qualified experts and given broad exposure—are those whose interpretations support the connotations useful to the dominant power structure.

Yet while Foucault insists on the multiplicity of interpretations, he does not hold all interpretations to be equally valid. And although he offers no criteria for accepting any one interpretation as "correct," he does hold that some are closer to "reality as it is" in a particular context than others. These are interpretations devised in full awareness of the ideology of the dominant system of knowledge, and, like his own interpretations, take into consideration ("pay attention to") those disadvantaged by the dominant system. They are more inclusive than the interpretations of the dominant system, which is by nature exclusionary.

As such, these interpretations do not erect an alternate ideology on the basis of their attention to the excluded; rather, their investigations undermine the validity of the system of knowledge that delegitimizes the "other," the "excluded," the negative component of a set of opposites, revealing that system as less than absolutely "scientific" or "true," showing that it could have been construed otherwise. Foucault calls scholars using this methodology "specific" intellectuals, as opposed to those involved in supporting the dominant exclusionary structure, with its claims to universal truth. The latter he refers to as "universal" intellectuals—those who claim their interpretations are essentially true. Universal intellectuals, in Foucault's analysis, are tools of the dominant power system, sometimes uncritically referred to as the state.[17]

Foucault sees power as ubiquitous in human relations. He does not attempt to change the fact that power is maintained through intellectual or ideological structures ("knowledge"), which rationalize, and justify, legitimize the status quo. "Power is not an evil," he says. "Power is strategic games."[18] Power relationships can always be reversed, since, he observes, wherever there is power, there is resistance to power. That is because power/knowledge is always exclusionary, but not completely so. It is only when power becomes dominance, attempting to interfere with efforts to modify it ("resistance"), that it becomes evil, when the natural resistance to dominant power is silenced, whether by being declared insane, criminal, or uncivilized. That is when excavating the sources of the kind of "knowledge" that allows or accepts that silencing becomes particularly important.[19]

Not surprisingly, Foucault's ideas have proven very controversial in Euroamerican academia. Within postmodern intellectual circles, Foucault and Jacques Derrida are probably the most influential intellectuals, their ideas considered revolutionary breakthroughs in the ongoing effort to interpret our world. However, a significant portion of academia maintains a modernist orientation—complete with accepted criteria of certainty and truth—as well as cherished models of civilized society and ways to determine who is not civilized, and how to either coopt or eliminate them. In that context, Foucault's ideas of the relativity of universal intellectuals' "truths," and their almost incestuous relationship with the dominant political-economic power structure, are naturally, considered revolutionary in another sense: they are considered subversive of Western culture.

Yet these same ideas of the relationship of scholarly treatment of "the other" and the resulting relativity of their interpretations are deeply embedded in Bandali Jawzi's *History of Intellectual Movements in Islam*. Jawzi considered it self-evident that interpretations change depending on their context, and that those interpretations that become canonized as knowledge, to be passed down through the generations, are those that are conducive to the maintenance of power in the institutions which produced them. This is the hermeneutic on which his work is based, and he applies it to both foreign cultures' interpretations of Arab/Islamic culture and to Muslims' interpretations of their own heritage.

By an interesting coincidence, one of the best known applications of Foucault's methodology was produced by Palestinian-American scholar Edward Said, particularly in *Orientalism* (1978), his searing critique of European scholarship of the Arab Islamic world. Said observed that differing sociopolitical contexts produce differing interpretations. Everyone works within a "culture" or a particular environment with its own intellectual "system," its own methodologies for determining what constitutes valid knowledge. But extrapolating from Foucault's description of specific intellectuals (the "resistance"), Said describes how individuals can straddle cultures and systems, allowing for unique perspectives that can give rise to cogent criticism.[20] His own work is a case in point. His dual (Palestinian and Euroamerican) perspective allows for a critical awareness of both cultures.

In *Orientalism,* Said's detailed analysis of modern European "knowledge" of the Arab/Islamic world demonstrates that despite its acceptance as legitimate, objective scholarship, most of the work produced in Europe concerning the Middle East has been radically biased so as to justify European imperialism. Until only very recently, Middle Eastern peoples were systematically presented in ways, usually implying their incompetence or immorality, that virtually demanded the European or Euroamerican corrective. In fact, for Said, the very effort to characterize the Middle East—to objectify it; that is, to make it into an object, an "other"—has been intimately related to an effort to dominate.[21]

As with Foucault, for Said there is no disinterested knowledge, no such thing as interpretations without presuppositions arising from the interpreter's specific context (the meanings s/he has learned, and her/his position within the dominant power structure).[22] Therefore, there is no ultimately true interpretation. This characteristically postmodern position frequently invites allegations of sheer relativism: if no position can be proven absolutely true, then all positions are relatively true. However Said, like Foucault, rejects such utter relativism. All positions are not equal to him. Clearly, some are more exclusionary than others. Some interpretations support political-economic policies hostile to an "other," while some undermine those policies. Establishing criteria by which to judge interpretations as more or less valid runs perilously close to the absolutism of modernity rejected by postmodernists. Still, unlike many postmodern scholars, Said is unapologetic about references to the desire for justice, truth, and freedom from oppression as a legitimate rationale for resistance. As such, Said is an example of the "specific" intellectual described by Foucault. His work undermines the power of the dominant system, not because of the mere fact that it is powerful, but because its power has been used to suppress those resistant to it. And Said maintains that, in the case of the Arab world, colonized and subjugated as it was by Europe with the support of America, resistance to that power was, and still is, perfectly justifiable. Said's *Orientalism* thus constitutes an examination of the power relations behind texts, and is informed by a critical consciousness aware of both the intricacies of the dominant system and the "brute reality" of the "lives, histories, and customs" of the subjugated people.[23]

Bandali Jawzi's *History of Intellectual Movements in Islam* clearly anticipates Said's analysis. His introductory chapter in particular, with its critique of European scholars' depictions of the Semitic world, which are skewed on behalf of existing or desired relationships of political-economic dominance, presents a brief glimpse of the kind of exhaustive analysis Said published exactly fifty years later. This certainly does not detract from Foucault's or Said's brilliance. Indeed, Jawzi neither articulates nor defends his methodology; he simply uses it. Furthermore, his subject is Islamic intellectual history; his critique of orientalism is sketchy and only secondary to his purpose. But Jawzi's work does raise an interesting question regarding the source of his hermeneutic. Why did it seem self-evident to a turn-of-the-century Palestinian and yet become the source of heated controversy in Euroamerican academia when it finally developed there in the 1960s and 1970s? What does Jawzi's work reveal about the hermeneutical context in which it arose? And does it indicate a commensurability between Euroamerican postmodern hermeneutics and the hermeneutics of Islamic reform utilized by Jawzi?

I believe an examination of Bandali Jawzi's hermeneutic reveals that it indeed shares with neohistoricism, as developed in the work of Foucault and Said, some key observations on the nature of intellectual production. An examination of the sources of Bandali Jawzi's hermeneutic (chapters 1 and 2) shows that the two are quite different in origin and implication. Neohistoricism has a long history in the transition from Europe's modernity, with all its absolutism, to the uncertainty of the postmodern, postcolonial world. Although he himself was not a Muslim, Jawzi's hermeneutic (chapter 3), is rooted in the Islamic heritage. Focusing on that hermeneutic in light of general trends in postmodern Euroamerican hermeneutical concerns (chapter 4) both provides a glimpse of the complex nature of Islamic reformist thought and opens the door to scholarly discourse among Euroamerican and Islamic scholars on shared issues and concerns.

I

COMMENTARY

1

Jawzi, Marxism, and Islamic Socialism

As noted in the introduction, Europe's betrayal of promises for Arab independence following World War I led to a loss of faith among Arab thinkers in classical liberal thought and a concomitant rise of interest in socialist ideology. This trend was coupled with the loss of faith in traditional Arab elites and the institutions they represented, both religious and political-economic, allowing for the rise of nontraditional and even non-Islamic elites. Perhaps the best evidence of this dual trend was the development of two of the most enduring sociopolitical organizations in the modern Arab world, Ba'thism and Nasserism. Ba'thism developed on Syrian university campuses in the early 1940s as an Arab nationalist movement. By that time, France and Britain had divided their portions of the Middle East allotted by the League of Nations into several mini-states. Besides Transjordan (which would eventually become present-day Jordan), Lebanon was separated from Syria by the French in 1920 (both Lebanon and Syria were formally recognized as independent by France in 1946). Ba'thism's "Arab nationalism" therefore was actually trans-nationalism: Ba'thists wanted the Arabs to work together for independence, development, equality, socialism, and above all, unity.[1] Nasserism, named for Gamal 'Abd al-Nasser of Egypt, would espouse virtually the same principles. Both groups enjoyed mass popularity during the 1940s and 1950s, and Ba'thism became powerful enough to gain control of both Syria and Iraq. 'Abd al-Nasser rose to the head of the Revolutionary Command Council, which ousted King Faruq in 1952, and was eventually successful in ridding Egypt of British control. The broad popularity of socialist Arab nationalism has clearly been eclipsed by Islamist opposition groups since the late 1960s, although their residual power remains. The leadership of Syria and Iraq is still at least nominally Baʿthist, and Nasserist parties can still be found in the Middle East. Nevertheless, in the early postwar era, Marxism and socialism were among the most popular trends in Arab intellectual circles. It is not surprising, therefore, that Bandali Jawzi's work enjoyed such success.

Arab Islamic Socialism

The way had been paved for Jawzi by earlier Arab socialists. Over a decade before Jawzi's *History,* Christian scholar Shibli Shumayyil (d. 1917) had popularized discussion of a socialist system wherein the state would be responsible for providing work for the unemployed, ensuring fair wages, preventing monopolization of public resources, and disbanding institutions that emphasize discord among social groups.[2] Similarly, Lebanese Druze scholar Amir Shakib Arsalan (d. 1946) articulated the "great socialist principles" that he believed were incorporated into Islamic law, making them therefore far superior to European socialism.[3] Even the conservative Muslim Muhammad Rashid Rida (d. 1935), although he rejected communism, begrudgingly accepted socialist principles: "[S]ocialism means the liberation of the workers from capitalists and oppressive governments. Muslims must hope for its success since they too are workers and suffer from the same oppression and if socialism succeeds the subjugation of peoples will end."[4]

As Maxime Rodinson, Olivier Carré, Tareq Ismael, and Issa Boullata, among others, have documented, socialist approaches to Islamic reform—with various degrees of Marxism—have been and remain a significant feature of twentieth-century Islamic thought.[5] Bandali Jawzi's work is therefore historically significant as the first full-scale Marxist analysis of the nature and development of Islamic thought.[6] But it is important to understand Jawzi's orientation toward Marxism. It was unique as Marxism goes, and specific to the Russian/Soviet-dominated Muslim environment in which Jawzi worked.

Sultangalievism

Jawzi had studied at Kazan University in Azerbaijan, at the time one of the centers of Muslim life in imperial Russia. The czarist-ruled Muslim community was, in the last quarter of the nineteenth century, enjoying a cultural revival parallel to that in the Middle East. This was due partly to the work of a Tatar mulla and historian, Shihabeddin Marjani (d. 1889).[7] Marjani called for a return to the pure Islam that had produced the golden age of Islamic civilization. To that end he advocated educational reform to cast off the stultifying effects of narrow dogmatism and traditionalism. He believed that Islam is perfectly compatible with modern science, and he encouraged the study of science and Western literature to release the Muslim world from its cultural isolation. Marjani's work was followed by that of many others, such as Rizaeddin Fahreddin (d. 1936) and Musa Yarullah Bigi (d. 1949), who similarly called for modernization and reform.

Initially confined to spiritual leaders, this movement eventually gained broad exposure, as well as vociferous defenders and detractors. By the turn of the century, a rift was clearly identifiable between those Muslims in favor of reform, known as the Jadids, and those favoring adherence to traditional patterns, known as the Qadimis. As would be expected, the Jadids enjoyed popularity among the urban intelligentsia, while the traditionalists maintained their hold among the rural population and the newly urbanized.[8] Yet as Russian domination of Muslim lands in the trans-Caucasus and Central Asia became more oppressive, active participation in reform movements became more widespread.

Muslims began organizing politically in Azerbaijan in the early years of the twentieth century. In 1904 and 1905, three Muslim congresses were held, resulting in the formation of the Muslim Union (*ittifaq al-muslimin*). The purpose of the union was to provide a unifying organization for all Muslims under Russian domination and to demand equality with the Russians. The Muslims of the Russian empire were mostly Turkic or of Persian heritage. The Russians were those who were heir to the Muscovite state that began its conquest of the Muslim lands of the trans-Caucasus and Central Asia in the sixteenth century. But the Muslims' demands for basic civil rights took the same form as demands by the Russian liberal bourgeoisie. Accordingly, the Second Muslim National Congress decided to align itself with the liberal Russian Constitutional Democrat Party. This move was made official at the Third Muslim National Congress. However, the failure of the Russian liberals' constitutional rebellion of 1905 to satisfy the Muslims' demands ultimately undermined the latter's confidence in the Russian liberal movement. The Muslim National Congress disbanded.

Thereafter, the Muslim movement in czarist Russia, and particularly in Azerbaijan, began to develop a unique approach to liberation. On the one hand, Muslims who were disenchanted with the ethnocentrism of the Russians looked to their own indigenous Islamic culture for a means to gain the strength needed to throw off the bonds of imperialism. On the other hand, some members of the intelligentsia were increasingly attracted to socialist principles. Thus, the Azerbaijan Muslim Social Democrat Party (Hummet) was formed in 1906. It was socialist, dedicated to the kinds of social reform its members believed Islam required. It was also nationalist in the sense that it called for independence of non-Russian peoples. Similarly, the Equality Party (Musavat) was formed in Azerbaijan in 1911 by Muslim intellectuals who presented both socialist and nationalist goals in an Islamic context. But the attempts of these parties to achieve equal treatment with the Russians were no more successful than those of the other Muslim national socialist organizations. Following the disturbances of 1905, the czarist regime had tightened its central control. Refusing any demands for concessions to non-Russians, the czar's government effectively galvanized opposition to the regime, vastly enhancing the popularity of the opposition Russian Communist Party. In this context, a significant number of Muslim activists and intellectuals lent their support to the Bolsheviks. Many, in fact, joined the Russian Communist Party.

Marxist doctrine, of course, involves internationalism and atheism. Ordinarily, these would have been as problematic for nationalists and Muslims as the latter's nationalism and religious orientation would have been for Marxist leaders. However, in the context of unified opposition to the czar, these issues troubled neither the Bolshevik revolutionaries nor the Muslim leaders. In fact, Lenin actively sought Muslim support, addressing their nationalist goals directly in 1913. He spoke of the "right of every nation in Russia to political self-determination—the right, that is, of separating from Russia and of creating independent governments."[9] If this formulation was ambiguous with regard to the extent of "self-determination" or the meaning of "separating from Russia," the Boshevik Social Democrat Workers Party appeared to leave no doubt about their support for nationalist claims in the 1917 conference declaration: "The right to voluntary separation and the right to create independent states must be recognized as belonging to all the nations forming part of Russia. . . . It is impermissible to confuse the problem of the right of nations to voluntary secession with that of the utility of the separation of a particular nation at a given time."[10] Even after the October Revolution, the provisional government directly sought the support of "the Muslim workers of Russia and the East" by promising them the right to conduct their own national life "freely and without hindrance."[11]

However, this conciliatory attitude would change, once the Bolsheviks gained power, in order to avoid the breakup of the empire. Following the October 1917 victory in the capital, the Bolshevik forces continued to face resistance from various sources, including loyalist counterrevolutionaries and sporadic mutinies within their own ranks. In the Muslim regions, autonomous movements continued to challenge the Bolshevik forces; in the trans-Caucasus, resistance was mounted well into the 1920s. The Bolsheviks continued to try to convince the Muslims of their sincerity, lest they follow the example of the Poles and Finns and try to break away from the empire. Besides this pragmatic desire to keep the empire intact, Marxist teaching held that socialism would overcome nationalism and that nationalist feelings were a function of the alienation produced by capitalism. Once the socialist revolution had succeeded, sincere Marxists believed, the Muslims' yearning for national independence would cease.[12]

Stalin therefore offered a pragmatic reinterpretation of the principle of self-determination, taking it from the arena of nationalism and placing it in the context of the class struggle. It was the workers, he said, not the Muslims as such, who had the right of self-determination, and their self-determination would ultimately produce equality for all the people of the Soviet Union.[13] But this self-determination could only occur after the reeducation and assimilation of the Muslims. In this process, the fully industrialized Leningrad proletariat would naturally take the lead. This gave theoretical justification for what, after 1918, became a political reality. With political victory in sight, the Bolshevik leaders reversed their policy of conciliation toward their Muslim allies. They no longer required their services (or, at least, their neutrality) and recognized the expedience of curtailing the Muslims' power in order to centralize their own. Thus in late 1918 Stalin, unable to accept the independence of the Muslim communists, which they demanded on the basis of their nationalist aspirations, declared himself their leader.[14]

The Muslims had aligned themselves with the Bolsheviks in the hope that the revolution would finally bring about their long-awaited liberation. Yet they had not abandoned their reformist ideals, which by the time of the revolution had become incorporated into a distinctive ideological framework. The Bolsheviks were at a loss as to how to deal with colonized peoples or national minorities. Their theories were geared exclusively for an industrial proletariat in an areligious context. The Muslims therefore had to adapt Marxist theory to accommodate both the Muslim minorities' nationalist aspirations and their religious orientation. Credit for developing this adaptation of Marxist theory is generally given to the Muslim Marxist Tatar Mir Said Sultan Galiev (d. 1939?).[15]

Sultan Galiev began with the principle that the true victims of oppression, even more so than the working classes in industrialized nations, were the colonized peoples of the world. They were oppressed not only by the bourgeoisie but also by the imperialist colonizers. This led Galiev to adjust the definition of "proletariat" to include all colonized peoples, regardless of the size of their industrial proletariat and including all social classes among them. The focus of revolutionary activity also required modification to include all movements for national liberation. Therefore, Sultan Galiev relegated the class struggle, considered of primary importance in mainstream Marxist thought, to second place, behind the nationalist struggle.

This formulation represents a rebuttal of the Weberian explanation for the failure of "eastern nations" to follow the Western model of capitalist development. In 1920 Max Weber had attributed that failure to what he considered the irrational nature of those under the influence of such "superstitious" religions as Islam. Weber believed that the "Protestant ethic" provided the essential foundation for the Marxist model of revolutionary progress.[16] Sultan Galiev believed that the

Marxist model would apply to the colonized, non-Christian world with just these few modifications. The goal remained a socialist revolution, based on the belief that socialist society was both just and conducive to the development of fully integrated individuals and communities. The difference between the mainstream Marxist model and Sultan Galiev's formulation lay, first of all, in the target of revolutionary activity. In industrialized society, the bourgeoisie oppressed the laboring class and therefore had to be overthrown. In colonized lands, however, all classes were oppressed by the imperialist power; the imperialist power, not its class orientation, therefore became the target of revolutionary zeal. That target included the newly liberated Russian proletariat.

The Russian revolutionaries had fought to liberate the industrial proletariat, but they had done nothing to liberate the preindustrial lands that had been colonized by the czarist regime. Furthermore, Sultan Galiev believed that the Russian proletariat, having emerged from the colonial tradition of bourgeois society, would overpower the preindustrial Muslim lands just as readily as had their bourgeois predecessors: "To replace the dictatorship of one class of European society, the bourgeoisie, by that of its adversary, the proletariat, will do nothing to change the situation of the oppressed part of humanity. In fact, if the change took place, it would simply mean, for the colonized peoples, the accession to power of another master." [17] Sultan Galiev therefore envisioned a "union of colonized peoples against the metropolitans," a "colonial international" that would unite all the Muslim national forces in a party, independent of the Soviet controlled Comintern, in which all classes of colonized peoples would struggle for independence. [18]

As noted, the other major difference between mainstream Marxist thought and that of Sultan Galiev was in their attitudes toward religion. Whereas mainstream Marxism saw religion as a tool of oppression, and therefore a hindrance to liberation, in the Muslim Marxist approach religion was a source of strength against oppression. Sultan Galiev advocated working with the indigenous culture of the colonized peoples, reinforcing it to a position of sufficient strength to cast off the colonial usurpers. At the heart of every culture, he believed, is its religion. Furthermore, for Sultan Galiev, Islam in particular was the key to throwing off the yoke of imperialism. Not only would it serve as a focal point for strength through unity, but its principal values of solidarity based on human equality and social justice were clearly the antithesis of imperialism. Therefore, once freed of colonial subjugation and reminded of their central beliefs, the Muslims could be free to develop in accordance with both their own egalitarian principles and the laws of economic development. In this condition of freedom and heightened Islamic consciousness, Sultan Galiev believed that economic development would be rapid, that the capitalist stage of industrialization accompanied by class conflict would be brief, and that industrialized Muslim society would emerge as a model of Islamic—and, coincidentally, socialist—values.

Sultan Galiev believed the 1917 revolution was a failure. Not only had it failed to produce a just and egalitarian society throughout Europe, but also it had failed to recognize that "the weak point of the capitalist world is in the Orient, not the Occident." [19] He did not believe Western Europe was ready for revolution. The only direction open to socialism was eastward, he thought, particularly in Muslim society, because of its insistence on social justice, which for him was the ultimate goal of socialism. Once liberated, the Muslims of the former czarist empire would become "the model, the hearth whence the sparks of socialist revolution would fly to the heart of the Orient." [20]

But the Bolsheviks did not agree, and as noted, their alliance with the Muslims was short-lived. For one thing, they saw Muslim independence as a threat to Soviet central authority and viewed the prospect of revolutions in the regimes surrounding the former Russian empire as an opportunity for consolidation of Western influence in the region. But beyond that, the alliance between the Muslims and the Bolsheviks had been built from the outset on mutual misunderstanding. In the words of Alexandre Bennigsen, "The Muslims were deluded into thinking that they could take advantage of the new regime in finally implementing their reformist movement. The Bolshevists entertained, falsely, the hope that they would be able to re-educate their fellow-travelers and make them in the long run good Marxists." [21] The Muslims met in 1920 in Baku for the Congress of the Peoples of the East. There, in response to Stalin's subjugation of the Muslim Communist Party, they called for jihad in the form of a general revolt in the colonies. Nothing came of the decision for lack of organization, but it did incite the Tenth Congress of the Russian Communist Party the following spring to declare the Muslims both anticommunist and anti-Russian. Thereafter began the merciless suppression of Muslim activists in the Soviet Union that culminated in Stalin's bloody purges in 1937–38. Included among the purged was Sultan Galiev.

Bandali Jawzi's insistence on the affinity between Islamic principles of social justice and the goals of socialism is clearly in keeping with the principles of Sultangalievism, as Soviet analysts called it. He could even be included among those in the vanguard of Sultangalievist Islamic Marxism who were "spreading the sparks of socialist revolution to the heart of the Orient." Perhaps the fact that Jawzi was writing from within a region that had been incorporated into the Soviet Union led some to think of him as an agent of the Soviet regime. As noted in the introduction, Muhammad Kurd ʿAli accused Jawzi of "surreptitiously [serving] the Communist regime in the lands whose civilization has influenced him." But although he obviously was enamored of socialism, Jawzi was not a communist in the sense conveyed by that term today, with its connotations of atheism, internationalism, and totalitarianism. His attraction was to egalitarian principles at all levels: class, religion, gender, and nation. As he makes clear in his dedication ("to the reawakening Arab youth"), Jawzi envisioned an independent Arab society, not one subjugated to the Soviet state, and one motivated by Islamic principles of social justice and tolerance. Perhaps more important, the key element in Jawzi's interpretive method—his recognition of the impact of specific sociopolitical and economic conditions on the development of Islamic intellectual heritage, and the resultant need for critical reevaluation of that heritage—reflects neither Sultangalievism specifically nor generic Arab/Islamic socialism. It shares far more in common with a dominant trend in Islamic reform, based on the juristic hermeneutic known as ijtihad, discussed in the following chapter.

2

The Hermeneutics
of Islamic Reform

Many scholars have discussed the persistence of themes of renewal and reform in Islamic thought. John Esposito, Yvonne Haddad, and John Voll, for example, drawing upon classic as well as lesser-known sources, have demonstrated that these themes are a perennial and defining feature of Islamic intellectual history.[1] But renewal and reform require a means, and perennial renewal and reform require built-in or institutionalized means. That is the subject of this discussion.

In Islam there are a number of approaches to perennial renewal/reform. For some, strict adherence to traditional Islamic institutions and practice assures constant renewal of society and reaffirmation of the commitment to moral righteousness and social justice. In some popular teaching this is the interpretation of the Sunna of the Prophet, the established way Muslims live based on the example of Prophet Muhammad: from ritual practice, prayer, and matters of diet, dress and personal hygiene, to specific rules codified over a thousand years ago regarding marriage, divorce, inheritance, and other matters of family law. If the Muslim community is in disarray, according to this model, it is because too many individuals have deviated from the established practice. The success of the community is seen as a reward from God for living by this unquestioned code. Another popular belief regarding the mechanism for continual renewal in Islamic society is that God will provide a gifted individual (called a *mujaddid,* or renewer) at the beginning of each century to lead specific renewal efforts.[2] According to this approach, if the Muslim community is in decline, only patience is required, for eventually the promised hero will appear. The mujaddid is frequently accorded the right to make innovative interpretations of Islamic principles, based solely on his having achieved popular recognition as a mujaddid.

These two approaches (strict adherence to the codified Sunna, and waiting for the mujaddid), often seen as complementary, are characteristic of traditional Islamic society, and are associated with a generally passive approach to Islamic renewal. They differ from the more critical and activist approach to Islamic renewal under discussion. According to the latter, the success of the Muslim community results from the collective effort to ensure social justice and maintain solidarity in ever-changing circumstances. Central to this approach is the belief that the call for justice and social solidarity are continually inspired by revelation, although determining the means to achieve these goals in various circumstances is the responsibility of each community and generation. This responsibility involves the critical reassessment of inherited Islamic practice and creative application of Islamic principles to new circumstances. In the view of many Islamic reformers, these means are incorporated into a hermeneutical principle essential to the development of Islamic institutions, particularly Islamic law: ijtihad.

It should be noted that ijtihad is not the only locus of Islamic hermeneutics. Frequently when scholars discuss Islamic interpretive methodologies they look to Qurʾanic exegesis, *tafsir*. Tafsir generally refers to a branch of Qurʾanic studies associated with materials transmitted over the centuries (hadith reports) which purportedly explain authoritatively the circumstances surrounding the revelation of Qurʾanic verses and establish the meaning of the verses. Heavily dependent upon philology, this branch of study is known as ʿilm al-qurʾan waʾl-tafsir, or knowledge of the Qurʾan and [its] exegesis. Among the most influential works of tafsir are those produced by al-Tabari (d. 923), al-Zamakshari (d. 1144), Fakr al-Din Razi (d. 1209), and al-Baidawi (d. ca. 1286). As the work of Andrew Rippin, Jane Dammen McAuliffe, and Fred Leemhuis demonstrates, the hermeneutic involved in traditional tafsir is quite different from that involved in Islamic law.[3] Most significantly, embedded in the notion of tafsir is the belief that the meaning of the Qurʾan can be fixed for all time by authoritative interpreters. Both ijtihad and tafsir accept the notion that the Qurʾan needs to be explained, at least in some passages. Both, in fact, refer to the same traditional reports that Prophet Muhammad himself engaged in such explanation.[4] But tafsir is generally understood to be simply a matter of revealing a meaning that already exists in the text of the Qurʾan. Ijtihad, by contrast, is an extension or interpolation of meaning. One determines—to the best of one's ability, and taking into account both traditional knowledge and ever new ways of understanding—the meaning of the revealed text in its own historic context. One then determines how to act in accordance with that meaning in changed circumstances.

It should also be noted that when we talk about Islamic law we are not talking about an obscure code of regulations that is marginal to the lives of ordinary believers, as would be the case, for example, with the Canon Law of Christianity. In Islam, law is an expression of God's will for humanity; it is the raison d'être of the community established by the Prophet Muhammad.[5] *Islam* means "submission," specifically to the will of God. One who submits is known as a *muslim*. That identification would be impossible, theoretically, without awareness of what God's will is. Thus the centrality of law in Islam. As Noel Coulson put it, "Law is the command of God; and the acknowledged function of Muslim jurisprudence, from the beginning, was simply the discovery of the terms of that command."[6]

Islamic law is derived primarily from the Qur'an, believed to be the word of God revealed for all people in all times. The second essential source of Islamic law is the Sunna, the normative behavior of Prophet Muhammad, as related in extra-scriptural reports called, individually and collectively, hadith. But early in the development of Islamic law it was recognized that revelation, which for Sunni Muslims culminated with the work of Prophet Muhammad, could hardly be expected to legislate specific behavior applicable in all cases for all time. Its function, rather, was to establish a moral imperative and to provide guidelines and some normative examples. While Prophet Muhammad was the leader of the community, his behavior and judgment could be considered normative. But following his death, Muslims had to determine some means for deriving the implications of the Qur'an and the Sunna for cases not specifically covered therein. In cases without direct precedents in the Qur'an and the Sunna, or in cases whose circumstances were significantly different, human beings had to exercise their own judgment to determine the appropriate course of action. That is the role of ijtihad.

The early founders of Islamic legal schools described ijtihad as the concerted effort to determine legal opinions in the absence of relevant precedents.[7] Yet this intellectual exertion (or intellectual jihad, as it has been called, since it comes from *jahada*, the same Arabic root as jihad, meaning "to strive" or "exert oneself") was to be exercised based on principles established in revelation. Therefore, interpreters had to distinguish between the normative elements in revelation and the merely descriptive or contingent, between legally binding enunciations and simple moral exhortations. They had to codify into actual, enforceable rules the Qur'an's insistent but sometimes elusive standards of justice, equity, and piety. This effort to determine the standards established by the Qur'an and the Sunna, and their implications for changed circumstances or those not expressly covered, became a third source of Islamic law.

As such, ijtihad is an essential component of Islamic law. As Wael Hallaq argues, "The primary objective of legal theory . . . was to lay down a coherent system of principles through which a qualified jurist could extract rulings for novel cases. From the third/ninth century onward, this was universally recognized by jurists to be the sacred purpose of *usul al-fiqh* [the roots of Islamic legislation]."[8] He also points out that ijtihad "was declared to be a religious duty (*fard kifaya*) incumbent upon all qualified jurists whenever a new case should appear."[9] He contends that "the practice of ijtihad was the primary objective of the methodology and theory of usul al-fiqh."[10] Yet the institutionalization of ijtihad had a rather problematic history.

The Institutionalization of Ijtihad

In the formative period of Islamic institutions, ijtihad was a relatively open practice. As Joseph Schacht put it:

> [D]uring the whole of the formative period of Islamic law, the first two and a half centuries of Islam (or until about the middle of the ninth century [C.E.]), there was never any question of denying to any scholar or specialist of the sacred Law the right to find his own solutions to legal problems. The sanction which kept ignoramuses at bay was simply general disapproval by the recognized specialists. It was only after the formative period of Islamic law had come to an end that the question of ijtihad and of who was qualified to exercise it was raised.[11]

In the period after the first two and a half centuries referred to by Schacht, the right to exercise independent judgment was gradually restricted, first to certain kinds of reasoning (*qiyas*, or analogical reasoning), and then to certain texts. It was restricted furthermore to individuals with specific qualifications, who reasoned in prescribed ways and with regard to prescribed sources.

This limitation was the result of a number of steps.[12] First was the institutionalization of legal scholarship, which began when a group of *fuqaha'* (specialists in fiqh) became critical of the Umayyad dynasty (661-750 C.E.). As members of the opposition, the fuqaha' were naturally favored by the ʿAbbasids (750-1258 C.E.), the dynasty succeeding the Umayyads, and came to play an important role in their administration. The Umayyads had introduced into their administration the office of judges (qadis), officials appointed by the political authorities who frequently had varied administrative responsibilities, including police and treasury work, but who were generally charged with settling disputes in accordance with local custom. They were accorded a high degree of leeway in this regard, exercising their own discretion concerning what was permissible in view of what they considered to be Islamic principles and administrative necessities. With the accession of the ʿAbbasids, however, legal scholars as such, drawn from the religious opposition to the Umayyads, became incorporated into the state system.[13]

By the time of the ʿAbbasids' accession, the Islamic community had spread far beyond its Arabian peninsular origins. Under the Umayyad administration, a wide variety of customs and practices had been incorporated into regional centers, and these were based on various interpretations of what was normative. In Medina, for example, a school of Islamic law was developing based on local practice and in view of the interpretations of scripture and hadith reports known locally. It was expressed in the work of Malik ibn Anas (d. 796), around which developed what is referred to as the Maliki school of law. Another center, with different local customs and different hadith reports, grew up in Kufa: the school of Abu Hanifa (d. 767), largely developed by Abu Yusuf (d. 798) and al-Shaybani (d. 804), known as the Hanafi school. The development of these schools was essentially democratic; determination of what was normative in the Qur'an and Sunna was based on local consensus, or *ijma*. And in cases where there were no apparently applicable precedents in the Qur'an or Sunna, legal scholars were to use their discretion to determine the implications of what they did find in revelation and tradition with regard to the novel situation. They were to practice ijtihad. The 'Abbasids' incorporation of legal scholars into the imperial administration, however, made the practice of determining issues on the basis of regional consensus—and the inevitable differences of consensual opinion among the various regions—problematic. The need became apparent for greater rigor in legal thought, with the goal of greater uniformity of practice throughout the empire. The scope of ijma, accordingly, was expanded geographically in theory, and limited demographically in practice. Al-Shafi'i (d. 820), founder of the third school of Sunni law, determined to systematize Islamic legal theory and regularize its practice, set out the Qur'an and the Sunna as the first two sources of legislation, and decided that only the consensus of the entire Islamic community, not just the various regions, was authoritative.[14]

Another major step in the process of limiting ijtihad, again resulting from efforts to regularize Islamic law, was the elevation of the Sunna from a source of precedent complementary to the Qur'an to an authoritative source of revelation in light of which the Qur'an was to be interpreted. Indeed, for al-Shafi'i, the third source of Islamic law was consensus regarding the meaning of the Qur'an as interpreted in light of hadith reports, themselves identified, interpreted, and determined authoritative on the basis of consensus, rather than local agreement on appropriate behavior in particular situations. Al-Shafi'i conceded that ijtihad could be practiced as a final resort, after exhaustive searches for precedent in the Qur'an and Sunna, but that any intellectual effort to determine the implications fo the Qur'an and Sunna was to be based on syllogistic reasoning (qiyas), rather than the freer exercise of independent juristic judgment called *ra'y* (juristic opinion), which was characteristic of the earlier schools of thought. The first premise of each syllogism, furthermore, was to be a principle already established as such by consensus; new principles were not to result from qiyas.

Al-Shafiʿi's point was to regularize the practice of ijtihad and to eliminate loopholes characteristic of what he considered less rigorous approaches to legislation. In the Hanafi school, for example, jurisprudents
were allowed to exercise their "juristic preference," that is, to make
exceptions to strict analogical reasoning when they determined that the
spirit of the law would not be served by following its letter. Similarly,
the Malikis maintained that legists must take into consideration the effect of strict application of precedent on the overall public well-being,
and, where necessary, reason independently to maintain it.[15] But al-
Shafiʿi stressed the need to find precedents. This naturally encouraged
an effort to collect, authenticate, and organize the hadith reports that
would constitute the body of precedents available. Of six collections of
hadith reports, all organized according to category, two were determined to be authoritative, that is, to contain reports that could be considered reliable on the basis of having been reported by authenticated
"chains" of trustworthy witnesses traceable to their original sources
(the Prophet or his closest companions). These were the collections of
al-Bukhari (d. 870) and Muslim (d. 875). The other collections, with
weaker claims of authenticity, were still instructive, but were to be used
with greater circumspection. Under the influence of the trend toward
greater rigor in juristic reasoning, these official collections of hadith reports came to represent for many the Sunna itself, the normative practice of Prophet Muhammad, and were for some, because of their interpretive role, more important than the Qurʾan.

Although there was a good deal of resistance to al-Shafiʿi's emphasis
on the interpretive role for the Sunna, a fourth school of Islamic law
eventually developed which placed even greater emphasis on the Sunna.
To al-Shafiʿi's student Ahmad Ibn Hanbal (d. 855) was attributed the
origin of what is now called the Hanbali school. In fact, Ahmad Ibn
Hanbal placed so much emphasis on the Sunna that he and his followers were not immediately known as legists, but rather as hadith collectors. Eventually, however, as they began to accept juristic reasoning, at
least in the absence of Qurʾanic or traditional precedent and in the form
of analogical reasoning (qiyas) described above, the Hanbalis were accepted as one of the four official schools of Sunni law.

In another development associated with the institutionalization of Islamic law, the qualifications for practice of ijtihad were themselves determined—again, by the consensus of those who had already determined themselves capable of establishing precedents binding on
subsequent generations. They include knowledge of the Qurʾan and hadith literature; the ability to verify hadith reports by examining the
claims of the transmitters; training in the principles of syllogistic reasoning; thorough knowledge of Arabic grammar and style; knowledge of
the customary law of the region in which the proposed legislation
would go into effect; knowledge of the precedents already established
at least in the school of law in which one was working; and knowledge

of God's attributes. Later accounts differed on minor details but maintained general agreement, particularly on the fact that the officially recognized legists were the only legitimate practitioners of ijtihad.[16] They were the ones to determine who could or could not engage in authoritative interpretation of the sources of Islamic law, a situation which made it unlikely that thinkers who disagreed with their opinions would gain the position from which to undermine them. Most scholars allowed that one could qualify for ijtihad by mastering limited areas of law, rather than by the more formidable method of gaining expertise in all areas of law, but the requirements for the practice of ijtihad as such remained virtually unchallenged until the present century.[17]

Furthermore, at some point, perhaps as early as the tenth century, the officially recognized legal scholars were able to institutionalize agreement that all the essential ijtihad had been done, that all the methodologies of Islamic jurisprudence had been articulated, and that the qualifications required for the kind of ijtihad necessary to initiate another school of law ("absolute" ijtihad) were no longer attainable. Legal scholars from the four officially recognized schools of Sunni thought in place at that time—the Hanafi, Maliki, Shafi'i, and Hanbali—apparently agreed among themselves that these four ways of looking at the Qur'an and the Sunna were sufficient to meet the needs of the community and guide them to fulfill the will of God for the rest of human history. As Joseph Schacht characterized it:

> By the beginning of the fourth century of the hijra (about 900 [C.E.]) . . . the point had been reached when the scholars of all schools felt that all essential questions had been thoroughly discussed and finally settled, and a consensus gradually established itself to the effect that from that time onwards no one might be deemed to have the necessary qualifications for independent reasoning in law, and that all future activity would have to be confined to the explanation, application, and, at the most, interpretation of the doctrine as it had been laid down once and for all.[18]

Such was the ultimate effect of narrowing the scope of ijtihad. Indeed, from the tenth century, so well established was the practice of legislating on the basis of precedent—known as *taqlid*—that even if a scholar exercised independent reasoning, which was inevitable, he attributed his work to a revered predecessor. The idea that all the really important reasoning in religious law had been done by the respected elders of the past became as pervasive in Islam as it still is in Eurocentric Roman Catholicism. Scholars debate about when the "door of ijtihad" closed—as this gradual restriction of independent reasoning is generally called—but there is little doubt that eventually the shift did occur.[19] Even though there were critics of this limitation of ijtihad as early as the ninth century, it appears that the lack of individuals capable of practicing ijtihad was gradually accepted, even if on a theoretical level ijtihad was still considered necessary.[20] Indeed, hadith reports began to circulate rationalizing the diminished vitality of the Muslim community resulting from taqlid.[21] This seems to have been the context in which the related hadith noted above, claiming that God will send a renewer (mujaddid) at the beginnning of each century, gained currency. Ijtihad may no longer be practicable, but, when necessary, God will provide patriarchal figures, as Pakistani revivalist Abu'l Aʿla Mawdudi described them: "[S]trong men, groups of men and institutions which could change the course of the times and bring the world round to bow before the authority of the One, Almighty."[22] Hallaq says belief in mujaddids was popular, especially among the Shafiʿis and Hanbalis, who maintained the belief in the need for ijtihad, since at least the eleventh century. According to Hallaq, that was their way of arguing for the continuation of ijtihad, since at least the mujaddid would have to be able to reason independently. But on the popular level, belief in a mujaddid served the opposite purpose: it relieved all others of the responsibility for ijtihad. In place of the self-confidence of ijtihad grew a dependence on the promised mujaddids.

In Support of Ijtihad

The negative effects of diminished ijtihad were obvious as early as the eleventh century, when Shafiʿi scholar al-Ghazali called for "revival of religious sciences" (*Ihyaʾ ʿulum al-din,* the title of his magnum opus).[23] But by far the most renowned advocate of the necessity of ijtihad for the vitality of the Muslim community was thirteenth-century Hanbali jurist Ibn Taymiyya (d. 1328). For Ibn Taymiyya, the distinction between Shariʿa (God's will for human beings) and fiqh (the laws human beings devise) was essential. He criticized those who confused the two:

People who [confuse Shariʿa and fiqh] do not understand clearly the distinction in the meanings of the word Shariʿa as employed in the Speech of God and His Apostle (on the one hand) and by common people on the other. . . . Indeed, some of them think that Shariʿa is the name given to the judge's decisions; many of them even do not make a distinction between a learned judge, an ignorant judge and an unjust judge. Worse still, people tend to regard any decrees of a ruler as Shariʿa, while sometimes undoubtedly the truth (*haqiqa*) is actually contrary to the decree of the ruler.

The Prophet himself said, "You people bring disputes to me; but it may be that some of you are able to put their case better than others. But I have to decide on evidence that is before me. If I happen to expropriate the right of anyone in favor of his brother let the latter not take it, for in that case I have given him a piece of hell-fire." Thus, the judge decided on the strength of depositions and evidence that are before him while the party decided against may well have proofs that have not been put forward. In such cases the Shariʿa in reality is just the opposite of the external law, although the decision of the judge has to be enforced.[24]

Ibn Taymiyya realized that the judgment of humans is fallible.[25] Furthermore, even a valid judgment is subject to amendment in light of new evidence. Therefore, Islamic law must remain flexible. For that reason, Ibn Taymiyya was opposed to wholesale taqlid, indiscriminate imitation of legal precedents. A devoted follower of Ahmad Ibn Hanbal, Ibn Taymiyya did not deny authoritative judgments—determined on the basis of consensus—by the eponyms of the four schools of Sunni law.[26] But he said that given the vast extent of the Islamic community by the time in which he was working, consensus among the legal scholars was no longer feasible. Even if it were, he said that would not relieve qualified jurists of the responsibility to examine all evidence in every case and all pertinent arguments in their own schools as well as others, and then determine on the basis of the Qur'an and the Sunna the most suitable judgment. If the jurist determines that there exists a precedent resonant with the spirit of revealed truth, that precedent should be applied regardless of the school of law in which it is found. If he does not find an appropriate precedent, he should not hesitate to judge independently—to exercise ijtihad—in accordance with the principles he has determined most conducive to justice.[27] The direct relationship envisioned here is between the jurist and revelation; no human authority should serve as a filter for the qualified jurist. Only those untrained in Islamic law are allowed (indeed, obliged) to follow the teachings of human authorities.

For Ibn Taymiyya, careful scrutiny of the cumulative tradition of Islamic law was essential to the life of the Muslim community. The fact that an opinion may have been suitable at a given time and place was no guarantee that it would be suitable in another time and place. That is why he rejected taqlid. To convince others of the point, he called upon the witness of the very scholars being imitated: "[T]he imams themselves have demonstrably admonished the people against their imitation and commanded that if they found stronger evidence in the Qur'an or in the Sunna, they should prefer it to their own."[28] In all cases, it must be the Qur'an that determines a judgment. In particular, he cites Malik and al-Shafi'i, as well as the first caliph, Abu Bakr: "Follow me where I obey God; but if I disobey Him, you owe me no obedience." The founder of his own school, Ibn Hanbal, is quoted: "Do not imitate me or Malik or Shafi'i or al-Thawri, but investigate as we have investigated."[29] Thus, ijtihad was for Ibn Taymiyya not only perennially possible but essential to the practice of Islam.

Such insistence on the necessity of ijtihad notwithstanding, the ethic of taqlid continued to dominate. Islamic law continued to be practiced, of course, but its scope and creativity were severely limited. Even those who argued for the continuation of ijtihad did so, with few exceptions, within the very restricted framework established by the legal scholars. They did not question the limitation of ijtihad to those trained and accredited according to the criteria described above, nor did they question the limitation of ijtihad to analogical reasoning on principles already determined by the respected ancestors to be normative, or the cessation of absolute ijtihad.

It is not until the eighteenth century that we find in the work of Ibn ʿAbd al-Wahhab (d. 1787/92) of the Arabian peninsula a revival of Ibn Taymiyya's rejection of taqlid and a call for the renewal of ijtihad. This theme was echoed in the subcontinent by his younger contemporary Shah Wali Allah of Delhi (d. 1762). But as twentieth-century ijtihadist Fazlur Rahman (Chapter 4) points out, their efforts tended to be self-defeating in that they involved a concomitant rejection of what was considered to be excessive intellectualism, such as that found among philosophers and other intellectuals not a part of the legal establishment.[30] The rejection of intellectualism, Fazlur Rahman believed, ultimately undermined calls for ijtihad, so that even these reformers became *muqallidun,* indiscriminate imitators of precedent. Furthermore, like other proponents of ijtihad, the Wahhabis were attacked by the ʿulamaʾ (religious scholars) for their rejection of the authority of the medieval heritage (rejection of taqlid). In any case, the Wahhabi movement was confined ultimately to the Arabian peninsula, and the state built upon ʿAbd al-Wahhab's alliance with Ibn Saud is generally known as one of the most conservative in the Muslim world. Shah Wali Allah of Delhi worked to reform Muslim education, extricating what he considered superstition and especially the nonrationality of taqlid.[31] But again, under the influence of Sayyid Ahmad of Rae Bareli, his movement was transformed into a more conservative one, emphasizing, as did the Wahhabis, "pure" Islamic practice, which became in effect imitative of a "golden age" of Islam.

Another scholar influenced by Ibn Taymiyya's ijtihadism was the Yemeni Shiʿi Muhammad b. ʿAli al-Shawkani (d. 1834). He claimed that ijtihad must and in fact does continue, but that since the twelfth and thirteenth centuries it has not been recognized as such, thanks to the ethic of taqlid.[32] Other reformers could be mentioned, such as Muhammad b. Ismaʿil al-Sanʿani (d. 1768) and Ahmad ibn Idris (d. 1837), who worked to unlock the doors of ijtihad. But again, as with the Arabian Wahhabis, their efforts were not sufficient to overcome insititutionalized taqlid. Indeed, with the onslaught of European colonialism came a further limitation of the jurisdiction of Islamic courts. Coulson notes that nineteenth-century developments in the Ottoman lands in particular resulted in the removal of criminal and commercial cases from Shariʿa courts.[33] The increasing westernization of law codes in the various regions under colonial domination left only family law and sometimes administration of *waqf* endowments (charitable trusts) to Shariʿa courts. Perhaps this further enfeebling of Islamic law is what led to intensified calls for the revival of ijtihad. Eventually, in a profound departure from earlier approaches and a shift that opened the floodgates

of intellectual renewal in twentieth-century Islam, even the limitation of
ijtihad to officially recognized religious scholars was questioned. Interestingly, this came from within the ranks of officially recognized religious scholars themselves, in the work of Egyptian scholar Muhammad
ʿAbduh (d. 1905).

ʿAbduh undertook a systematic exposition of the Qurʾan and, as Ibn
Taymiyya had, identified its core teaching as *tawhid*, literally "making
one," but generally taken as referring both to monotheism and to God's
simple or unitary nature. The concept had always been at the core of
kalam, Islam's scholastic theological tradition.[34] But ʿAbduh refocused
Muslim attention on tawhid. Extrapolating from the theological level to
the practical, he identified the rationality of the universe as a reflection
of divine unity. Rather than being incomprehensible or separate from
the sphere of spiritual endeavor, the world for ʿAbduh was preemi-
nently the proper sphere of Islamic endeavor. Accordingly, exercise of
the human capacity to understand was a form of worship, an integral
part of Islamic practice. Conversely, failure to exercise human rationality comprised religious laxity. He held that we not only can but must
scrutinize our surroundings. Divinity manifests itself in the natural
world; the challenge of human existence is that we make divinity manifest in the world of human device. In this context, ʿAbduh identified
reliance on simple imitation of precedent (taqlid) over the exercise of
reason as the essential failing of pre-Islamic religious communities:

> So the Qurʾan directs us, enjoining rational procedure and intellectual en-
> quiry into the manifestations of the universe, and, as far as may be, into its
> particulars, so as to come by certainty in respect of the things to which it
> guides. It forbids us to be slavishly credulous and for our stimulus points
> [to] the moral of peoples who simply followed their fathers with complacent
> satisfaction and were finally involved in an utter collapse of their beliefs and
> their own disappearance as a community. Well it is said that traditionalism
> can have evil consequences as well as good and may occasion loss as well as
> conduce to gain. It is a deceptive thing, and though it may be pardoned in an
> animal, is scarcely seemly in man.[35]

ʿAbduh believed that ongoing rational endeavor, particularly critique
of tradition and creative response to historical circumstances, reflects
the true spirit of Islam. But he thought that spirit had been suppressed
through traditionalism, with drastic consequences. Criticizing the idea
popular among conservative ʿulamaʾ that successive generations of
Muslims are divinely predestined to become increasingly degenerate, he
says, "They took to assuming that there was an inherent impracticabil-
ity in [religion's] commands."[36] The "custodians of religion" became
an elite, and the rest of the people fell into "slavish imitation of the
ancestors." This, with the encouragement of misguided leaders who
said, "'Nay! We will follow what we found our fathers doing' (Surah
31:21) and 'We found our fathers so as a people and we will stay the

same as they' (Surah 43:22)."[37] By contrast, ʿAbduh believed that Islam actually liberates the "authority of reason . . . from every kind of taqlid enslaving it." Indeed, he believed Islam perfected humanity, precisely by allowing the exercise of free will and by demanding "independence of thought and opinion."[38] He acknowledged that not everything is subject to human comprehension. He noted that such things as the divine attributes and details regarding modes of worship were not simply matters of empirical deduction. However, he cautions, "[T]his must be in such wise as not to shake man's confidence or deprive him of his assurance about reason as a God-given power."[39]

ʿAbduh was well aware of the discrepancy between his vision of Islamic rationality and the reality as it had developed by the late nineteenth century. He was also aware of the unsuccessful efforts by earlier scholars to counter the stultifying ethic of taqlid. He therefore took a critical step beyond the traditional calls for reactivation of independent reasoning by jurists. Jurists, he believed, were responsible for the stultification in the first place. "The larger part of the specialists," he says, "are afflicted with the disease of traditionalism (taqlid)."[40] Referring to them as "temple custodians," he says that they jealously guard against reason. "Sleep on," he paraphrases their advice to would-be practitioners of ijtihad; "the night is pitch dark, the way is rough and the goal distant, and the rest is scant and there's poor provision for the road."[41] He felt, therefore, that there was no choice but to challenge their monopoly on independent reasoning. In support of his challenge, he calls upon the Qurʾan: "[The Qurʾan] characterizes [the friends of truth] as those who weigh all that is said, irrespective of who the speakers are, in order to follow what they know to be good and reject what gives evidence of having neither validity nor use."[42]

ʿAbduh goes on to specify that anyone who accepts Islam's basic ethical teachings, and specifically those relating to reward or punishment in the afterlife, is capable of understanding the Qurʾan, which for him means "rational exegesis" or interpretation.[43] This does not mean, he adds, that such people's interpretations are binding on others. But this is a codicil added only in light of the religious scholars' belief that there are such things as fixed, unalterable, ultimate interpretations of revelation. In fact, ʿAbduh proclaims, Islam rejects the idea of fixed interpretations of revelation. All individuals are at least potentially capable of independent reasoning and must work to be able to achieve that potential: "Islam laid upon every adherent of religion the duty of taking seriously the knowledge of revelation and of God's law. It finds all men [*sic*] equally so bound and able, on condition of the necessary readiness—a condition readily attainable by the vast majority of believers and in no way confined to a particular class or a peculiar time."[44]

Perhaps more than any other single development, this revolutionary challenge to the religious establishment's monopoly on ijtihad set the stage for twentieth-century reformist thought in Islam.[45] By the time of ʿAbduh's generation, Muslim thinkers had been grappling with the challenges of institutionalized religious thought for ten centuries. The achievement of Islam's goals of social justice seemed to demand practical involvement in social structures. But how to maintain the necessary openness to change and responsiveness to new circumstances within an institutional framework? The proponents of ijtihad throughout the centuries found the answer in a hermeneutic that recognized the impact of practical considerations on human judgment and therefore stressed the need for continual reassessment of the community's intellectual heritage. But until the twentieth century their persistent pleas had not been sufficient to overcome institutional inertia. And the Muslim world had lost its vitality, eventually being overcome by foreign powers. ʿAbduh's Egypt was actually controlled by Britain, despite being nominally still a part of the Ottoman empire. British India had designs on Iraq and the lands surrounding the Persian Gulf. Much of North Africa was under French control, and France had established a strong foothold in Ottoman Syria as well. European Zionists' increasing immigration into Palestine appeared to be part of the same pattern. The Islamic world was clearly in steep decline, and virtually every intellectual of note addressed the obvious questions that condition raised. It was in this context that Muhammad ʿAbduh struck at the very heart of the institutionalized lethargy, his own religious elite, who had naturally resisted challenges to their authority. His immediate inspiration had been the fiery anti-imperialist Jamal al-Din al-Afghani (d. 1897), and ʿAbduh was succeeded by a number of other capable advocates of renewal in Islam—such as Farid Wajdi, ʿAli ʿAbd al-Raziq, and Qasim Amin—all looking for the key both to Islamic society's original strength and its current weakness.[46] But ʿAbduh breaks with traditional advocates of ijtihad by challenging the monopoly held by religious scholars on legal thought. Still, that challenge is in the spirit of the earlier reforms, and in many ways merely a logical extension of them.

The same kind of development occurred in the subcontinent in the work of Muhammad Iqbal (d. 1938). Iqbal, who had studied at Cambridge and Heidelberg universities and had completed his doctoral degree in philosophy at Munich, was well versed in European philosophy. As he makes clear in *The Reconstruction of Religious Thought in Islam* (1934), he accepts fully the cognitive uncertainty that characterizes postmodern thought, and advises that the search for cognitive certainty is bound to fail; the proper human goal is moral certainty rather than cognitive certainty, and that is to be found only in the realm of spiritual experience. But even for Iqbal, of equal importance are the practical aspects of life. And in that sphere what is necessary is the revival of Islamic thinking—as his title, reminiscent of al-Ghazali's twelfth-century *Revivification of the Religious Sciences*—indicates.

Muhammad Iqbal wants to make Islam "essentially a mode of actual living" again, in the face of the stagnation that has overcome it. He claims, "During the last five hundred years religious thought in Islam has been practically stationary."[47] Therefore, "Surely, it is high time to look to the essentials of Islam." Again, "The Qur'an opens our eyes to the great fact of change, through the appreciation and control of which alone it is possible to build a durable civilization."[48] But Islam's essential responsiveness and adaptability were replaced with inertia. This Iqbal attributes to "localization," whereby the interpretations produced in specific places and times were assumed to apply to all places and for all times.[49] But this localization is contrary to the spirit of Islam: "[E]ternal principles when they are understood to exclude all possibilities of change which, according to the Qur'an, is one of the greatest 'signs' of God, tend to immobilize what is essentially mobile in its nature."[50] A corrective is needed, he felt, in order to recapture Islam's dynamism: "What then is the principle of movement in the structure of Islam? This is known as ijtihad."[51]

Iqbal, like his predecessors as far back as Ibn Taymiyya, was convinced that ijtihad is an interpretive principle integral to Islam and essential for its social role.[52] Discussing the sources of ijtihad, Iqbal refers to several early legal authorities and relates one of the most common traditional justifications:

> When Mu'adh was appointed ruler of Yemen, the Prophet is reported to have asked him as to how he would decide matters coming up before him. "I will judge matters according to the Book of God," said Mu'adh. "But if the Book of God contains nothing to guide you?" "Then I will act on he precedents of the Prophet of God." "But if the precedents fail?" "Then I will exert to form my own judgment."[53]

Iqbal therefore questions the restriction of ijtihad—even absolute ijtihad—to the founders of the official schools of law by means of qualifications "hedged round by conditions which are well-nigh impossible of realization in a single individual." He chastises the jurisprudents' "fear of rationalism," which he believes is at the heart of Islam's stagnation. He says it resulted from their concern for social solidarity and control, a concern heightened by the fall of Baghdad in the thirteenth century. He also criticizes the Sufi mystics' excessive emphasis on inner meaning, which resulted in a lack of concern with the practical world.[54] He criticizes as well the relegation of Islam's ongoing renewal to the mujaddids, which he believes emerged only in the sixteenth century.[55] And he finds fault with the Wahhabi movement's uncritical rejection of the finality of the four official schools of fiqh. "While it rises in revolt against the finality of the schools, and vigorously asserts the right of private judgement, its vision of the past is wholly uncritical, and in matters of law it mainly falls back on the traditions of the Prophet."[56] What he wants to promote is "healthy conservative criticism."[57] In his view, "The teaching of the Qur'an that life is a process of progressive creation necessitates that each generation, guided but unhampered by the work of its predecessors, should be permitted to solve its own problems."[58]

Iqbal also rejects, as had ʿAbduh, the idea of decline in later generations' capacity to exercise ijtihad. He quotes approvingly Shafiʿi jurist Zarkashi (d. 1392):

> If the upholders of this fiction mean that the previous writers had more facilities, while the later writers had more difficulties in their way, it is nonsense; for it does not require much understanding to see that ijtihad for later doctors is easier than for the earlier doctors. Indeed, the commentaries on the Qurʾan and the sunnah have been compiled and multiplied to such an extent that the mujtahid [practitioner of ijtihad] of today has more material for interpretation than he needs.[59]

Similarly, Iqbal believes qiyas (the use of analogical reasoning to determine the application of Islamic teachings) is in need of certain correctives. He believes life is too complex and unpredictable to "be subjected to hard and fast rules logically deducible from certain general notions." Besides, he believes the inclusion of qiyas in the first place was "a mere disguise for the mujtahid's personal opinion."[60] Indeed, he continues, the true meaning of qiyas, "as Shafiʿi rightly says, is only another name for ijtihad which, within the limits of the revealed texts, is absolutely free." He concludes with perhaps his most pointed statement on ijtihad:

> [I]ts importance as a principle can be seen from the fact that, according to most of the doctors, as Qadi Shaukani tells us, it was permitted even in the lifetime of the Holy Prophet. The closing of the door of ijtihad is pure fiction suggested partly by the crystallization of legal thought in Islam, and partly by that intellectual laziness which, especially in the period of spiritual decay, turns great thinkers into idols. If some of the later doctors have upheld this fiction, modern Islam is not bound by this voluntary surrender of intellectual independence.[61]

Therefore, Iqbal believes the ongoing practice of ijtihad among an educated populace can and should be made part of the institutionalized Islamic world. Again, it was for political reasons that it was not done in the early days of Islam: "It was, I think, favorable to the interest of the Umayyad and the ʿAbbasid caliphs to leave the power of ijtihad to individual mujtahids rather than encourage the formation of a permanent assembly which might become too powerful for them."[62] He calls for "transfer of the power of ijtihad from individual representatives of schools to a Muslim legislative assembly." That, he believes, is the only way to secure ijmaʿ, consensus, which is necessary for Islamic legislation. It will also put responsibility for ijtihad where Iqbal thinks it belongs, with laypeople "who happen to possess a keen insight into affairs."[63]

The work of ʿAbduh and Iqbal is very representative of the mood of the Muslim world at the time when Jawzi wrote. It was an era charged with intellectual energy and demands for critical reassessment of the

Islamic heritage in light of changed circumstances, and that critical reassessment is just what Jawzi produced. He was no doubt influenced by Islamic socialism in general and Sultangalievism in particular. But these provided neither the motivation nor the essence of Jawzi's analysis. Owing to the openness of the intellectual atmosphere, Marxian analysis was an acceptable tool, but it was only a tool. As the following survey of *The History of Intellectual Movements in Islam* shows, Jawzi's goal was to help the "Arab youth"—to whom he dedicates the work—understand their heritage in order to direct their society toward a future in keeping with Islamic goals of social justice.

3

Bandali Jawzi's Hermeneutics

Bandali Jawzi's *Min Taʾrikh al-Harakat al-Fikriyyah fiʾl-Islam* (*"The History of Intellectual Movements in Islam;* Jerusalem, 1928) is part one ("The Social Movements") of what was intended to be a two-part work. It consists of five chapters, tracing the nature of Islamic social values and their fate at the hands of various regimes from the Umayyad and ʿAbbasid caliphates (661–750 c.e. and 750–1258 c.e., respectively) to the constitutional movement in Iran in the early twentieth century. Throughout, Jawzi characterizes Islam as a social reform demanding the end of oppression. The exigencies of power politics under the dynastic caliphates, according to his portrayal, vitiated and actually distorted that message, until it was virtually unrecognizable in any practical form. But Islam's egalitarian spirit was kept alive, Jawzi argues, in various reform movements throughout Islamic history.

Jawzi focuses in particular on the Babakis, the Qaramatis, and the Ismaʿilis. These movements were motivated, Jawzi argues, by demands for social justice entirely in keeping with Islamic principles. They challenged the caliphal authorities because of inequities in the imperial system. Jawzi considers it perfectly natural that the official historians and heresiographers of the eras in question would condemn these movements as rebellious; those whose reports were promulgated and passed down through the ages to become the accepted wisdom of later scholars were actually spokespeople for the caliphal authorities. Just as naturally, reports sympathetic to the rebellious movements, such as their own manifestos, would be marginalized or suppressed. The bulk of

Jawzi's analysis, therefore, is devoted to efforts to reconstruct descriptions of the three subject movements that are untainted by caliphal political concerns. In that process, Jawzi takes to task the official reports in places where they deviate from what he considers more reliable evidence.

Jawzi introduces his book with a chapter entitled "The Unity of Social Laws," in which he criticizes European scholarship of Islam and makes clear his own approach to the texts. Using historians Barthold Georg Niebuhr (d. 1831), Leopold von Ranke (d. 1886), and Friedrich Schlosser (d. 1861) as examples of defective work, he criticizes first of all their ignorance of "the East" or "the Orient." Because of their lack of information, he says, they based their opinions on the history of the West, assuming it as a model of development. Jawzi's history, he believes, will help correct some of the misinformation spread by these "orientalists."

But beyond their simple ignorance, Jawzi points out a number of methodological errors made by the orientalists. The first is exemplified in a statement he attributes to Schlosser: "The most important difference between the history of the West and that of the East is that religions and religious rites and literature, state and civil organization, even the arts themselves, are based in the eastern states—charged as they are with the spirit of autocracy and religious authority—on the rejection of social and cultural evolution, as well as the influence of Western civilization." (All quotations herein from Jawzi's work are taken from the translation, part II in this volume.) Allegations that an entire people are "charged . . . with the spirit of autocracy and religious authority" and reject "social and cultural evolution," are automatically suspect to Jawzi. Such sweeping generalizations are patently oversimplifications at the very least; Jawzi does not even bother to refute the statements on factual grounds. More importantly, he sees them as a kind of error of synecdoche. Synecdoche (taking a part to stand for the whole) may work as a figure of speech, but it is utterly out of place as a historical methodology. As he puts it: "According to this view, then, one need know only a short period in the life of an ancient eastern nation; one can extrapolate from that to discover its overall conditions, regardless of how long it has existed or how many internal changes it has undergone."

Jawzi then quotes (without attribution) a description of the method he is criticizing: "For there is no need to know the history of a nation in its entirety in order to understand its social condition in a long period passed under the rule of one dynasty and one sky." He dismisses this approach as preposterous. For Jawzi it goes without saying that every age has its peculiarities and that generalizations about one age that are based on another age are bound to be inaccurate.

In the same vein, he discusses the view of "another historian, renowned for his studies on the history of the ancient Near East" (probably Gustave LeBon or Hugo Winckler) that all Arabs believe in astrology, reject empirical investigation, and base all their judgments on the authority of revered ancestors. Again, the problem with this kind of analysis is that it assumes that entire civilizations can be judged on the basis of samplings from a single era or locale. It may well be that some Arabs believe in astrology or reject the authority of scientific method, but that does not mean that all Arabs do so.

On a more specific level, Jawzi continues his critique of the methodology:

> Now, the teaching of the above-mentioned scholars was on the history of ancient [near] Eastern nations, like Babylonia, Assyria and Egypt, etc. But can this be applied to modern history as well, or even to the Middle Ages? Some [historians], influenced by the thoughts of Schlosser and [German archaeologist Hugo] Winckler, tried to do just that: to judge the medieval history of Eastern nations, even their modern history, and particularly the history of Islam, on the basis of ancient history. The best known of those who attempted this was the French orientalist Ernst Renan, in some of his lectures on Judaism and Islam, particularly "Islam and Progress" and "The Position of Semitic Nations among Other Nations." Here is what he said in the latter with regard to our subject: "Islam detests science and calls for the destruction of civil society. It is nothing but the terrible simplicity of the Semitic spirit which oppresses the brain of man and obstructs the way of all free thought and scientific investigation, exchanging for all that the boring repetition of the *shahada* [Muslim declaration of faith in God and Prophet Muhammad]."

Jawzi's criticism therefore goes beyond mere rejection of negative stereotypes. He attributes the formulation of stereotypes in the first place to what he believes to be the interpretive error of letting the part represent the whole. The second error of the orientalists is related to the first: the failure to recognize that societies change from place to place and through time. As Jawzi put it, "[T]he inability [of the orientalist scholars] to analyze the available historical materials" results from "bas[ing] their judgment of the future of Eastern nations on their social and cultural situation in the past." He considers this "totally inaccurate in the view of rational people. . . . It is as if a Muslim Arab of the tenth or eleventh century were to visit Europe at that time and, seeing the ignorance, religious fanaticism, and poverty of its inhabitants, pass sentence on their future by saying that they would never have social life in the modern sense of the word." In Jawzi's view, it is clear that peoples change through history. In order to understand any given report, one must understand the material and cultural conditions of the time and place in which the report was produced, as well as the position of the reporter within that context.

This last refinement is closely related to Jawzi's third conviction regarding appropriate historical methodologies: that all societies are equally affected by historic conditions and that similar conditions tend to result in similar social developments. He considers Schlosser's statement that "[t]here has never been and will never be for the nations of the East 'history' in the sense accepted today among European scholars" to be ridiculous. He paraphrases another Western scholar, probably Renan, in a similar vein: "The factors affecting Western society are different from those affecting the history, culture and lives of Eastern nations." In both cases, Jawzi sees a failure to recognize that the same kinds of factors affect all societies.

Referring specifically to Renan, Jawzi quotes another example of the kind of analyses resulting from failure to accept this principle:

> "The Arian peoples have had from the dawn of their history an ancient code of rights. . . . But as for the life of the Arabs and (ancient) Jews, they have always been subject to other laws." Elsewhere: "The religious development of the Semitic nations has always been based on other laws." And, "The Arab or Muslim today is without exception more remote from us than ever. For the Muslim and the European today are two different personalities, sharing nothing in common with regard to modes of thought and feeling, as if they were of two different worlds." Renan repeated these ideas in his second lecture even more vehemently, but we have confined ourselves to the above.

Jawzi considers it fortunate that "no one today accords [such opinions] much importance." As anyone who has read John Esposito's *The Islamic Threat: Myth or Reality?* will recognize, Jawzi's optimism was somewhat misplaced. Nevertheless, he found many scholars in his day had overcome the problems that afflicted the early orientalists, and indeed makes use of the works of some European scholars in his own analyses.

In contrast to Renan's view, Jawzi presents the view of Soviet historian V. V. Bartol'd:

> He said in his book *History of Research on the East in the West and Russia*: "If the Eastern nations approached anything like the simplicity and lack of dynamism that some historians of the West attribute to them, the investigation and understanding of Eastern history would be easier than that of Western history for orientalists who study the later ages, to whom more historical sources are available than to their predecessors. [But in fact] they see that the number of people of perfectly monolithic character in the East does not exceed their likes in the West. Their religion and its rituals, just as in the West, necessarily conform to the actual conditions of life, more so than vice versa. And often there arose under the banner of religion movements whose sources were economic or political factors, not religious, as we had previously thought."

Furthermore, continues Jawzi:

> More important than that, most European scholars are now beginning to declare that religion had no effect on the decline of civilization in the Eastern nations. This temporary decline was due to factors other than religion, the most important of which were the following: immigration and conquests by Barbarian nations (the Mongols, Turks, etc.); the Crusades; the growth of

new cultural centers far from the old ones; the shift in trade routes. These and other factors are familiar even to students in secondary schools.

Jawzi's point is that responsible histories must be based on universally applicable principles of social change, among them, that historic conditions affect how people think about things and organize their lives. In fact, Jawzi describes this conviction as one of his reasons for writing the book in the first place:

> [T]he history of the East, the social and intellectual life of its people in general, and that of the Islamic people in particular, are subject to the same laws and factors to which the life and history of the Western nations are subject. The nations of the East have passed and will continue to pass through the same social stages and changes as Western nations. For there is no difference in this sense between the East and the West, and one is not innately superior to the other. This is in part what we will try to elucidate in this book.

In other words, it is not so much what people think that determines their history, but their history that determines—at least partly—what they think. This was by way of refuting orientalists' claim that Islam, or something else endemic to Semitic consciousness, accounts for current conditions in the Muslim world. Europeans like Max Weber believed that "the Protestant ethic" was necessary for economic development; Muslims' preindustrial economies were therefore considered to be a permanent condition resulting from a lack of that ethic. Jawzi was convinced instead that Muslims' preindustrial condition was a result, at least in part, of waves of foreign invasions and their subjugation to foreign powers.

Yet Jawzi is not a complete economic or material determinist. He does not underestimate the power of ideology to influence people's actions. In fact, throughout his analysis he expresses admiration for those who withstood the lure of power and remained true to Islamic principles of social justice. Although they were in the minority, for Jawzi they are far more representative of Islam than the majority who succumbed, intentionally or by default, to the dominant power system. Clearly, in Jawzi's view, devotion to higher principles can be effective against indoctrination.

Furthermore, at the conclusion of his analysis he expresses confidence in what he regards as his contemporary Arabs' "cultural reawakening and heightened consciousness." He is referring to renewed commitment to the Islamic principles central to his own discussion, as well as that of other reformers active in his time. He believes that in this state of objectivity and clear understanding of their own heritage, Arabs will be able to cast off the bonds that have kept them subjugated in preindustrial conditions. He considers it clear that Arab Islamic society is about to embark on industrialization, which will inevitably involve social changes, as it did in Europe. Among those developments, his socialist orientation implies, will be exploitation of labor. But, he predicts, given the example of Europe's industrialization and Muslims' renewed commitment to social justice, the Arabs' era of unfettered capitalism will quickly give way to socialism:

> It seems to me that what I have mentioned regarding the social and socialistic movements in Islam—only a small part of the whole—is sufficient to satisfy the unprejudiced reader that the Eastern nations in general, and the Arab Islamic ones in particular, have passed through the same social stages as the nations of the Christian West. We are therefore convinced that our Arab people must pass in the near future through the same social stage now being experienced by Western nations—our brothers in humanity who have preceded us due to their good fortune and historical role. And we hope, based on the cultural reawakening and heightened consciousness we see today in the East, that it will be short.

Within this framework, Jawzi embarks on his analysis of Islamic reform movements and their negative characterization by historians who were accepted as authoritative. Despite his introductory critique of orientalists and their methodologies, the bulk of his criticism is reserved for Muslim historians themselves, who he believes misrepresented reform movements in ways consistent with the demands of the power structures dominant in their respective eras. Jawzi believes that both European orientalists and official Muslim heresiographers—or more accurately, the power structures in which they were involved—were motivated by a natural tendency toward self-preservation and aggrandizement. In the case of the Europeans, he says, the effort to marginalize or delegitimize "the East" resulted from "nationalistic or political objectives." His analysis of canonization within the Islamic world of reports marginalizing or delegitimizing groups that challenged the caliphal authority is based on the same estimation of the way power structures work. Both were functions of extant or desired power relationships.

Jawzi's analysis of Islamic intellectual movements, therefore, is offered not only as a corrective to orientalism but to Muslims' misapprehension of their own heritage. He seems convinced that, in addition to foreign invasions and subjugation, Muslims' lack of socioeconomic development has resulted from lack of attention to their own tradition. Helping to overcome that is the ultimate aim of his book, as expressed in his dedication: "To the reawakening Arab youth; to those who are liberating their minds from the influence of irrational beliefs about social, religious, and national affairs; to those with healthy understanding and vibrant minds, I dedicate this part of my book, *The History of Intellectual Movements in Islam*."

"The Economic Bases of Islam"

Jawzi begins his first chapter, "The Economic Bases of Islam," by explaining his reasons for considering economic issues in a discussion of Islam: "For it has been well established that Islam, like all other great religions, is not only religious thought but a social and economic matter as well—or, more precisely, more so than it is religious thought." This could be considered a reflection of Jawzi's Marxist orientation toward religion in general: he believed that, like all ideologies, religion arises from and reflects socioeconomic conditions. But this statement should not be taken as a denigration of religion in general, nor of Islam in particular, especially in light of Jawzi's repeatedly expressed admiration of Islamic principles. Indeed, this comment is more accurately understood in view of that admiration. What clearly appeals to him in Islam is its central and very practical concern with social justice. Islam is not concerned simply with spiritual or nonmaterial matters. It calls for an end to oppression and injustice, both of which result from socioeconomic conditions. Social solidarity, as well as economic justice, is fundamental to the vision of Islam. This is the point Jawzi seeks to establish in chapter 1.

Describing socioeconomic conditions in Mecca at the time of Prophet Muhammad (sixth to seventh centuries c.e.), Jawzi emphasizes the wealth of Mecca's elite and the poverty and oppression suffered by those upon whose labor that wealth was built. Relying on classic studies such as those of French historian Henri Lammens and German scholar Martin Hartmann, he stresses what he considers to be the two practices most indicative of social and moral degradation—usury and female infanticide. Both were accepted practices: the first was a means of exploiting the already impoverished; the second, a tragic statement on the position of women in society.

Into this milieu Prophet Muhammad was born and emerged, Jawzi tells us, as the voice of social reform. Having been born into poverty, and, upon the death of his parents, exposed to wide disparities in wealth within his own family, no one could have been more suited to this role. In any case, Jawzi continues, social reform was the core of the Prophet's message, and the key to understanding the economic bases of Islam:

> These differences in poverty and wealth among the members of one tribe were what called the attention of the Arab prophet to the social strife found among the classes of people in his community and [led him] to search for its sources. They were what caused him to declare a war of words against the class of shameless oppressors who monopolize the resources of wealth and capitalize on the burdens of the poor and artless dwellers of the desert.

Jawzi characterizes the source of the social strife criticized by Prophet Muhammad as the monopoly of resources by the wealthy. He notes that some analysts have therefore described the Prophet's reform measures as essentially socialist. But he disagrees. He states that we cannot "force the Meccan reformer among the socialists or communists who say that his call was aimed at socialist or communist goals." Elsewhere: "The opinion of some—that the Prophet intended to abolish private ownership of property and make it common, that is, the property of the community or nation—is false; such extreme communistic thoughts did not occur to the Prophet except in the first stage of his social life." (It should be noted that when Jawzi uses the term "communism," he means a community sharing all its material possessions and conducting its economic activities in common, as in a convent; it has neither political nor religious connotations for him, such as the totalitarianism and atheism of the Soviet system.) Jawzi does not elaborate on what reforms "in the first stage" of the Prophet's social life he would characterize as socialist or communist, but he does contend that the Prophet did not seek to revolutionize the Meccan economic system. Instead of prohibiting or even limiting private ownership or enterprise, the Prophet simply set such endeavors into a new perspective. He held that those who seek wealth for its own sake are courting disaster. The Prophet conceded that wealth is essential as a means toward the goal of social justice, but its acquisition through exploitation ultimately renders wealth an obstacle to its owners' spiritual well-being.

Thus, Jawzi describes the Prophet as the champion of the poor and oppressed, "the orphans and the helpless and pitiful people." The Meccan elite clearly recognized a threat to their economic power, and therefore fought the Prophet's reforms.

That the Prophet, realizing the Meccans' determination, willingly transferred his nascent community to Medina is significant for Jawzi. It provided the opportunity for the Prophet's community, no longer under the Meccans' constraints, to develop in accordance with divine prerogative. Jawzi believes we may look to the Medinan Muslim community for the true nature of Islam:

> The Arab nation began to carry out [the Prophet's] orders and defer to his judgment in all matters. Thus it became easy for him to carry out his promises and realize the social reforms he had been called to implement in Mecca; to apply his long-cherished ideals of justice, brotherhood, and freedom for women and slaves; and to fight the causes of suffering among the citizens of his community, indeed, in all the Arab communities.

However, Jawzi warns, we must not look to the Medinan community for the precise form of Islamic socioeconomic organization. The Prophet did not establish a specific system—social, political or economic—that would sustain humanity for all time. Rather, he described the basic principles upon which any and all Islamic societies must be based: freedom, justice, and equality. But social reform is a practical process; it must be workable. Reforms must be suited to their times. And, Jawzi believes, the Prophet's reforms were just that. This is why the Prophet did not prohibit private property, for example. Jawzi believes that in industrialized society, private ownership of the means of production is at the root of oppression. He believes that it would have been possible for the Prophet to outlaw private property for all time, and thus eliminate what would eventually become a source of economic oppression.

He could have eliminated other perennial sources of oppression as well, Jawzi continues, by prohibiting slavery definitively and by establishing unequivocally the equality of women and men. But the Prophet's mission was to establish the basic principles of social justice and a model of their effective application in a particular time and place. In the society established by Prophet Muhammad, there was no perceived exploitation of any sort, whether economic, gender-, or class-based. The record of those principles and that model, then, constitute a source of inspiration upon which every generation of Muslims may draw in their efforts to organize their societies in accordance with the divine will. In other circumstances, implementation of the same system could well result in exploitation. Removal of the sources of exploitation in every time and place, according to its specific conditions, is the prophetic imperative, the divine challenge. Those communities that fail to meet that challenge—who fail to draw inspiration from the Prophet's example and who mistake the form for the substance—inevitably deviate from Islamic principles. And this is how Jawzi describes the history of the caliphates.

"Arab Imperialism and the Vanquished Nations"

In chapter 2, "Arab Imperialism and the Vanquished Nations," Jawzi describes the results of successive generations of Muslims' failure to heed the spirit of the Prophet's reforms. After the death of the Prophet, those whom the Prophet sought to benefit—"the poor, the prisoners, the orphans, the widows"—were once again plunged into their former plight. Implementing only the letter of the law, Jawzi points out, the Islamic administrators used the money which was supposedly collected for the benefit of the needy "mostly for the needs of the state." Accordingly, he concludes:

> [I]t was as if the call of the Prophet and his social revolution, his labors and those of his early caliphs, were only to strengthen his adversaries, indeed to augment their wealth and power. And even stranger, it was as if the Meccan merchants of the past benefited from the Islamic movement and its ideas and principles, and that they had established one of the greatest states in the world, between which and the nation the Prophet founded there was scarcely any resemblance.

Jawzi thus presents a picture of Prophet Muhammad as a divinely-inspired social reformer who envisioned a society based on universal principles of human equality and solidarity. Yet due to his followers' greed and insensitivity to the Prophet's example, the society they created sank back into depravity soon after his death. Still, the spirit of justice and equality survived, Jawzi believes, most evidently in the revolutionary struggles to return to the norm established by the Prophet that punctuate Islamic history. He treats in detail the Babakis, the Isma'ilis, and the Qaramatis.

"Babak's Movement and His Socialist Doctrine"

In "Babak's Movement and His Socialist Doctrine," Jawzi argues
against the interpretations of traditional historians and heresiographers.
Against those who assert that Babak's movement was a rebellion representing the desire of the Iranian people to reassert their Persian culture,
Jawzi argues that had it not been for the failure of the prevailing regime
to provide a suitable social and economic environment, the Babaki
movement would never have gained popular support. He accepts the
testimony of Muslim historians al-Tabari and al-Baghdadi that Babak's
movement embraced the communistic system of Mazdak. Having described the condition of the peasants in Iran under Islam as no better,
and perhaps worse, than that under their former (pre-Islamic) masters,
Jawzi considers the peasants' desire for economic justice through communal ownership to be reasonable. Their sustenance lay in the land to
which they were enslaved by large landowners. It was therefore natural
for them to consider their freedom to lie in the freedom of the land
they worked.

Jawzi allows that some illegal activities may have been carried out
under the cover of revolutionary movements like that of the Babakis.
And he recognizes that the Babakis were lenient with regard to the
drinking of wine and certain marriages disallowed by Islam. However,
he argues that beyond these issues there is little accuracy in the accounts
of those who denounced the Babakis as thieves and godless brigands. In
particular, he says, their attitudes toward women were misrepresented.
Apparently relying on the analysis of Soviet historian Belyaev, Jawzi
claims that the Babakis sought to raise the social status of women by
giving them rights and responsibilities on a par with those of men.[1]

Following a detailed history of the military and strategic aspects of
their twenty-year campaign against the caliph's forces, Jawzi assesses
the ultimate failure of the Babakis' movement. Two factors, he says,
account for their downfall. First, their movement would have had
greater chance for success had they not limited their sphere of activity
to the Iranian people. They were further weakened by the inclusion of
certain people more concerned with power and personal fortune than
with the movement's call for justice. Both factors were to be overcome,
Jawzi continues, through a more highly developed system of proselytization and indoctrination. These were the forte of the Isma'ilis, to whom
Jawzi devotes his fourth chapter.

"The Isma'ilis"

Jawzi does not commit himself to a direct link between the remnants of
the Mazdaki-Babaki movement and various elements of Shi'i Islam, but
he asserts that there was at least an "ideological relationship" between
the two groups, based on their shared social goals.[2] He believes that the

Isma'ilis consciously avoided the exclusivity of the Babakis, and therefore represent an advanced stage in the development of those goals. Rather than attacking injustices only in the system to which they were subject, as the Babakis had done, the Isma'ilis attacked the ideological bases of all oppressive political systems, Jawzi continues, including those operating in the name of the caliph. Furthermore, the Isma'ilis were careful to develop a method of proselytization conducive to group solidarity through utter faith in group leaders. Initiates were taught to trust no one except their teachers. Yet this tendency toward secretiveness, Jawzi believes, engendered suspicion on the part of the government and, as a result, official heresiographers accused the Isma'ilis of everything from atheism and materialism to nationalism, anarchy, and general debauchery. Extreme caution must be used therefore, Jawzi warns, with regard to sources of Isma'ili teaching. Credibility must be accorded only to Isma'ili sources themselves.

Jawzi argues further that readers must be aware that Isma'ili teachers frequently addressed different audiences in terms suited to each one's particular background and orientation. Their teaching, he explains, had both esoteric and exoteric levels of meaning, and their detractors frequently confused the two. The Isma'ilis placed their overall message centered on social values at the heart of both levels. Accordingly, Jawzi believes that Isma'ili teaching is more properly called a school of thought or philosophy than religion, by which he means it was an ethic applying to all humanity rather than to a particular community alone.

The Isma'ili social vision, as Jawzi describes it, was based on two principles: equality of the sexes and abolition of private property. He bases this appraisal, however, partly on extrapolation from the teaching of the Qaramatis, assuming somewhat questionably that they were representative of Isma'ili teaching. He is on surer ground when he relies on the Isma'ilis' own "Epistles of the Brethren of Sincerity." In that source, the privileged classes (wealthy merchants and rural landowners) are attacked through satire. Their condition, the Epistles describe, is "worse than that of the wretched slaves and the poor and weak, their minds constantly tormented by worries about their wealth."[3] This is the source of their moral depravity, which allows them to watch "their poor neighbors and orphan children of their brother, the downtrodden among their people, fallen in the roads, hungry and ailing and afflicted and crippled, begging for a crust of bread . . . while they do not pay any attention to them or pity them."[4]

Such criticisms of wealth do not necessarily justify calling Isma'ilis socialists, as Jawzi does.[5] Similarly, gender equality, even by Jawzi's own admission, was certainly not accepted by all Isma'ilis. Yet Jawzi's description of the Isma'ili emphasis on Muslim solidarity—or, as Jawzi puts it, "internationalism"—is accurate. The Isma'ilis clearly preached against religious fanaticism, and appealed to Muslims of all sects as well as to Christians, Jews, Mazdakis, Manicheans, Mandeans, and Sabians.

This "internationalism" is of particular importance for Jawzi. Unfortunately, Jawzi reports, the Isma'ilis' potential success was severely undermined by the combined effect of Turkish and Christian inroads in their region. Still, he sees their impact in the work of the great philosophers, mentioning al-Farabi, Ibn Sina, and Ibn Tufayl by name, as well as in the science of Qur'anic exegesis (tafsir) and in the Sufi works of al-Hallaj, al-Ghazali, and Ibn 'Arabi. Most importantly, he sees their teaching culminating in the system established by the Qaramatis of Bahrain, that group of Isma'ilis which actually can be called socialist. In Jawzi's final chapter, the Qaramatis are described as the greatest of the Isma'ilis.

"The Qaramatis"

Jawzi does not concern himself with whether the Qaramatis were mainstream or dissident Isma'ilis. Instead, he concentrates on their internal order, which he describes as egalitarian and socialistic. He notes that the Qaramati government was by a sort of administrative council. Although the six members of the council were from a single leading family, they ruled in consultation with their deputies, and policy was made only with the consensus of the entire council. He implies that this system of government by a council of first-among-equals is an ideal form of Islamic government. (He also notes, interestingly, that this was the system employed by the Soviets at the time he wrote, although he does not dwell on the comparison. He simply focuses on the lack of elite in both cases and on the fact that both systems were born of a revolution by oppressed classes.)

After summarizing the Qaramati tax structure, Jawzi examines the topic of private property among the Qaramatis. He observes that individual ownership of property at the time was not an issue, but refers to the "communistic character" of property administration. Fields were bought with common funds, there were no individual taxes, and those in need were advanced funds without interest, as were newcomers into the area (at least those with skills). Grain was processed by state-owned and -operated mills, and commerce was carried on with token money that could not be exported. All of these elements, Jawzi thinks, were designed to provide for economic justice in the community and to prevent exploitation. What he does not deal with, although he mentions it, is the government's use of slave labor. Persian historian Nasr Khusrow reports that the Qaramati governing council owned some thirty thousand Black slaves for agricultural work. While there is no reason to assume that these slaves were mistreated, slave labor of any sort is clearly not in keeping with principles of equality and social solidarity. Therefore, Jawzi presents the Qaramatis as not fully "communist" but as a community that implemented, at least to a limited extent, principles of distributive justice.

As he did with the Babakis, Jawzi concludes his treatment of the Qaramatis with a defense of their morality and sincerity, as against official historians' assertions to the contrary. He acknowledges some of the atrocities they committed, particularly in Mecca, but he explains them in terms of the Qaramatis' rejection of idolatry. In general, their treatment of those they considered their enemies does not disturb Jawzi. He prefers to judge them on the basis of their internal order. In that context he describes them as just, generous, and temperate, and he denies their apparent duplicity concerning the Fatimid regime in Egypt. He explains that at one time they had supported the Fatimids and then turned against them, but only because of their disillusionment with the Fatimid leader al-Muʿizz and his apparently excessive concern with wealth and power. In breaking with the Fatimids, then, the Qaramatis believed they were defending their revolutionary principles of justice. Nor should the Qaramatis be rebuked on the basis of shallow devotion to the family of ʿAli, the traditional leaders of Shiʿism. At the core of Qaramati beliefs, he claims, was social justice. Tribal loyalty and cultic practices were of secondary importance. The Qaramatis did not prohibit religious ritual, but they considered ritual worship unimportant relative to the practice of social justice.

"Conclusion"

In his conclusion, Jawzi reiterates his regard for Islamic goals of social justice and his belief in their enduring impact on society, despite the deviations by caliphal authorities. He extends his treatment briefly to include the Babi and Bahaʾi movements, noting again an "ideological link" between them and Ismaʿilism. He further speculates on the influence of Ismaʿili social doctrine and organizational techniques on the development of the Jesuit Christian religious order, the Freemasons, and trade and craft guilds. Overall he believes he has demonstrated, contrary to European orientalists' opinions, that it was not backwardness that prevented Islamic society from developing economically as European society did. Rather, Islamic society was led astray, and in fact overcome, by foreign powers when its fundamental principles were ignored. Only then were the invaders able to hinder the progress of Islamic society. Nevertheless, Islamic principles have been kept alive, particularly in the sort of reform movements he describes. Thus, once freed of imperial and colonial forces, and once Islamic principles are implemented in ways suitable for changed circumstances, Jawzi is convinced, Islamic society will indeed progress through the same stages of economic development as the West; in fact, because of the Islamic concern with social justice, it will avoid much of the exploitation characteristic of the capitalist stage of economic development.

Summary of Jawzi's Interpretive Methodology

In general, power politics has a very strong influence on intellectual production, on what gets canonized as truth or knowledge in any given context. Those whose subjugation is considered necessary to maintain the status quo, as well as those considered a threat to the status quo, are characterized by those in the dominant power structures as somehow defective, aberrant, deserving of marginalization, or even eradication. Among the devices used to produce accounts conducive to that goal is stereotyping, based on letting one element in a society stand for the whole. This is a methodological error, Jawzi asserts; he focuses on the need for attention to the uniqueness of circumstances surrounding all historical reports. Furthermore, Jawzi continues, sometimes a kind of synecdoche is practiced by allowing a single moment in history to represent a people's entire history. But this involves a further methodological weakness: the failure to recognize that societies change and develop over time, with changing circumstances. Finally, the factors that affect change and development are the same for all peoples.

These are all elements Jawzi employed in his introductory criticism of European orientalism, as well as in his criticism of Muslim historians who marginalized any group that challenged the caliphal authority. But there are two further dimensions to Bandali Jawzi's hermeneutic, implicit in his explanation of the contrast between Islamic principles and what actually happened in Islamic regimes after the death of the Prophet. Prophet Muhammad established Islamic principles of equality, justice, and social solidarity. He also established and led a community that exemplified those principles. But he did not establish specific organizations or institutions that would guarantee those principles' application throughout history. It is each generation's responsibility to figure out the best ways to realize those principles in changed circumstances, based on the example of the Prophet as described in the Qur'an and in reliable reports elucidating the Qur'an. Jawzi displays a conviction that each generation must therefore return to the sources of revelation for inspiration regarding Islamic principles, trusting in the Qur'an's continuing ability to inspire and in their own ability to understand; then they must critically evaluate the institutions in which they live, the collective heritage of previous ages, representing earlier generations' efforts to determine and implement Islam's moral/ethical norms. Where they find discrepancies, as Jawzi has in his analysis, they must devise more suitable practices—again, as he has suggested—in accordance with prevailing conditions.

4

Conclusion

Like others before and after him, Jawzi tried to determine the source of the original strength of Islamic society and to figure out what had gone wrong. The methodology he used was based on the assumption that various elites had devised ideologies that were nominally Islamic, but that in reality were suited to their group or class interests. His goal was to dismantle those ideologies, to reveal the power interests involved in their construction and to show how those with vested interests had managed to delegitimize competing ideologies. His awareness of the incestuous relationship between power structures and intellectual formulations—between knowledge and power, as contemporary sociology of knowledge has it—was unlabored. Beyond his introductory comments about European orientalists and their jaded interpretations, Jawzi did not find it necessary to articulate, much less justify, his hermeneutic. It apparently seemed self-evident to him that ideological formulations were influenced by political-economic—that is, power—interests. Muslims had been calling for reassessment of their heritage for centuries, and ijtihadism (the movement calling for reactivation of ijtihad as the means to revitalize Islamic society) had finally been mainstreamed with the work of Muhammad ʿAbduh. Jawzi's critical rethinking of Islamic heritage, in view of the relationship between ideology and power in his history of Islamic intellectual movements, seems to reflect the intellectual tenor of his time. His use of a Marxist paradigm is historically significant. But Jawzi's socialist orientation is not essential to his methodology. His belief that Islamic principles would best be served in the twentieth century through a socialist economic structure results from his concern with distributive justice, not hermeneutical issues.

Ijtihadism continued to develop in the twentieth century, for example in the work of one of Iqbal's proteges, Abu'l-A'la Mawdudi (d. 1979), founder in 1947 of the influential resurgence group Jama'at-i Islami. Mawdudi believed that God's will has been revealed in the Qur'an and the Sunna and is therefore accessible to all, not just to a privileged elite.[1] All citizens have the right to participate in legislation in the Islamic state, not just those of a particular class, family, or profession.[2] Their legislation is bound by the eternal principles of the Shari'a, of course, and this is why he sometimes calls the Islamic political system he envisions a popular vicegerency, to distinguish it from a secularist "popular sovereignty." (At other times he calls it a theo-democracy.) But the mechanism of that vicegerency is ijtihad. People must determine the best way to implement eternal Islamic principles of social justice in specific circumstances. As he put it, "Every Muslim who is capable and qualified to give a sound opinion of matters of Islamic law, is entitled to interpret the law of God when such interpretation becomes necessary. In this sense, the Islamic polity is democratic."[3] The exact form of the legislature will vary with the needs of the time. But whatever the form, Muslims will be charged with interpreting the best way to implement Islamic principles in light of changing circumstances, evaluating traditional interpretations and superseding them when necessary.

Sayyid Qutb (d. 1966), the major ideologue of the Muslim Brotherhood in Egypt, agreed with Mawdudi. When he talked about the pitfalls of taqlid (imitation of precedent), he generally referred to those who blindly imitated European intellectual styles. Yet he too stressed the need for flexibility in the interpretation of Islamic teaching, which was necessary because of Islam's social role and was made possible by its emphasis on the responsibility of human reason: "The Islamic system has room for scores of models which are compatible with the natural growth of a society and the new needs of the contemporary age as long as the total Islamic idea dominates these models."[4] Sayyid Qutb stresses that the Qur'an is not a philosophical system, nor is it a book of science or history.[5] Its purpose is to instruct and inspire human action in accordance with divine prerogatives. Accordingly, Qutb in his commentaries describes the specific historical situations that are addressed in various verses.[6] He rejects the modernist European approach to historical studies of religion, and relies generally on hadith reports and traditional Qur'anic exegesis (tafsir) to determine the historical context of verses (shu'un or asbab al-nuzul, as they are called in traditional Qur'anic studies). But his interpretive principle is nonetheless one that relies on historical context in order to understand the attitude and action the verses intended to inspire.

Like those reformers before 'Abduh, Sayyid Qutb sometimes seems to restrict the right of interpretation to men trained in the traditionally recognized religious sciences. This, to him, is what guarantees that legislation will be "from God" rather than from human beings. But for him that does not mean rule by a religious elite:

> The kingdom of God on earth will not be established when religious leaders supervise sovereignty on earth as was the case under the power of the church, nor by men who pontificate in the name of gods as was the case under "theocracy" or divine rule; rather it is established when God's law has sovereignty and all matters are judged in the light of God's will as evident in his Shariʿah.[7]

Indeed, Sayyid Qutb specifically rejects the idea of an intellectual elite: "Allah did not teach us through the form of a theory or a theology, nor in the style common to our scholastic writings on the subject of tawhid (the Oneness of Allah)."[8] Sayyid Qutb himself was trained as a literary critic and an educational administrator, but he produced one of the most influential contemporary interpretations of the Qurʾan, the 24-volume *Fi Zilal al-Qurʾan* (In the Shade of the Qurʾan). He believed that those with sincere intentions and proper education were capable of receiving guidance directly from revelation. He quotes the Qurʾan as proof: "And for those who strive in us, We surely guide them to our Paths."[9] For them what is required is a dynamic fiqh, one that responds to the Qurʾanic imperative in ways that are suitable for changed circumstances.[10]

Although the issue of ijtihad is handled differently in Shiʿi Islam than in Sunni Islam, even popular Iranian ideologue ʿAli Shariʿati (d. 1977) stresses ijtihad and the need to reinterpret the application of Islamic principles. Originally, he says, ijtihad was the means by which jurists maintained the dynamism of Islam, balancing Islamic principles with new historic contingencies. But it fell into disuse, he says, and as a result, Islamic society fell into stagnation. Shariʿati's father had established the Center for the Spread of Islamic Teachings, a school dedicated to ijtihad through "critical examination of the sources of revelation, and reinterpretation of its historical setting."[11] Shariʿati's work as a university lecturer (he was trained at the University of Paris) continued in this vein. Following Iqbal, he stressed Muslims' need to participate in the creation of a just social order. All Muslims have the responsibility to exert themselves—to practice ijtihad—in order to allow society to face new challenges, yet maintain ultimate Islamic principles. Societies that fail to respond to changing needs will become extinct, he warned. Through ijtihad Muslims must "recognize the conflict between the traditional interpretation of Islam and the demands of the contemporary life" and come up with new, suitable applications.[12]

The point here is not that these thinkers are progressive or even univocal on the issue of ijtihad, who can exercise it, and how. Support for ijtihad in some contexts does not preclude essentialism or reactionary attitudes in others. However, these references do demonstrate the pervasiveness of the concern with overcoming intellectual stagnation in the Muslim community, and doing so by means of critical assessment of Islamic intellectual heritage. A thinker like Jawzi, therefore, need not have ventured outside the Islamic intellectual world for his hermeneutic. The context in which Jawzi produced his *History of Intellectual Movements in Islam* was one of "intellectual independence," in Muhammad Iqbal's words, exercised in search of the causes of the decay of the Islamic world. Jawzi's critical analysis of the political-economic power concerns that influenced not only European orientalists' negative assessment of Islamic culture but, more importantly, the Islamic intelligentsia's marginalization of reform movements that stressed egalitarianism at the expense of caliphal power, was based on an interpretive methodology with roots deep in Islamic tradition. It had been contested and was itself open to diverse interpretations. Nevertheless, ijtihad has had proponents since the earliest days of institutionalized Islam and had gained widespread support by the beginning of the twentieth century.

Yet considering Jawzi's education and historic position in the czarist-Soviet empire, it is interesting to speculate whether or not he was also influenced by some of the trends current in Russia—particularly a school of thought known as Russian formalism—that are considered important in the development of Europe's postmodern thought. The background of Russian formalism is somewhat complex. It began with the concern with language and meaning that had developed in the fields of theology (particularly Protestant) and philosophy throughout the nineteenth century. By the twentieth century, intellectuals in the fields of linguistics and literary criticism had joined in. Linguistics was a relatively new field in the early twentieth century, developing out of traditional philology. Philology was the classical field of language study, focusing on specific languages—their grammar, syntax, and so on—as well as on the historical development of meanings of words. The goal of philological studies was better understanding of the meaning of historical texts, particularly religious texts. Its method was diachronic, meaning across or through time, historically. Linguistics, as it developed in this century, is the study of language itself, its structure, and how it works in the first place. Its approach is synchronic, meaning that it is not concerned with historical developments in meaning, but with language as a structure.

Credit is generally given to Swiss linguist Ferdinand de Saussure (d. 1913) for developing structural linguistics, the analysis of the various elements of language and their interrelationships or patterns (what he calls *langue*; rather than with everyday meaning systems, which he calls *parole*). Saussure established the now classic description of language as a system of arbitrary signs (signifiers) that correspond not to things as such but to mental images (signifieds). (The things that signs are supposed to point to in the real world he called "referents"; the relationship between them and the system of signs of which language consists was of no concern to Saussure since linguistic signs bear no direct connection whatsoever to their referents in the real world.) The choice of one signifier over another, and the relationship between the signifier and the signified, is purely conventional; it is a function of the way people, over time, have set up their systems. Furthermore, the signs—the signifiers and their associated "signifieds"—are presupposed in any given use of language. People generally do not concoct meanings and then assign signs to represent them; they receive sign complexes (meanings) in the languages they learn. Finally, signs work, according to Saussure's articulation of the obvious, because they are different from one another. (Using the same sign for multiple images would not serve the purpose of language.) Saussure calls this kind of meaning functional; it does not matter what marker (sign) is used for any particular image, as long as it is different from the markers used for all the others.[13]

Saussure's treatment of language as a structural system operating independently of the real world, combined with German philosopher Wilhelm Dilthey's (d. 1911) observations concerning the givenness of meaning in language, had profound implications for the field of literary criticism. Traditionally, literature had been taken—to various extents— as the expression of an author's intentional meanings, and "good" literature was considered a reflection of universal truths. The assertion that language presupposes meaning, rather than creates it, implied that the author's words were a product of the language s/he was given in the specific time and place s/he was writing. And the observation that we are all locked in our language systems, complete with their temporal matrices, implied that try as we might, we can never even be quite sure what the meaning was of the language the author had been given. We could attempt, in terms used by German philosopher Hans Georg Gadamer, to fuse our matrix (horizon) of meaning with the author's, but there were neither guarantees nor clearly identifiable ways to determine that our interpretations were accurate. Therefore, the proper object of study in literature, for some, became the structure of the work. Derivation of meaning became a function of the various juxtapositions or systems of relationship among the linguistic elements.

One of the first literary schools to find affinity with these implications of Saussure's ideas was that known as Russian formalism. Developing in the years before the 1917 Bolshevik Revolution, Russian formalism eventually developed a variety of approaches to literature.[14] But the central focus was on the words themselves and how they affect readers, rather than as vehicles of various sorts of meaning or ideas. The authors were therefore considered artists or craftspeople; words were their material, and literary devices were what they used to make their products, which were distinguishable from ordinary use of language in that they had no practical purpose as such.

This approach to literature was criticized as early as the 1920s by a faction of Russian formalists known as the Bakhtin school, after Mikhail Bakhtin. Bakhtin's critique of formalism was first presented in texts published in 1928.[15] It focuses on the failure to recognize the influence of specific historical realities on the production of meaning. The critique was particularly concerned with ideologies stemming from the economic interests of various groups or classes. For Bakhtin, language was the vehicle of ideology, and it reflected the dynamism evident in the class struggles that play themselves out in ideologies. He did not reject the notion of language as a system of signs, but insisted that the correspondence between the signifier and the signified was neither isomorphic (one to one) nor static. Meanings are contested—for Bakhtin, along ideological lines—so that the same term can have different meanings in different ideological contexts. These differences in meanings can only be discerned by considering the social context of the linguistic usage, only by considering the dialogue in which the terms are being used, the "discourse," as language-in-use is now called. Nor did Bakhtin reject the givenness of language, the idea that meanings are learned rather than created by individuals. But he believed the emphasis on the synchronic elements of language resulted in overlooking the central feature of language use: the social struggles for which language provides a battleground.

Bakhtin's insistence on considering the political-economic and ideological context of language in order to understand a text seems resonant with Jawzi's hermeneutic. The fact that Mikhail Bakhtin's criticism of Saussurean linguistics was published in 1928, the same year Jawzi's *History* came out, raises questions regarding possible influence of Bakhtin or his school on Jawzi. But the fact that Jawzi simply makes use of the methodology, arguing neither for its necessity nor its validity, indicates that he did not see himself as a participant in the European debate. Instead, the similarity seems to indicate a level of compatibility between the critical postmodern methodology developing with Bakhtin's work, one element of which is neohistoricism, and the ijtihadism which so clearly influenced Jawzi's work.

That impression is heightened by the fact that, as noted, Euroamerican neohistoricist Edward Said produced an analysis of European scholarship on the Middle East very similar to that sketched in Jawzi's introduction. It is further heightened by the explicit references to the work of Derrida and Foucault in the work of thinkers in the contemporary Muslim world trying to encourage critical analysis of Islam's intellectual heritage.[16]

Moroccan sociologist and litterateur 'Abd al-Kabir al-Khatibi, for example, conducts what he calls a "double criticism" of world culture.[17] He is concerned that, despite the official end of direct political colonization, there remains the intellectual residue of colonization. He finds that residue particularly in the Arab world's assimilation of Euroamerica's binary world, its culture of exclusivity ("us" versus "them"). In this context he criticizes—as did Bandali Jawzi—both Euroamerican culture and Arab culture for their marginalization of "the other." Unlike Jawzi, al-Khatibi includes Marxist culture in the hegemonic West. He believes it has maintained the modernist absolute typologies, despite the fact that "Marxism presents itself as, claims to be, and is applied—in one way or another—against imperialism."[18] Calling on Derrida, al-Khatibi characterizes Marxism's universalist (hegemonic) claims as logocentric, no less so than capitalist imperialism.[19] Both the capitalist and the socialist West insist on a single socioeconomic system. But al-Khatibi is particularly harsh on Marxism because of the false hope it held out for liberation. Reminding readers that it was Marx who grouped more than half the world into the category "the Asiatic mode of production" and called for "the annihilation of the old Asiatic society" in India, he concludes: "One may therefore read Marx in the following manner: the murder of the tradition(s) of the other and the liquidation of its past are necessary so that the West, while seizing the world, can expand beyond its limits while remaining unchanged in the end."[20] Still, al-Khatibi cautions strongly against an anti-West, anticapitalist, or anti-Marxist orientation. That would simply be further logocentrism. More importantly, it is a prime example of the very cultural colonization that concerns him. It reflects assimilation of the West's own exclusivism:

That is why the "thought of difference" that we call for is neither Marxist in the strict sense nor anti-Marxist in the narrow sense of the term, but does recognize the limits of its potential. For we want to uproot Western knowledge from its central place within ourselves, to de-center ourselves with respect to this center, to this origin claimed by the West. This should be done by operating in the sphere of a plural and planetary "thought of difference" that struggles against its own reduction and domestication.[21]

Therefore, using Foucault's terminology, al-Khatibi calls for an achaeological search into the Western body of knowledge, revealing its inherently oppressive exclusivity. In the same way, he criticizes Islam's insistence on a single truth, a single way, its culture of unity; that is the source of its own logocentrism, and it must likewise undergo a deconstruction of its heritage in order to construct a pluralistic culture, one tolerant of "the other."

Jawzi's socialist orientation, by contrast, made him see capitalist greed as the culprit in colonial oppression, and deviation from Islam's egalitarianism as the source of elitist caliphal institutions' marginalization of challenging groups. He clearly does not see Islamic principles as essentially exclusivist. Just the opposite, in fact; though he does not engage in the tawhidist (unitarian) discourse that has become popular in contemporary Islamist movements, he is no doubt convinced that Islam's universalist claims are in fact inclusivist, pluralist, and above all, tolerant of "difference." Therefore, while al-Khatibi stresses that today's Arabs must break with their exclusivist heritage (including the exclusivist elements in Islamic ideology), Jawzi stresses that Islamic society must return to Islamic solidarity through egalitarianism. A difference of emphasis, perhaps; both thinkers reject universalist systems that result in oppression of an "other" and both conclude the necessity of reevaluating cultural heritage based on recognition that intellectual constructs are the creations of individuals operating under the influence of specific historical circumstances.

Similarly, Muhammad ʿAbid al-Jabiri makes facile use of postmodern, particularly Foucaultian, observations concerning the nature of intellectual production. Al-Jabiri analyzes the development of Arab/Islamic philosophical heritage, demonstrating the partisan political concerns in its institutionalization.[22] He also criticizes the incarceration of the Arab Islamic intellect by such thinkers as eighth- and ninth-century legist al-Shafiʿi and ninth- and tenth-century theologian al-Ashʿari, whose insistence on intellectual production in the fields of Islamic law and Qurʾanic exegesis was based on imitation of earlier ideas. Al-Jabiri then bases his denunciation of taqlid on recognition of the historicity of ideological and epistemological constructs. The Arab Islamic world has developed and maintains a fractured intellectual heritage, both in its formative stage and today, in its borrowing from foreign models to legitimize positions assumed as a result of power politics. In the formative period, it was based on Greek philosophical models; today, it is both classical Islamic and European intellectual models. But in all cases, given that intellectual constructs are a function of specific historic concerns, the Arab Islamic world saddles itself with intellectual formulations unsuited to the concerns of its own historic and geographic setting. Therefore, al-Jabiri calls for a reassessment of both Arab Islamic and Western intellectual heritage based on recognition of their historicity.[23]

Al-Jabiri's approach is similar to that of Moroccan scholar ʿAbdullah al-ʿArwi, although the latter is critical of Foucault. Al-ʿArwi also criticizes both the adoption of Western ideological models and the indiscriminate acceptance of medieval Muslim ideology. Their incorporation into contemporary discourse leaves Muslims in a disjointed state of separation "from the real world . . . by intellectually inhabiting another world, the world of the past or the world of the Other, which [they turn] into absolute reality."[24] Al-ʿArwi insists on a "conception of truth as an indefinite process," rather than accomplished fact. He therefore rejects the idea of "apparent intelligibility which is that of the event." He believes that kind of thinking is responsible for philosophies of history and other tendencies "which all seek a point of departure other than that of political event." He includes among these tendencies historicism, "sociologism," cultural anthropology, and "epistemologism," all of which he believes become enmired in historicism as if it were "alone real."

For al-ʿArwi, historicism (*al-taʿrikhaniyya*), in the sense of recognizing the temporality of various components of intellectual heritage, is a necessary corrective to traditionalism. But he criticizes the sort of nineteenth-century European historicism, with its Hegelian legacy, which privileges itself and tends to reduce non-Eurochristian histories to cultural constructs.[25] What he prescribes instead is "factual history," which he says is the source of all progress. "Factual history," for al-ʿArwi, is not absolute truth; instead, it is a recognition of the impact of economic concerns on the formulation and adoption of ideologies. Discovering that influence, he continues, is "the sole means of achieving a certain objectivity."[26] In this context, al-ʿArwi insists on the distinction between "fact" and "theory:"

> [E]verything comes to us in a framework of culture and ideology: we have a theory of religion and few evidences of the actual lived religion, a political theory and few political documents, a theory of history and few specific dates, a theory of social structure and few indications of actual social behavior, an economic theory and few series of economic data, etc. We are in constant danger of confusing theory with fact.[27]

Al-ʿArwi's emphasis on the impact of (in his Marxian view, economic) power structures on the production and adoption of intellectual formulations, as well as his insistence on the need to critically assess that impact, are clearly in the ijtihadist tradition. Despite his specific criticism of Foucault, the ease with which he engages in postmodern discourse in the same discussion is another indication of similarities between neohistoricism and ijtihadism.

Perhaps the best known of contemporary Muslim thinkers integrating postmodern and ijtihadist terminology is Algerian/French scholar Mohammed Arkoun (Muhammad Arkun). Again we find an emphasis on the need to recognize the impact of political debates in the past on the ideological formulations that have become the revered tradition of today—the archaeology of knowledge (in Foucault's phrase), or in Arkoun's terminology, recognizing its historicity (*al-taʿrikhiyya*).[28] He not only accepts but vigorously advocates making use of social sciences and generally multidisciplinary methodologies developed in the West. In an essay dealing with the work of tenth-century thinker Abu-l Hasan al-ʿAmiri, for example, he expounds on the nature and effects of "logocentrism" in Islamic thought.[29] In his description of logocentrism, he refers explicitly to Derrida's *Of Grammatology*. Elsewhere he calls on Foucault in his effort to dismantle both Euroamerican orientalist and Muslim traditionalist essentialization of Islam. Both result, he says, from failure to recognize the integral relationship between historical circumstances and intellectual production. Lifting an ideology from its historical (sociopolitical and economic) context and imposing it on a different context inevitably threatens cultural integrity.[30]

Arkoun obviously does not feel that in referring to Derrida's or Foucault's work he is doing the same thing (adopting foreign discursive models inappropriate for the contemporary Muslim world). He specifically places his methodology in the context of ijtihad. It is ijtihad as it could and should be practiced by contemporary Muslims, in his view.[31] His theme is the need for ongoing evaluation of Islamic intellectual heritage in light of the impact of historical circumstances on interpretations. Ijtihad today, Arkoun continues, must focus on the critique of intellectual heritage.[32] Indeed, in his essay on al-ʿAmiri, Arkoun argues for the permanent necessity of ijtihad.[33] All the activity of the Prophet in establishing a successful community, at once religious and political, was possible, he says, "because the Qurʾan recapitulated the new religious symbolism in non-systematic language, which allowed the generation of appropriate significations in even the most changing historical circumstances."[34] The Prophet himself was inspired and interpreted his inspiration in ways most effective for his historical context, and his companions and witnesses experienced his words and deeds and then commited them to text. The historical circumstances upon which the understanding of each interpreter was conditioned must be scrutinized in the effort to understand and appreciate the Islamic heritage.[35] In order to resolve the tension between those who hold doctrinal authority and the specialists challenging their interpretations (shades of Foucault's general and specific scholars), he says, "I will continue to incorporate the techniques of argumentation, the contents of tradition in a global analysis which allows rights of critical epistemology to prevail for the Pious Ancestors and for us today."[36]

The compatibility between Euroamerica's neohistoricism and ijtihad-ism was explicitly recognized by one of the late twentieth century's most vocal proponents of ijtihad, Fazlur Rahman (d. 1988). Unlike scholars such as al-Khatibi, al-Jabiri, al-ʿArwi, and Arkoun, Fazlur Rahman began his advocacy of ijtihadist hermeneutics completely outside of postmodern discourse. In 1965 he published his seminal work on the subject, *Islamic Methodology in History*. In that work Rahman begins his treatment of ijtihad with the notion of the Sunna, or the normative example established by the Prophet. He distinguishes between the concept of the Sunna and the content of the Sunna. The former, he wrote, is the general idea that the Prophet's actions were interpretations of Islamic principles for application in the specific context of seventh-century Arabia. Prophet Muhammad set the example of responding creatively and on an ongoing basis to specific situations on the basis of principles expressed in revelation.[37] The "content of the Sunna" is also the result of interpretation: the interpretations by early generations of Muslims of the Prophet's "situational interpretation[s]" in the fixed form of specific hadith reports.

Rahman sees the root of ijtihad, for him the interpretive principle of Islam, in both senses of the Sunna. Indeed, the notion of interpretation is essential to Islam, he believes, contrasting active, situational interpretation (the "concept of the Sunna") with passive acceptance of ahistorical statements of truth (the "content of the Sunna"). Revelation consists largely of contextualized examples of basic principles put into action. While the basic principles are relatively straightforward, the challenge is putting them into practice in ever-changing situations. And that is what Prophet Muhammad's behavior, recorded in both the Qur'an and Sunna, represents. That the Qur'an and the Sunna of the Prophet are historically and geographically contextualized interpretations of divinely revealed principles is what Fazlur Rahman calls the historicity of revelation. They establish a precedent of interpreting that itself becomes normative. Muslims, deriving inspiration from revelation about essential Islamic values, must continue to exercise every effort to determine the most effective ways to implement those values in their specific contexts. As he put it, the message of revelation "must—despite its being clothed in the flesh and blood of a particular situation—outflow through and beyond that given context of history." [38]

The Sunna, therefore, is a "behavioral" term for Fazlur Rahman. This means that the message of the Qur'an is one that requires response in activity (as opposed to simple intellectual assent or belief). Every instance of proper response to the Qur'an is in behavior or activity. But behavior is situational: it is bound to the specific circumstances of the time and place in which it takes place. Therefore, no particular instance of behavior can be taken as normative without due consideration of its historic context. In Rahman's words, "[S]ince no two cases, in practice, are ever exactly identical in their situational setting—moral, psychological and material—Sunna must, of necessity, allow of interpretation and adaptation." [39]

This is how Fazlur Rahman explains that the concept of Sunna, as the ongoing response to spatiotemporal situations inspired by Islamic principles, is essentially interpretive, or ijtihadist. [40] Like the ijtihadists mentioned, he believes that the historic decline and current decrepitude of the Islamic world are the result of the cessation of the practice of ijtihad in any meaningful way. [41] Through a gradual process, the early Islamic community's vibrant historicist (situationally responsive) approach to ethical behavior was replaced with an ahistorical one, one accepting behavioral norms as such, with virtually no consideration of the contexts in which they arose or in which they were to be applied. What is necessary now, Rahman concludes, is to regain the concept of the living Sunna—the ongoing responsiveness to changing circumstances in light of Islamic principles. The Muslim community, he believed, must undo the "total fixation" on the content of the Sunna. The creativity of Islam was stifled "because the *content* of this structure was invested with a halo of sacredness and unchangeability." The Prophetic Sunna "ceased to be living *sunnah,* that is, an ongoing process, and came to be regarded as the unique incarnation of the Will of God." [42] Therefore, he says, mixing his metaphors, "[t]he present need undoubtedly is to reloosen this formalism and to resume the threads from the point where the living Sunna had voluntarily emptied itself into the hadith dam." [43]

He calls for "a revaluation of different elements in hadith and their thorough reinterpretation under the changed moral and social conditions of today."[44]

In this way, Fazlur Rahman, like those scholars mentioned who worked within the postmodern Euroamerican intellectual milieu, concludes for the necessity of critical analysis of all aspects of traditional Islamic learning in view of the historical circumstances—particularly those associated with the concerns of power—in which they developed. This analysis emerged in a strictly Islamic context.[45] However, in one of Fazlur Rahman's last works, *Islam and Modernity: Transformation of an Intellectual Tradition,* it is clear that he had discovered postmodern discourse. There he reiterates his argument that Islamic society finds itself weak and in disarray because it failed from the start to institutionalize continuing ijtihad, and this time he notes the affinity between his ijtihadist hermeneutic and certain aspects of Euroamerican postmodern discourse on the subject of interpretation. He cites with approval postmodernists' recognition of the impact of historical context on intellectual production (interpretation). He agrees with Gadamer's criticism of what he calls the objectivity school, which neglects the importance of historical circumstances in understanding the meaning of a text. And he applies his observation to the issue of Qurʾanic interpretation: "This, of course, admits of varying degrees, but certainly in the case of the Qurʾan, the objective situation is a *sine qua non* for understanding, particularly since, in view of its absolute normativity for Muslims, it is literally God's response through Muhammad's mind . . . to an historic situation."[46] Rahman also agrees with Gadamer that "all experience of understanding presupposes a preconditioning of the experiencing subject and therefore, without due acknowledgement of this fact . . . any attempt to understand anything is doomed to unscientific vitiation."[47] However, he disagrees vehemently with what he considers Gadamer's conclusion: that "there is no question of any 'objective' understanding of anything at all." He calls this view "hopelessly subjective." As his use of the phrase "objective situation" in the above quote indicates, he believes that, given sufficient study and adequate material, we can determine fairly accurately the circumstances that surround not only the delivery of Qurʾanic verses but also their interpretation in various times and places by various historical figures. Nevertheless, on this issue, the question of certainty, Fazlur Rahman reverts to the Iqbalian position. He observes that "the wish and search for certainty are extremely powerful motives in man."[48] But one will seek in vain for the source of certainty in positivist formulations of the past, he says, like Iqbal, distinguishing between cognitive and moral certainty. The latter is to be sought in the realm of faith. The former remains quite elusive.

Indeed, Fazlur Rahman believed that Islam's unique contribution to the monotheistic tradition was that it "has taken society seriously and history meaningfully" for the betterment of this world.[49] He was utterly opposed to those revivalists who seek the solution to the Muslim world's "acute sense of deterioration and failure" in a return to specific practices of the past. "A simple return to the past is, of course, a return to the graves."[50] It is absolutely essential to realize not only that the Prophet's behavior was itself interpretive of Islamic principles but also that the reports of that behavior are themselves interpretations. We are therefore at least two interpretations removed from the essential teachings of revelation. And since all interpretations are historically and geographically contextualized, Muslims must exert every effort to understand those contexts in order to be able to distinguish the essential from the contingent.

There is, therefore, at least a perceived affinity between postmodern Euroamerican thinkers' concern with the nature of interpretation, as well as with the relationship of power to intellectual production and the need to critically analyze it, and the ijtihadist hermeneutic of Islamic reform. (There is also a perceived difference: in response to the nagging question of uncertainty, considered by many the predominant characteristic of postmodern theory, Muslim hermeneuticists suggest searching elsewhere for self-affirmation.[51] It is only the modernist emphasis on the certainty of human reason that prompts us to look for certainty in intellectual products anyway. The Muslim analysts mentioned here instead suggest seeking certainty in the spiritual realm). It is not surprising, then, that later Islamic scholars might find congenial the work of a Derrida, a Foucault or Said. For some Muslim analysts, reference to these scholars in their work results not so much from having discovered a novel approach to understanding their own heritage as from recognizing a shared approach to human intellectual heritage in general. This is not always the case, of course. Not all Muslim scholars working in the postmodern context juxtapose ijtihadist and postmodern terminology as Mohammed Arkoun and Fazlur Rahman do. Some Muslim analysts are more familiar with Euroamerican postmodern theory than with Islamic heritage in the first place, having been educated in the Western-dominated intellectual atmosphere of twentieth-century academia. Some are familiar only with exclusivist formulations of Islamic thought—such as those represented by the popular refrain, "Islam is the solution"— and therefore see postmodern analysis as an important corrective to a potentially hegemonic ideology. Yet, as this discussion has tried to show, one need not have been tutored in Western academia to engage in a critique of cultural heritage based on concern for the relationship of intellectual products to the historically conditioned socioeconomic and political constructs in which they were produced.

There is an interesting dynamic set in motion when Islamic ijtihadist and Euroamerican postmodern hermeneutics are juxtaposed. ʿAbd al-Kabir al-Khatibi notes the irony of "borrowing" from the imperialists methodologies in order to deconstruct the ideology on which their imperialism was based. He quotes Derrida in this regard: "We are dealing with the need to explicitly and systematically present the problem of the status of a discourse that borrows from a heritage the resources necessary for the deconstruction of that very heritage. It is a problem of economy and strategy."[52] The deconstruction methodology itself, no doubt, is an articulation specific to Derrida's unique sociocultural and historical position. But in light of the foregoing discussion, the term "borrow" does not seem appropriate to describe the Islamic scholars' use of what Euroamerican scholars recognize as their own postmodern concern with the sociology of knowledge. Perhaps Gadamer's "fusion of horizons" is a more appropriate way to describe the result of Muslims and Westerners joining in a common discourse.[53] Perhaps both ijtihadist and neohistoricist analysts are working in a context that transcends or obfuscates, perhaps obliterates, the distinctions that identify the "one" and the "other."

In any event, that is the spirit in which this work is offered. Bandali Jawzi's *History of Intellectual Movements in Islam* is an erudite and fascinating work in its own right, and is historically significant as the first Marxist interpretation of the origin and development of Islamic tradition. But beyond that, it is important in that it calls attention to the apparent affinities between two methodologies which, albeit for differing reasons, are equally concerned with the need to criticize the intellectual heritage upon which the world's present tenuous state of affairs is based. Whether or not one accepts Jawzi's interpretation of the essential Islamic principles and his recommendations for their effective implementation in twentieth-century industrialized society, his work offers an excellent example of the ijtihadist hermeneutic, and suggests the possibility of discourse among Euroamerican scholars and those of the Islamic world on shared concerns regarding the nature and use of intellectual products.

II

THE HISTORY OF INTELLECTUAL MOVEMENTS IN ISLAM: THE SOCIAL MOVEMENTS

Bandali Jawzi

Translated by Tamara Sonn

Dedication

To the reawakening Arab youth;
to those who are liberating their minds
from the influence of irrational beliefs
about social, religious, and national affairs;
to those with healthy understanding
and vibrant minds, I dedicate this part of my book,
The History of Intellectual Movements in Islam.

Author, Jerusalem, 10 August 1928

Introduction:
The Unity
of Social Laws

We know that the first to set out the principles of historiography and the methods of historical criticism were Western historians such as Niebuhr, von Ranke, and Schlosser, among others. But those historians—ignorant, for the most part, of the history of the East—based their opinions on the history of the West alone. It is therefore easy for us to determine the extent to which the work of such historians actually pertains to the history of the East and how much of it is sheer fancy. For example, consider the ludicrousness of the following: "There has never been and will never be for the nations of the East 'history' in the sense accepted today among European scholars. The methods of historical research which Western scholars have established cannot apply to the history of the East.[1] [Bracketed endnotes are added by translator. Regular notes are those of the author as they appeared in the 1928 Jerusalem text.] Or could there by any greater ignorance than to say, "The factors affecting Western society are different from those affecting the history, culture, and lives of Eastern nations"?[2]

Had such bizarre ideas emanated from medieval historians or from people imbued with religious or nationalist prejudice and political or imperialist goals, there might have been an excuse for them. But when they have (and sometimes still do) come from the ranks of scholars and historians of the nineteenth and even the twentieth century, is there any excuse for them?

Schlosser, the above-mentioned historian, says:

The most important difference between the history of the West and that of the East is that religion and religious rites and literature, state and civil organization, even the arts themselves, are based in the Eastern states—charged as they are with the spirit of autocracy and religious authority—on the rejection of social and cultural evolution, as well as the influence of Western civilization.[3]

According to this view, then, one need only know a short period in the life of an ancient Eastern nation; one can extrapolate from that to discover its overall conditions regardless of how long it has existed or how many internal changes it has undergone. "For there is no need to know the history of an [Eastern] nation in its entirety in order to understand its social condition in a long period passed under the rule of one dynasty and one sky."[4] This statement is so obtuse as to require no explication nowadays. But worse yet, consider the views of another historian, renowned for his studies on the history of the ancient Near East, and Babylon in particular. In an attempt to corroborate this fruitless idea (with proofs not acceptable today even among school children), he claimed that Eastern peoples believe what happens in this life on earth is "nothing but a mirror image of what happens in the heavens. The life of human societies must be organized to run in accordance with the movements of the heavenly planets."[5] This abstruse statement implies that there is a marked difference between the mentality of the Eastern peoples and that of Westerners, to wit: Eastern peoples do not believe in the fundamental principles of evolution and empirical investigation. "These together form the foundation of modern science, yet [Eastern peoples] give them no weight. Furthermore, general laws, according to them, are not based on logical conclusions, but on the thought or theory of a preceding age, on whose controlling authority all their thoughts and deeds depend."[6]

That is the opinion of some Western historians on the history of the Eastern world and its mentality. It is no wonder, then, that they deny any development in the history of the East. They believe the life of the Eastern nations, in all its stages and manifestations, is controlled by one cause or factor, that is that these nations have no history in the scientific sense of this word. And that is precisely what some of them have said.

Now, the teaching of the above-mentioned scholars was on the history of ancient [Near] Eastern nations, like Babylonia, Assyria, Egypt, and so on. But can this be applied to modern history as well, or even to the Middle Ages? Some [historians], influenced by the thoughts of Schlosser and Winckler, tried to do just that: to judge the medieval history of Eastern nations, even their modern history, and particularly the history of Islam, on the basis of ancient history. The best known of those was the French orientalist Ernst Renan, who attempted this in some of his lectures on Judaism and Islam, particularly "Islam and Progress" and "The Position of Semitic Nations among Other Nations."[7] Here is what he said in the latter with regard to our subject:

"Islam detests science and calls for the destruction of civil society. It is nothing but the terrible simplicity of the Semitic spirit which oppresses the brain of man and obstructs the way of all free thought and scientific investigation, exchanging for all that the boring repetition of the *shahada*."[8] Having said that, he might just as well have claimed that the life of Eastern Islamic nations is based on laws and factors different from those on which the life of Western nations depends. In fact, he, did say that in the same lecture: "The Arian peoples have had from the dawn of their history an ancient code of rights. . . . But as for the life of the Arabs and (ancient) Jews, they have always been subject to other laws." Elsewhere: "The religious development of the Semitic nations has always been based on other laws."[9] And, "The Arab or Muslim today is without exception more remote from us than ever. For the Muslim and the European today are two different personalities, sharing nothing in common with regard to modes of thought and feeling, as if they were of two different worlds."[10] Renan repeated these ideas in his second lecture even more vehemently, but we have confined ourselves to the above. I believe that if Renan and those who share his views had lived to this day and seen with their own eyes the effects of the intellectual movements in Arab lands and the East in general, they would have recanted their statements on the intelligence and psychology of the Eastern peoples. [In any event,] since this view is now passé, we do not see any benefit in refuting it; time itself takes care of refutations. Suffice it to say that the source of these mistaken ideas is, first of all, the paucity of knowledge of Eastern history on the part of their author, and his inability to analyze the historical materials which were available at that time. Secondly, the above-mentioned writers based their judgment of the future of Eastern nations on their social and cultural situation in the past. This is totally inaccurate in the view of rational people. It is as if a Muslim Arab of the tenth or eleventh century were to visit Europe at that time and, seeing the ignorance, religious fanaticism, and poverty of its inhabitants, pass sentence on their future by saying that they would never have social life in the modern sense of the word.

However, it pleases us to be able to say that the majority of scholars of the history of the East—those who are above nationalistic or political objectives—do not share the opinions of Schlosser or Renan and their ilk. But for fear of boredom, we would present statements from many of them so that the reader could see for himself that no one today accords them much importance. We therefore will confine ourselves to Professor Bartol'd, a member of the Petersburg Academy, and considered today one of the greatest historians of the Middle East, if not the greatest. He said in his book *History of Research on the East in the West and Russia*:

If the Eastern nations approached anything like the simplicity and lack of dynamism that some historians of the West attribute to them, the investigation and understanding of Eastern history would be easier than that of Western history, [especially] for orientalists who study the later ages, to whom more historical sources are available than to their predecessors. They would see that the number of people of perfectly monolithic character in the East does not exceed their likes in the West. Their religion and its rituals, just as in the West, necessarily conformed to the actual conditions of life, more so than vice versa. And often there arose under the banner of religion movements whose sources were economic or political factors, not religious as we had previously thought.[1]

He said in another place:

For a long time, the West considered the religions of the great Eastern nations, like Buddhism, Brahmanism, and Islam, the only source of knowledge of their states and social systems. Scholars built on them alone their knowledge of the past, present, and future of these nations, and tried to use them to explain the causes of the fall of the nations which were and still are followers of these religions.

This great scholar [also] said in an article on the revolutionary movement that occurred in Samarqand in the year 1665, "We can demonstrate decisively that it is easy to apply to the history of the East the conclusion to which historians arrived in the West, i.e., that there is a strong connection between the development of social consciousness and the development of the two classes of tradesmen and artisans."[2]

More important than that, most European scholars are now beginning to declare that religion had no effect on the decline of civilization in the Eastern nations. This temporary decline was due to other than religious factors, the most important of which were the following: immigration and conquests by Barbarian nations (the Mongols, Turks, etc.), the Crusades, the growth of new cultural centers far from the old ones, and the shift in commercial routes. These and other factors are familiar even to students in secondary schools. (Some of them were indicated in an article published in the Russian language some thirty years ago under the title "Islam and Science.")

It follows, therefore, that the history of the East, the social and intellectual life of its people in general, and that of the Islamic people in particular, are subject to the same laws and factors to which the life and history of the Western nations are subject. The nations of the East have passed, and will continue to pass, through the same social stages and changes as Western nations. For there is no difference in this sense between the East and the West, and one is not innately superior to the other. This is in part what we will try to elucidate in this book. If we succeed, it will be our great good fortune. If not, we must [nevetheless] try.

ONE

The Economic Bases
of Islam

To say that Islam is merely a religious idea, that its triumph over Arab paganism, its rapid spread, and the widespread victories of the Rashidun and Umayyad caliphs are all traceable to religious zeal or fanaticism, is considered ridiculous today. Such views have been disproven by historical and economic research by the likes of Professor Wellhausen, Prince Caetani, Professor H. Lammens, T. Nöldeke, and V. V. Bartol'd, among others. For it has been well established that Islam, like all other great religions, is not only religious thought but a social and economic matter as well—or, more precisely, more so than it is religious thought. Prince Caetani said, "Islam was not a religious movement except outwardly; its essence was political and economic." [1] Part of the genius of the founder of Islam was that he comprehended the source of the economic and social movement which appeared in his time in Mecca, capital of the Hijaz. And he knew how to turn it to profitable account for his lofty religious and social ideals.

Caetani says, "Islam is the last emigration of the Arabs and its incentive was the same as that which induced similar movements previously in the Arabian peninsula, i.e., the continuing dessication of the land and its consequent depression and poverty." As the well-known Dutch orientalist M. deGoeje said, "The cause of the appearance of the Islamic movement was religion; however, the Arab tribes and the inhabitants of Mecca and Medina turned toward it and entered into it for reasons other than religion." [2] That is, the founder of the Islamic religion, like

75

those of the other great religions before and after him, used religion as a means of achieving other goals not originally connected to the religion (or only peripherally connected). In any event, there is no doubt that the Islamic movement was a child of its time and the offspring of the Meccan social environment in the end of the sixth century A.D. Therefore, if we want to understand the origin of this movement which led to the appearance of Islam, it is necessary for us to know that milieu and those social bases upon which the life of Mecca and her neighbors in the Hijaz were built.

It is known that Islam appeared in Mecca and could not have appeared elsewhere. For the conditions necessary for its appearance did not exist at that time and in such abundance in any other city in the Arab world. Of these many conditions, we have isolated the following.

Before the fifth century A.D., Mecca was a small community, a stopping place for the caravans returning from the South with goods from India and the Yemen to Syria, Palestine, and Egypt. In the late sixth century, it became a rich commercial city, providing foreign and domestic goods to the residents of the Hijaz. Its markets were frequented by Arabs from all parts of the peninsula and from Syria, Iraq, and the rest of the Arab countries. This development of Mecca depended, in the first place, on its central geographic location, and on the existence there of water. Secondly, it became, perhaps from the beginning of the fifth century, an important religious center for a great number of Arabs. They made pilgrimages every year, coming by the thousands from all parts of the Arab world to visit the sacred Ka‘bah and to perform the religious duty of the Hajj for a period of three months.[3] They also came to trade in the markets of the Hijaz, especially the ‘Ukaz market which was held every year near Mecca and was attended not just by Arab traders and poets but by Persians, Syrians, Abyssinians, and others, as well.

I do not consider it an exaggeration to say that this market, along with the horse racing, poetry competition, and other varieties of amusement and entertainment, provided a greater impetus to visit Mecca than the ancient religious ceremonies (which Islam has preserved for us to this day). For the residents of Mecca—that is, a small class of them (the custodians of the Ka‘bah and members of the city council, known as the *mala*’)—took advantage of the days of the Hajj, its rites, and such markets as ‘Ukaz, al-Majanna, dhu’l-Majaz, and Mina. They exploited them for personal gain, and they drew from them their influence among the Arabs; that is, their political and spiritual power, which was based on their financial power.

The inhabitants of Mecca knew the source of their wealth and power in the Hijaz, and they devoted themselves to commerce to the exclusion of other kinds of work. Thus Mecca became an exclusively commercial city, her people thinking only of trade and concerned only with amassing wealth and profit by all means, legally permissible or otherwise. One only has to read the Qur’an to understand the commercial activity in Mecca and how its inhabitants devoted themselves to it. There one will also discover the effect this enduring market had on the Holy Prophet and his teachings, and on the meaning of his words at the beginning of his call (indeed, throughout all phases of his life). If you ponder the verses of the Qur'an you will see that the number of people "whom neither buying nor selling distracted from the remembrance of God and performance of prayer and giving of alms" (Surah 24:38) was very small in Mecca. The number of those caught up in trade—running in the markets of Mecca, inquiring after the prices of goods and the value of [various] currencies—was very great. Indeed, some of the followers of the Prophet who journeyed with him to Medina left him while he was praying, to seek news of the caravans and to ask about the prices of goods. [See Surah 62:12.] For some of those who traveled with him to Medina became traders, competing with their adversaries in Mecca.

It is not surprising that the inhabitants of Mecca were preoccupied with trade and the exploitation, by any means, of what wealth they had. Their town, which the Qur'an describes as "settled but uncultivable" (Surah 14:38), was not suitable either for cultivation or industry. Its people were therefore obliged to live on imports from other lands. Their life and welfare depended on trade and *mudarabah* partnerships [a form of silent partnership which allows one to contribute capital, rather than labor, to an enterprise for the sake of profit]. Mudarabah was, in their view, simply a type of commerce. Were it not for trade and mudarabah, they would have had to abandon their territory, which they had grown to love despite a life of hardship there. Their situation in that age was like that of their brothers today, living on the pilgrimages and by them, and borrowing money from neighboring tribes at usurious rates.

In addition, the number of pilgrims and visitors to the markets of the Hijaz was great. It was therefore necessary and expedient for the Meccans to concern themselves with them, to provide them everything they needed in terms of food, drink, and commodities. They were obliged, as a result, to make provisions in advance, to prepare goods before the months of the Hajj and the opening of the 'Ukaz market. They had two trips per year, the summer journey and the winter journey (Surah 106:3), to Syria, Palestine, and South Arabia to buy commodities and to sell some of the products of their land such as dates, leather, currants, and so on. It appears that the capital in the hands of the traders and caravan owners of Mecca sometimes exceeded hundreds of thousands of dinars.[4] It was not, however, in the hands of one individual, but was collected from numerous persons among the inhabitants of Mecca and Ta'if, according to specific conditions.[5] It was the owners of caravans (and others among them who were entrusted with their money) who benefited from it. This is not surprising since most of the inhabitants of Mecca were involved in the annual caravans, and they chose as their escorts to the borders the best guards and men who were known for their skill in trade and political sophistication, such as Abu Sufyan and others of the council of Mecca. And the more capital they invested in the caravans, the more their concern over it increased. In addition, the task of the leaders and agents was made difficult by the fact that the caravan routes were always open to tribal raids and attacks by groups of vagabonds. These people wandered in the desert wreaking havoc, living by plundering and robbery. So it was difficult for the caravan owners to reach the borders of Syria and Palestine with their goods without encountering some resistance en route. In fact, not all caravans did reach their goals, and not all Meccans offered their company and leadership. Leadership was restricted to people well known for their self-possession, strength of purpose, political keenness, and ability to arbitrate between the interests of the wealthy of Mecca and the greed of the tribal leaders who controlled the caravan routes and were hired for their protection. They won them over at times with money, at times by marriage, and sometimes by intimidation and armed power. Thus, the owners of the caravans and the wealthy of Mecca had to employ a great number of people to protect their goods and to maintain them on the road. Most of those protectors were Abyssinian or African slaves whose numbers increased yearly, so that eventually they comprised a regular army supported by the Meccan traders. This indicates that trade was very profitable and that the gains were significant. Otherwise, they would not have been able to meet their expenses and amass great wealth besides, as it is well known that they did.

Our proof is that some of them had hundreds of thousands, in fact millions [of dinars]. Their banks were full of gold and silver coins, indicating that Meccan traders exported more than they imported. This is not surprising. Like the Arab tribes of the sixth century, it is known that in the past, peoples of Russia and Central Asia sold more goods than they purchased, because their needs were simple. This explains the discovery of large stores of Arab coins in central and southern Russia, whose Barbarian tribes sold the Arabs products such as fur, honey, and various kinds of wood for high prices, and bought from them what they needed in their simple lives.

Money, therefore, was abundant in Mecca and Ta'if, and many were wealthy. We have a number of indications of this in the Qur'an, in pre-Islamic poetry, and in the stories of the Prophet's life. The best proof, however, is the existence of a large class of moneylenders and bank owners in the beginning of the seventh century. For a variety of reasons, they indulged commonly in *riba* [the charging of interest]—indeed, it was so common that it was a second source of wealth and influence for many Meccan merchants. It was also one of the reasons that the people resented them. For the interest was exorbitant, fluctuating between 40 and 100 percent, as it does today in many countries.[6] But for this, the Qur'an would not have launched its well-known attacks on usurers and usury, nor would it have cursed usury and usurers on every page of the Meccan chapters.[7]

Whoever studies the Qur'an carefully and researches what appears in the verses dealing with usury and usurers cannot deny that the number of usurers in Mecca was very large in the days of the Prophet. And their negative effect on the social order was in proportion to their number. "For woe betide whomever falls into their snares and perish whoever the conditions of life force to take refuge with them. Because this kind of people are concerned only with amassing wealth. They do not understand the meaning of mercy and cannot see the difference between trade and usury" ([paraphrase of] Surah 2:276). That is because merchants and usurers at that time treated both trade and moneylending as one transaction with one and the same goal—to amass wealth by any means. For example, "When they received measures from the people, they took full measure; and when they gave them measures, they skimped" (Surah 83:3–4). They also speculated in silver and gold coins and foreign currency, at times increasing their value and sometimes decreasing it, depending on their personal interests and in accordance with their well-known greed. They would also flagrantly violate the terms of debts, postponing them or hastening them [as they chose], or increasing them. Whatever means they chose, it was always at the expense of the debtor, and led to his [virtual] enslavement. The Prophet very correctly described this as follows: "Oh you who believe, when you borrow from each other for a fixed period, write it down and let a scribe write it down between you justly.[8] Do not let a scribe refuse to write it down as God has taught him. Let him write and let him who incurs the debt dictate. And he should fear God his Lord and not diminish anything from it. If the person who incurs the debt is a fool or weak or unable to dictate, then let his guardian dictate justly and call two male witnesses, or if not two men, then one man and two women, as you like" (Surah 2:283).

The result of this type of oppressive burden was the subjugation and exploitation of the debtors in various ways, inspired both by the corrupt consciences [of the wealthy] and by the customs of the times in that debased environment. Among these was a custom that debts were borne by the wife or daughter of a debtor. When there was no other way to pay, and the debt was increasing daily, even hourly, through onerous interest rates, [the wife or daughter was often forced to turn to] prostitution in order to fulfill the debt of her father or husband[9] (Surah 24:34). There was no [other] way to repay the debt. Most debtors were forced either to flee into the deserts and join up with the vagabonds and bands of wanderers, or become slaves. This latter was the fate of the majority, as can be concluded from certain verses of the Qur'an and the Prophet's numerous calls (after the Hijrah) both for the release of the slaves and the betterment of their condition.

The outcome of this social situation was the existence of two classes of disproportionate size: that of the wealthy, bank owners, and custodians of the Ka'bah, that is, the aristocratic class or "council of elders," or the honorable, as the Qur'an calls them (Surah 63:9); and the class of wandering beggars (proletariat), the poor, the slaves and outcasts (Surah 26:112), those whose lives and happiness depended on the will of the wealthy. Indeed, it appears from a careful reading of the Qur'an that this class in Mecca was very large relative to the wealthy class, and that relations between the two groups were not much different from what they are today or, [for example], in the Byzantine empire when Islam appeared.[10] These relations are well known today, so there is no need to go into detail on the condition of the poor in Mecca and Ta'if at that time. We can simply describe their condition in general by saying that they owned nothing, not even themselves. For the right of legislation was restricted to the upper class, and its members enacted only the laws that coincided with their interests. Since the members of this class had no compunctions of conscience preventing them from exploiting and abusing the poor, the life of the poor was always subject to peril, suffering, and hopelessness. No laws dealt with them, and no legislation sympathized with their plight or tried to rescue them from the hell of everlasting slavery and social death. They lived in the back reaches and remote areas of the community in wretched, squalid houses, in difficult circumstances, and in constant hunger, while those who lived off their burdens resided in the center of town, in splendid houses near the Ka'bah and the council headquarters, the two sources of wealth and power.

This is a brief sketch of the situation of the poor in Mecca at the beginning of the seventh century, a picture characterized by desperation and resentment. These conditions necessarily brought about grievances and protests and, at times, rebellion. This was particularly true in times of commercial or agricultural crisis, when the condition of the worker, farmer, and slave worsened for lack of jobs, and because of oppression by the estate owners. Is it surprising then that the poor left Mecca and tried to improve their lot by any means they could? And is it any wonder that the Bedouin poets—the spokesmen of the state of the nation and mouthpiece of the majority—heaped censure on the wealthy, denounced the acts of the nobles of Mecca, appealed to them for kindness toward the poor, and reminded them of their duty toward the poor and oppressed? Goading the wealthy to help the poor, Bishr b. al-Mughaira said:

All of them had filled their stomachs,
But a man's satiation becomes meanness if his friend is hungry.

And al-A'sha said:

You spend the night in the winter pasture with full stomachs,
While your hungry neighbor women go to bed emaciated.

Yet these few outcries and feeble protests had little effect to speak of because they were not directed toward the elimination of the disease that sapped the vigor of the social body in Mecca, engendering the disharmony among the classes which we discussed above. The resistance to these social diseases required a more effective remedy, more powerful means, and more persistent men, men more effective than the Bedouin poets. And it was also necessary to wait for a suitable time to declare war on the Meccan elite and the usurers. The time, when it arrived, would itself provide a man of the age, a hero for the times.

If we look back and ponder for a moment the social work of the Prophet in the beginning of the seventh century A.D., we cannot fail to see that the social reformation—indeed, the social revolution that originated among the people of his homeland—was a more important, greater, and deeper revolution than called for by any Arab before or since the Prophet.

We do not want to get into a [long] discussion of the personal characteristics of the Arab reformer which compelled him to set out on this treacherous path and travel that difficult and dangerous but noble road. (I say dangerous because it usually leads those who take it to Calvary.) It is enough for us to know that the social system in Mecca at the end of the sixth century had prepared a place for one person sharing in it who had the strength and other necessary characteristics, such as sensitivity, kindness, farsightedness, good-heartedness, understanding, political adeptness, willingness for self-sacrifice for the sake of the common good, and the realization of his lofty principles.

The name of the man so richly endowed was Muhammad b. ʿAbdullah."[11] It was he who was called to become the reformer of his country, or, as the Qurʾan calls him, the warner and messenger of his people. And he obeyed the call gladly. His assignment was not by chance; it was in recognition of his spiritual power (which we have mentioned briefly) and his willingness to follow this call, as well as his knowledge of the social milieu in which he was born and had lived some twenty years before the call. He lived first as a poor orphan, suffering hunger and sometimes degradation while serving others. Then he became an employee or deputy in the commercial enterprise of a Quraishi widow who was like a mother to him. This position required him to travel all year and mix with the people. He entered into families and listened to their grievances. He contemplated the causes of the hardships of so many of them, and considered ways to lighten the burden of the poor and oppressed. These trips, then—this mixing with the people and attention to their situation—became a veritable school for him. It prepared him to be that social agent and reformer known to history today.

No doubt the Arab prophet apprised the people of his city and nation of the social diseases and how to resist them. For he had contended with them himself for a long time and had spent years observing and contemplating. He had spent a long time in the school of life; it taught

him its secrets and exposed its wretchedness to him. He came to understand the meaning of life and the causes of happiness and misery. And
he wanted to reveal that secret to the people of his city, his homeland—
indeed, the whole world. So he began his work without any weapon
but a sincere devotion of will and utter faith in God, who had "found
him an orphan and sheltered him, who found him lost and guided him,
who found him poor and enriched him" (Surah 93:7–9). What school
could be more useful than to start out as a poor, contemptible orphan
and then become, through earnestness and integrity, wealthy, beloved,
and respected? [It was thus that the Prophet] understood the meaning
of life and the sources and remedies for social disease. With all the
intellectual and moral powers granted him, he resisted [the temptations
of] the environment which he wanted to reform, and he [overcame] the
other political and cultural obstacles at the time. He had to rise above
them if he was to achieve the great goal placed before him.

No doubt poverty and its effects on the personality were the greatest
education for the Arab reformer. Our proof is that whenever this phase
of his life was mentioned, he drew new strength from it, seeking help
against his adversaries and overcoming the difficulties that were placed
in the way of his reforms. When he forgot this stage, his lord reminded
him of it, saying, "Have we not opened your breast and taken from you
your burden which nearly overpowered you, and exalted your reputation?" (Surah 94:2–5). In addition, he was orphaned as a boy and was
influenced during his childhood by the talk in the family and tribe about
his parents. His father had died while returning from Syria accompa-
nying the caravan of a wealthy Meccan trader as a simple laborer. He
did not profit from the caravans because he was very poor. He served
the wealthy in Mecca with menial labor, and was not able to provide
for the needs of his family. The Prophet's experiences in the house of
his uncle, Abu Talib, who gave him shelter after the death of his parents, were even harsher. As we know, Abu Talib was not [even] as
fortunate as his brother, 'Abdullah; he was forced to employ his
nephew and relied on him in many difficult matters. We must remember
that there were among the relatives of the orphaned boy some who
were extremely wealthy, such as his uncle Abu Lahab, the well known
and wealthy merchant "who was not benefited by his money and what
he had acquired" (Surah 111:3), or his other uncle, 'Abbas, who had a
great deal of money which he had gathered through usury at the expense of the Bani 'Abbas. But he did not benefit from the Qur'an and
the deeds of the Prophet. None of these rich uncles was concerned with
the matter of their poor nephew. Nor did they know much about him
before his call, before he began to threaten their wealth. Thus the
Prophet came to understand that there was a great contrast in wealth
between his uncles. He thought about it and about its sources. He also
pondered the techniques of commerce, the methods employed in trade
and by those entrusted with the people's property. All these had the

greatest effect on the sympathies of the man and his personality. These differences in poverty and wealth among the members of one tribe were what called the attention of the Arab prophet to the social strife found among the social classes in his community and led him to search for its sources. They were what caused him to declare a war of words on the class of shameless oppressors: those who monopolized the resources of wealth and capitalized on the burdens of the poor and artless dwellers of the desert.

This viewpoint on social strife was firmly rooted in the soul of the Arab reformer. What he observed daily only served to strengthen and intensify it. When he became a merchant—that is, a commercial representative for his wife, Khadija—he was exposed to the deceit and fraud in trade, the lack of concern for the property of orphans, the free play in measures, the luxury and affluence of the upper classes at the expense of the poor and the laborers, and the shortcomings of commerce and speculation. Thus his goal became to fight these social disorders at whatever cost to his own comfort. So the origins of the Prophet and his social milieu strongly affected his later life, his call, and the content of his words; not only in the beginning, but in all phases of his life. There is no truth to the reports that describe him otherwise which have appeared recently in Russia and West Europe, or to those that try to make the Arab prophet a rich man who defends the rights of the wealthy and powerful and their material welfare in his country. Nor can we call the Meccan reformer a socialist or communist, or say that his call was aimed at socialist or communistic goals, as some Western writers imagine.[12] But we believe that social factors—which scarcely appeared in the Semitic Near East without the thick veil of religion—had a powerful effect on his call. He threw his complete support behind the poor and the oppressed, openly defending their welfare, exposing himself to danger, and no more mindful of the moral or religious results than of the economic or material.

The weapons of the Prophet in this civil war—which he waged by himself, especially in the Meccan period—were the weapons of reformers of former ages, such as Socrates, Buddha, Zoroaster, Jesus, and other Semitic prophets. Indeed, he followed their example in all phases of his life, from the day of his call to its early termination. These weapons were [at first] sincere words: calling, warning, asking for mercy, and later threatening and intimidating. He did not fear the censure of a critic, but spoke the truth, even to himself and the people closest to him.[13] He expressed his opposition to his own uncle, Abu Lahab, denigrating his deeds, arousing the people against him, cursing him and his wife, and threatening them "with blazing fire," where his wife would tend the fire "and on her neck [would be] a rope of palm-fiber" and where "he will not benefit from his money or profit" (Surah 111:4–6). Another of his uncles, al-Mughaira b. Walid, one of the most powerful and wealthy men in all Mecca, opposed the Prophet, and began to harass him as he pursued his great task. But the Prophet feared neither his uncle nor the power of his wealth. The Prophet criticized al-Mughaira to his face and threatened him with everlasting damnation in a place where his money, "which he had collected and amassed," would not benefit him. These are but a few indications of the Prophet's boldness of spirit and disdain for danger, and are examples of some of the statements for which the wealthy of Mecca were not prepared. Most effective (and those requiring greatest courage) were the words he directed toward the merchants of Mecca. He accused them of greed and avarice, misuse of the money of orphans and other helpless and pitiful people, deceit in measuring, and other reprehensible practices which were among the chief sources of their wealth[14] (Surah 63:1–3; 81:10).

The prophet branded all of them depraved and disgraceful, and threatened them with the worst punishments in the afterlife (Surah 83:2; 72:18–23; etc.). On the other hand were those who "feed, for love of Him, the poor, the orphaned, the prisoner," and feed them "for God's pleasure," not demanding "from them reward or thanks" (Surah 76:9–10). And those who prepare for them "walled gardens and grapevines and young women companions and overflowing cups where they hear no nonsense or lies" (Surah 78:33–36).

> Resting there on couches where it is neither too hot nor too cold, and its shade shields them, and its many fruits are in easy reach. Vessels of silver and glass goblets are passed to them, bright as glass but made of silver, which they measure according to their own choice; they will be given a cup flavored with ginger from a spring called Salsabil and ageless youths will wait on them who, when you see them, you will think they are scattered pearls. You will see bliss and a great kingdom, and they will wear robes of fine green silk and brocade and bracelets of silver, and their lord will give them a pure drink. (Surah 76:14–22)

This was the language of the Prophet in that time. It was all he had to promise the faithful and threaten the infidels who did not heed his call or defer to his judgment for the solution of social and religious questions.[1] Later, neither the Isma'ilis nor their brothers the Qaramatis, the communists of Islam, approved of this language. In fact, they scorned and criticized it. Today we consider it simple-minded; its effect is lost on us. But this does not change the fact that in the days of the Prophet, and coming as it did from him, it had the greatest effect on his listeners. They had never heard such language before, because no one before him had used it in Mecca. So it is no wonder that these expressions caused a good deal of commotion among the Meccans, especially among the poor classes. The poor were delighted by talk of truth and justice. They began to accept the religion of the new prophet, embracing his words and aspiring to his ideals. In fact, those who followed the Prophet first, for the most part, were from the class of the poor, the slaves, and the uninfluential, as is well known[15] (Surah 15:29, 26:112).

And this is precisely what frightened the upper class in Mecca. As they put it, "We see that none follow you except the lowest of us" (Surah 11:28). Therefore, they scorned him and his group, and ignored him, until his call became so strong that it began to win over the elements of society that were dissatisfied with their lives. When the wealthy and powerful sensed this, and realized the danger that was threatening them, they began to consider ways to eliminate him. No doubt the first thing they thought about was not the danger to their religion, to which the Prophet objected strenuously in his Meccan chapters, but material danger, and perhaps danger to their administrative authority. That is because religion was not important to this class; they were known for their tendency toward skepticism in all important religious matters (Surah 36:38; 22:6; 64:8). Rather, their fear was for their material wealth and for their power. They understood that the attention of the poor of Mecca to the new call would mitigate their influence in the community and their wealth, built on the hajj [pilgrimage] to the Ka'bah and the markets of the Hijaz. For among the results of the spread of the new call was the end of the Ka'bah and the rites of the pagan hajj. They were not sanctioned by the new religion. [They also felt] it portended the end of Mecca and the old religion, the end of all its residents, and especially the wealthy and powerful. That is what the powerful of Mecca understood when the Prophet said that he wanted to eject them from their homes (Surah 2:78 247; 4:69; etc.). This is precisely what caused them to resist the new Prophet before he got out of their control. Thus they took whatever measures they could—threats, intimidation, warnings, boycotts, defamation, ridicule—to prevent him from spreading his destructive opinions and to limit his revolutionary call in the community, or at least weaken its effect on the poor and slave class. What is more, their efforts and plots would have succeeded had the Prophet not been somewhat tolerant toward his adversaries and [eventually] answered them with attacks stronger than theirs.[16]

When the council of Mecca saw that they were powerless to deter the Prophet or force him to agree to the well-known conditions they proposed, they planned to kill him or run him out of their city (Surah 8:31). But the Prophet was aware of their plans and urged his companions to leave Mecca for Medina. He had already communicated with some of Medina's inhabitants, and he was related to one of them by a maternal uncle (or some such relationship). So they left Mecca and went to Medina [beginning] on the night of the sixteenth of July in the year 622. The Prophet and his closest friend, Abu Bakr, were the last to leave the city.

No doubt the hijra of the faithful and their Prophet to Medina opened a new phase in the life of the Prophet and, indeed, in the life of Islam. Among the most distinctive characteristics of this new phase, in my opinion, is that the Prophet became, after lengthy conflict between his old adversaries and his new protégés, chief of his people and leader of his clan. Indeed, he became head of the state from end to end, having started out as a simple preacher, exhorting, cautioning, and bringing a message of peace. And the Arab nation began to carry out his orders and defer to his judgment in all matters. Thus it became easy for him to carry out his promises and implement the social reforms he had called for in Mecca. He began to realize his long-pursued principles of justice, brotherhood, and freedom for women and slaves, and to fight the causes of suffering and poverty in his community—in fact, in all Arab lands.

If we look back now and study the reforms the Prophet accomplished, we cannot deny that he fulfilled most of his promises and realized a large portion of his trusts. Had he lived longer, the reforms he brought into the life of the Arab nation would have been even greater and more far-reaching. Nevertheless, what he did in those few years in Medina—despite the wars and personal rivalries, the schemes, and the envy and deceit of the "hypocrites"—was very great. Only the obstinate, arrogant, or blindly fanatic would deny this. Among the reforms he introduced into the life of the Arab nation and placed among its foundations was the destruction of ignorant fanaticism. He attempted to consolidate the bonds of love, equality, and brotherhood, even if only among the Muslims, on a new basis: that of moral principles founded on religious tenets. He improved the condition of the poor, first by means of *suffa* [leader's share in the pre-Islamic tribal system] and then the *zakah,* the first tax the Arab reformer put on wealth and affluence for the benefit of the poor and the destitute. This socialistic tax brought with it great benefit for the poor, even though—after the death of the Prophet and his first four caliphs, and despite their wishes and practices—it came to be spent mostly for the needs of the state, rather than for the poor, prisoners, orphans, and widows. This new economic innovation which the Prophet devised while he was in Medina, was not the type that socialists and communists today use to solve economic and social problems. The zakah was a limited tax, not meant to remove wealth from its owners and distribute it to the needy equally, or to attain equality in means, as some imagine. As far as I am concerned, other reforms the Prophet devised were of no less significance than the zakah. Among them were improving the position of women; prohibiting usury; introducing laws designed to [eventually] eliminate slavery whatever the circumstances (Surah 5:91; 58:3; 4:94; 90:14, etc.); prohibiting or restricting the right of blood vengeance (Surah 17:34), the greatest evil in the Arab system; and prohibiting female infanticide, which was practiced by some of the barbaric tribes (Surah 81:9–10; 6:152; 17:32), as well as other progressive social laws.[17] Seen in the context of the age, these new practices strike us with their similarity to the laws of Rome, Constantinople, and other such civilizations. Yet we must recognize that, for all their progressive elements, they were not intended to kill the roots of the social diseases against which the great Arab reformer fought. There are a number of reasons for this, of which we limit ourselves here to the following.

No doubt the Arab prophet did not intend by his words and deeds in Mecca and Medina to uproot the causes of social evil and kill all its roots, as socialist groups today try to do. Rather, his goal was to lighten the burden of these illnesses on some classes, specifically those [whose labor was the source of] a great deal of wealth and who were defenseless against slavery. If he had wanted to kill the roots of all social disorders, he would have resorted, once he became a man of unlimited power in the Arabian peninsula, to other means, as we have mentioned. In this sense, the Prophet was like the rest of the prophets who preceded him, especially the prophets of Israel. He preferred to use moral means (except in unusual circumstances), unlike the means of some European political reformers today such as Lenin, the Russian communist leader, Mussolini, and others. That does not detract from the reforms the illiterate Arab reformer did introduce to this backward, ignorant people. For it is not fair to seek in the first quarter of the seventh century means of reform unheard of until the middle of the nineteenth century, means whose effectiveness hadn't even been demonstrated until today. To every season its flowers and to every age its men, as the Russian saying goes.

We can say that Muhammad excelled in describing and enumerating the diseases of Arab society, more so than in remedying them and uprooting their causes. And, indeed, his descriptions of these diseases often served to prompt a solution. It created in the minds and imaginations of his listeners an indelible impression. But his remedy for the disease was not as effective as his description of it, although there are exceptions to this. For example, the Prophet was the first to realize that the discontent of the lower classes in Mecca and Ta'if was due to their economic and social situation, and to recognize the reasons for this discontent. Nevertheless, that did not cause him to completely kill the causes of discontent by prohibiting, for example, personal trade, and putting it completely under the control of the government he had founded in Medina; by prohibiting slavery definitively; by taking property from its owners and making it the property of those who worked it; by monopolizing the rest of the sources of individual wealth which were (and still are) the source of social evils; or by using other means demonstrated by some socialists in this century.[18] This is because the Prophet was not an enemy of personal wealth or banking, nor was he against the accumulation of most of the land in the hands of a few. Indeed, he was not in principle an enemy of slavery, nor an advocate of the necessity of complete equality of women (Surah 4:12, 35, 177, 2:283) in terms of rights and duties. He was only against inequity in the operations of these social systems and their excesses (Surah 4:38; 43:18). That is obvious from the fact that the Qur'an and Sunna are devoid of words that clearly suggest the abolition of the above-mentioned systems and introduce others. The opinion of some that the Prophet intended to abolish private property and make it common— that is, the property of the community or nation—is false. Such extreme communistic thoughts did not occur to the Prophet except in the first stage of his social life. In fact, the problem of property was not at that time and in that milieu an important one, because the tribal system (which prevailed among the Arabs in that time) prevented the wide-spread accumulation of land by one owner who could capitalize on it through the burdens of others. Moreover, rental fees were very low, as was the situation, for example, in Europe, Asia, and Egypt in the feudal age, or as it is today in many of these areas. Therefore, we can conclude that in the days of the Prophet there was no special class of land-poor in the Hijaz. Nor did the discontent that we mentioned above emanate from this class, although we did see its effect (as well as that of other causes of poverty in Mecca) in the Qur'an. This view is also corrobo-rated by the fact that the lands that the Prophet and the Muslims after him conquered became, within a short time, the property of individual Muslims who administered it as they chose. It did not become the prop-erty of the nation or the caliphs who represented it. We do not deny that the lands of the Arabian peninsula, which the Arabs acquired through peaceful means—as well as some of the lands outside the penin-sula, which they acquired by the sword but did not divide among them-selves on the basis established by the Prophet (Surah 8:42; 59:8)—did become the property of the nation. But it does not necessarily follow that the administration of these lands (al-fay' and al-waqf) was like the administration of common lands; that is, that the Islamic nation ex-ploited them on communistic principles. (That is the situation, for ex-ample, today in Russia. They depend on land which the government keeps for itself rather than distributing to the peasants, for a variety of reasons we need not mention here.) It is well known that most of the lands taken by force remained in the hands of those who worked it and that the kharaj [tax] was levied on such lands. Thus, little of it was taken over by the government and made administrative property (fond territorial) or divided up among those who wanted it as their own property.[19]

Therefore, there is no basis to dispute whether or not the Prophet considered calling his people to a new system of land distribution, whether termed, albeit loosely, socialist or communist. The Prophet was neither a socialist nor a communist in the modern sense of these two terms, nor in any other sense. The reasons for this are complex, but turn for the most part on both the lack of the necessary conditions in that milieu and at that time, and on the personality of the Arab re-former. For, unlike Mecca, whose inhabitants were wealthy merchants and traders, the new environment to which the Prophet moved in 622 A.D. was, as we mentioned, very different. Most of the residents of Me-dina were poor peasants. Therefore, language appropriate in Mecca was not considered appropriate in Medina. Indeed, it was not understood there. And the goal the Prophet sought and worked toward realizing in Medina was different from his goal in Mecca. In addition, his policy toward the Meccans changed drastically in Medina.

A number of factors contributed to this change, such as the trials and tribulations experienced by the Prophet in the new circumstances and his love for his birthplace and family homeland, as well as other psychological and political factors, which appeared after the two battles of Badr and Uhud, and the siege of Medina. Accordingly, the Prophet began to mitigate his policies toward his Meccan brothers. Concurrently, the leaders of Mecca decided—after their defeat at Badr and their subsequent commercial losses—to be conciliatory in many matters with the Prophet, on the following conditions: that the status of the Ka'bah, the Hajj [the Islamic pilgrimage], and 'Ukaz revert to what it was before Islam; that they be granted general amnesty (except for a few); and that they be allowed to participate in [the Prophet's] new administration, which they anticipated would be beneficial for them as well. Perhaps among their mutually accepted conditions was that the Prophet remain in Medina and not speak against [the Meccans'] financial affairs. Thus, the Treaty of Hudaybiyyah became possible, as well as the "God-given victory" and the policy of "reconciliation of the hearts" (Surah 9:60)— in short, the policy of mutual tolerance and reconciliation (compromise). The people began "to enter the religion of God en masse." It was not because of their belief in the truth of the new religion, which they scarcely understood, but because of a desire to be near the new leaders and to preserve their ancient centers and the wealth which they had accumulated over the generations. It appears to me that among the conditions agreed to by the two sides, whether at Hudaybiyyah or elsewhere, was that the Prophet refrain from challenging the Meccan council and inciting the poor and slaves of the Hijazi capital against them. This appears to me to be the reason for the absence from the Medinan chapters, especially those which came in the final stages, of any biting criticism or rebuke of the Meccans. And there is another reason, no less significant: the social situation of the Prophet in Medina changed markedly, as is known, leading to a change in his emotional makeup. This is not unnatural. One of the results of this change was that some of the Prophet's social and religious reforms were incomplete, owing to something the Europeans call tolerance (compromise). It is possible that the personality of the Prophet and his ethnic characteristics had an effect on that [process] as well, the exact nature and extent of which, however, is difficult to define precisely. For we Arabs are known to be prone to excess in everything: self-sacrifice and excessive egotism; "Platonic" love and promiscuity; exemplary devotion and friendship and intractable vindictiveness; godlike idealism and extreme materialism; true democracy and personality cults; excessive self-confidence and a ready inclination to despair in the face of difficulties. In other words,

in the Arab people there are great powers which sometimes cause the
most noble deeds, and at other times, the lowest and most contemptible.
The reason for that, it appears to me, is that this great, clever, and
intelligent people, in general, lives by its strong feelings—more so than
by its intellect—and is motivated in its daily life and activities by personal interests. This our history shows us: we are a people of intelligence, capability for action, and far-sightedness, but we are easily im-
pressed and thrown off balance. How quickly we sink into desperation
when disaster befalls us! When good comes along, we fly on the wings
of euphoric happiness. With rare exceptions, this judgment applies to
all of us, individually and collectively, to young and old, educated and
ignorant.

It is among the teachings of the socialists that personal feelings and
perceptions accord with one's surroundings and social situation. Therefore, if one's surroundings or social situation change, so, usually, do
one's feelings, thoughts, and behavior. It is thus that the Prophet, his
personal situation having changed at Medina, followed in the second
half of his social and political life a path different from that which he
had followed at Mecca. At Medina he followed a policy directed by the
new conditions and his personal reactions to them.

The Meccan stage was one of preparation, of unfolding a new call
among the classes of the nation. It was a stage of antagonism and controversy, between a man devoted to his principles and work and a class
of people who, realizing the danger to their wealth and position in the
country, opposed that man and declared him an enemy. It was, however, a stage of efforts and dreams, all of which, if realized, would have
completely changed the country. How suitable this stage and how great,
and how sweet those dreams and the efforts expended in their realization! As for the second stage, it was one of work and ordering, a stage
of wars, the beginning of the political activity that led to compromise
between the two sides. The meaning of compromise in this example of
social revolution is the surrender of some demands or principles and the
retraction of some ideas, or putting them in a form acceptable to both
sides. This was the decree of the Prophet and the sophisticated and
experienced president of the republic of Mecca who spoke for the council of Mecca: The latter acknowledged the spiritual and secular rule of
the Prophet, gave up its idols, and agreed to pay the zakah and perform
the *salat* [required Muslim prayer]. The Prophet, on the other hand,
promised to leave Mecca and its leading thinkers a place in the administration of the new spiritual republic, and to let them continue in their
trade and to live as they chose. As for the third group—those for whose
sake the war had been waged and for the betterment of whose condition
the call had appeared—they were gratified in the beginning by such
things as alms and the zakah. But after the death of the Prophet and
the first caliphs, they were forgotten and returned to worse than their
former position. The council of Mecca became, from the caliphate of

'Uthman b. 'Affan, the unlimited power in the country. And the sons of Abu Sufyan, head of the council and greatest enemy of the Prophet, became the secretaries and agents, the heads of the victorious armies and functionaries in the lands conquered by Muslim swords. Then they became the unchallenged masters of those countries. Thus, it was as if the call of the Prophet and his social revolution, his labors and those of his early caliphs, had been only to strengthen his adversaries, and indeed, to augment their wealth and power. Stranger still, it was as if the Meccan merchants of the past had benefited from the Islamic movement and its ideas and principles, as if they had established one of the greatest states in the world, between which and the community the Prophet had founded there was scarcely any resemblance. That is proof of the brilliance of the Umayyads and of the breadth of their vision and political sophistication, which cannot be ignored except by the most ignorant arrogance and reprehensible bigotry.

TWO

Arab Imperialism and the Vanquished Nations

This is the import of the foregoing chapter: The great problem and most important issue with which the greatest leaders of the past age were concerned, and with which the scholars and leaders of this age still deal, is the issue of reconciliation between the welfare of opposing classes; that is, between the welfare of the rich and the poor, of the elite and the destitute; between the owners of the means of production and land, and the workers and farmers. This problem, with which the Arab reformer dealt, and which he tried to solve to the extent that the conditions of that time allowed him, shifted after his death to his caliphs. However, there were some changes, for political and social problems became more complex after the great Arab victories in the days of the first four caliphs (Rashidun) and the Umayyads and the incorporation of other ancient civilizations and different religions. The result was a new social situation in which relations among classes in Islamic society were strained. This tension reached a degree that threatened the outbreak of severe clashes, which would have meant the virtual collapse and death of the Arab state. Among the factors contributing to these tensions were the imperialist policies of the Arabs in general, and their economic policies in particular.

No doubt the preoccupation with conquering and settling other lands, with the resulting influx of properties confiscated and collected in various ways in the Arab peninsula, and the scattering of the Arab tribes throughout the conquered lands, distracted the Arab leaders from thinking about the social problems that had been the most important motives for the Islamic movement and had become, indeed, the source of their wealth; perhaps it made them forget. And there is no doubt that those victories and the occupation of new capitals outside the Arab peninsula helped change the center of the intellectual movement from Mecca and Medina to other great, ancient cities, and from the Arabs to the defeated nations. This was not because these nations were more capable of speculation than the Arabs, or more deeply rooted culturally. Nor was it because the conquered peoples were familiar with social or socialist movements before the Islamic victory and so were more inclined to grasp them, or more capable of understanding the reasons for their appearance than the Arab nations, who had never heard of them until the beginning of the seventh century, and then only in a small part of their country. Rather, it was because the conditions necessary for the appearance of those movements were more abundant among the non-Arab and non-Muslim peoples than among the Arabs at that time. The focus of the conditions there was the economic and moral condition of these countries.

If I tried to classify exhaustively here the condition of the conquered peoples in the Arab period or the period of the Islamic caliphate, along with all the manifestations of their social, religious, and moral life, or tried to speak of all the factors that forced the people at various times to attack the dominating nation and resist these disorders, as the Prophet had begun to do, I would need more pages than there are in this book. Therefore, I am forced to limit myself to only a few of them and refer the reader to scholarly sources for a more comprehensive view.

Indeed, the system of taxes which the Prophet established, combined with the changes and additions instituted by his calĭphs (especially ʿUmar b. al-Khattab, actual founder of the Arab empire and its constitution and system, and then the Umayyads), was a heavier burden on the shoulders of the vanquished nations than on the victors. This was because the former nations, like the Copts, Syrians, Persians, and Turks, had to pay, in addition to land taxes (the kharaj and *jizyah*), other taxes on trades and crafts which were frequently more burdensome than the kharaj and the jizyah. For they were not specifically limited to or based on a rational framework. Their extent and the time of their payment depended on the caliph's envoys and tax collectors. The kharaj and jizyah, on the other hand, were limited and known from before; their range was not up to the functionaries, nor were they heavier on farmers or debtors than on others. In addition, those who paid the jizyah did not suffer humiliation and abuse once they had "paid it out of their hands and were subjugated" (Surah 9:29). If you want to understand the true meaning of this expression and know what happened once the *ahl al-dhimmah* [protected peoples, that is, those who chose not to convert to Islam but to abide by its laws in return for full citizenship rights;

also referred to as dhimmis] paid the jizyah, simply peruse the books of history and law. Read what Abu Yusuf, Ibn Adam, and others wrote about the kharaj and jizyah.[1] For since there was no way to escape this burden except to accept Islam, the Iraqis, Persians, and Turks entered the religion of Allah in droves. Thus in Egypt, for example, during the caliphate of ʿUmar b. al-Khattab, there were practically no dhimmis who had to pay the kharaj, and the treasury was almost depleted in the days of ʿUthman and ʿAli, whereas it had been plentiful before. This is what forced the Umayyad caliphs—ʿUmar b. ʿAbd al-Aziz and his functionaries in the East and West—to abolish the practice of ʿUmar I and take jizyah even from those who entered Islam. That was one of the causes of dissatisfaction with the Umayyad state, as is well known.

No doubt the conversion to Islam of the people of the conquered lands in the first half of the first century A.H. led to the material and moral improvement of the condition of the peasants, even though they were not put on the level of the Arabs, their brothers in religion. For the Arabs regarded the converts to the religion and Arab nationality with contempt. This was contrary to the noble principles which the Prophet instituted, the principles of equality in rights and duties and brotherhood among all Muslims regardless of their nationality, social class, or personal situation. Nevertheless, no one can deny that the social status of those converts, as we said before, was better than that of their brothers in the past who continued to preserve the religions of their ancestors. We have plentiful historical evidence that the situation of those others gradually worsened, and that the government and its functionaries began to consider them as little more than milch cows, as was the case with the Jews in Europe and the Middle Ages and in some parts of Russia before the last war.

It appears that the abuse in land taxes and the levying of taxes on non-Muslims began in the last days of the caliphate of ʿUmar b. al-Khattab. This may be concluded from the numerous complaints against him, such as that of the Persian slave Fairuz, who came to Medina to complain about the governor of Kufa, Mughirah b. Shuʿbah; the emissary of the governor did not treat him well, so Fairuz killed ʿUmar in the mosque. He was the first martyr in Islam who was killed as a victim of its administrative system and economic policies.

It is said that ʿUmar b. al-Khattab, known for his justice and strength, was opposed to the injustice of his officials, and always encouraged them to pursue just means. He called them to compassion toward their subjects and threatened them with severe punishment, including dismissal and confiscation of their property, if they violated their duties.[2] Nevertheless, these measures did not prevent the property of the subjects, and especially the dhimmis, from flowing into the hands of the officials. Nor did they prevent the accumulation of great wealth in the hands of a few or the appearance of a new class of wealthy in Medina. Thus, the capital of the new kingdom was quickly transformed from a small community to a large city, complete with crowds and great markets full of foreign goods, as well as new social classes that did not exist in that city before Islam.

The great caliph, reformer, and victor died near the age of sixty, having spent the last decade of his life establishing the great Arab empire and introducing laws necessary for its preservation and security from the ravages of time and the foolishness of men. After long arguments and a controversial crisis, he was succeeded by the son-in-law of the Prophet and one of his first converts, ʿUthman b. al-ʿAffan, one of the wealthy Umayyad nobles, and one of the few educated men of the age. ʿUthman was acknowledged as caliph at an early age despite his weakness of will and his dependence on family and relatives to govern the great new kingdom for him. He was forced to surrender its administration to the Umayyads, sons of his uncle, who were the most capable in administrative matters at that time. This displeased many of the companions of the Prophet and the old Muslims, as well as a group from the family of Abu Bakr and ʿUmar. All of them began to oppose the caliph and his family and to plot against them and incite the people against them. Thus, the condition of the kingdom worsened, especially the condition of the lowest classes. Political parties appeared or, more precisely, were established, as is well known. They killed the third caliph, and the caliphate transferred to the second son-in-law of the Prophet and his cousin, ʿAli b. Abi Talib. His caliphate was full of war and struggles, and ended after six years with his murder. Then the caliphate passed in 661 A.D. to the Umayyads, opponents of the Prophet and Islam until the year 628 A.D.

It was hoped that the situation of the farmers and workers among the dhimmis and others would improve during the caliphate of the Umayyads. Many of them were known for being politically farsighted and levelheaded, to have determination moderated by constraint, and for their habit of considering the feelings of the common people. Nevertheless, their love of money, which they inherited from their ancestors, Meccan traders, and their urgent need for it, compelled them to execute great political exigencies and to undertake far-flung and difficult conquests in addition to battling their enemies within the country. These factors, combined with others, caused the social changes that appeared in Islam in later years. They were forced to demand money in all ways, that is, to increase taxes on their people and to collect them by more severe methods and, in general, to overburden the classes paying them.

We do not deny the positive effect of the Umayyads on the Arab nation. For example, they improved the ancient administration of the Persians, based on the disparity of classes, and treated the Copts, Syrians, and Christian Arabs well, lifting the religious yoke of the Byzantine government and lightening their overly oppressive taxes. Nevertheless, that does not prevent our saying that the situation of the poor classes worsened in the latter days of the Umayyads. Those caliphs were forced, for the reasons we mentioned, to levy taxes and to use methods of collecting them which were not pleasant to some classes of people. We must draw attention, accordingly, to their abrogation of the Sunna of the Prophet and rightly guided caliphs who were devoted to the rights and privileges of all dhimmis and *kafirs* [unbelievers] who accepted Islam. For their way had been to exempt these classes of people from the jizyah and kharaj, unless the land had been subject to the kharaj since the day of Islamic conquest. The Umayyads—except 'Umar b. 'Abd al-Aziz—forced the class mentioned to pay the jizya and kharaj, as if they had not accepted Islam and received its justice. The result of this economic policy was that the number of converts to Islam decreased and the discontent of those who converted among the Meccan tribes increased, so much so that they left the new religion and worked with the rest of their enemies toward its downfall. The Coptic nation, for example, which had received the conquering Arab army with a contingent to rescue them from the hands of their enemies and which helped them conquer the country, did not hesitate to turn away from them. They began to distrust them and to complain about their internal financial policies because they saw things that aroused their anger and made them long for the days of their former servitude. The Copt writer Sawiris [b. al-Muqaffa'] complained about the condition of his nation at the end of the Umayyad caliphate: "Many of the rich and poor of our country deny the Muslim religion in order to escape from the kharaj and the rest of the oppressive taxes."[3] There is other written evidence which leaves no room for doubt that the dissatisfaction of the conquered nations with the policies of the Umayyads did not stop with complaints, protests, objections, and imploring. It sometimes extended to attacks on the state and its workers and the use of the sword. Among these incidents we mention the attack of the Turks in Central Asia against the Arabs. Those in power there refused to be tolerant in financial matters and broke their promises. They levied a heavy tax on the Turkish tribes, which had entered the religion of Islam not out of devotion but out of hope for a decrease in the collection of jizyah money. This was the pattern of those who entered Islam in the age of the Rashidun caliphs. If it had not been for the discretion of the caliph's administrators and the heads of his army, as well as the money they gave freely, this revolt would have crushed the Umayyad power in all the Turkish lands. In that year (728 A.D.) there remained in the hands of the Arabs only Samarqand and Al-Dabusia, and they almost lost them in the year 730 A.D., after long wars with the greatest Turk Khaqan and those petty kings and princes who gathered around him. It added to the gravity of the situation that some of the Arabs of the *a'imma al-marju'ah*, who had led the Turks into the religion of Allah and made promises in the name of the government of Damascus, joined forces with the Turks.[4] They censured the sultans and their representatives in this country for placing love of money above love of country. Money made them forget the Sunna of the Prophet and the first four caliphs.

These were the results of the financial policies of the Umayyad caliphs, not only in the countries we mentioned but in non-Arab countries, the Caucasus, and beyond, and the rest of the conquered lands, as we shall see in the following chapter. These were dangerous results that had a devastating effect on the rule of the Umayyads and the brilliance of their career.

The new system of land administration that the caliphs brought in when they assumed power bore similar negative effects. The essence of this system was that they gave a free hand to whomever among the Muslim Arabs wanted to acquire lands outside the Arab peninsula. This had been forbidden in the days of Abu Bakr and ʿUmar. Accordingly, there was a rush of the wealthy and powerful among the Arabs to take possession of lands in Iraq, Egypt, and other regions known for good land and abundant waters. They began to work the land and to profit from it with whatever means they had at the time. This led to the shift of most good lands to individuals or small families, who became owners of great wealth. Not fifty years of the reign of the Umayyads had passed before the lands of Egypt and Iraq became fertile at their hands, and at the hands of those who followed them and their clients. It is said, for example, of the lands of Khurasan and beyond, that the most fertile and wide-ranging lands, like Muqan and the desert of Shirvan, passed into the hands of a small group of Arabs very close to the rulers, or members of the royal family itself. They capitalized on it by means of the lowest classes of the country, or African negroes, who arrived by the thousands from their country and were forced to work in the marshes of Egypt, Iraq, and trans-Caucasus, where malaria, fever, and hunger decimated their ranks, just as their brothers were annihilated in the southern states of America until the first half of the last century.

If you want to know how these lands passed from the hand of their original owners to the hands of the above-mentioned groups of Arabs, you must read the Arab historians like al-Baladhuri, al-Yaʿqubi, al-Tabari, and others. There you will find a great deal of information about the holdings of the Umayyads and their clients, as well as the methods of exploitation of those lands and the conditions of the laborers on them.

There was another cause that sometimes led to hostile movements against the ruling powers, not only among the forsaken dhimmis and kafirs but also among the Muslim Arabs. That was the law enacted by ʿUmar b. al-Khattab under which kharaj lands—that is, lands that paid the kharaj tax, not the tithe, at the time of the Arab conquest—continued to pay this tax even after the conquest and after a large portion of it had passed to the hands of the Muslims. True, this law was not introduced by the Umayyads themselves, but they preserved it, and not out of respect for the ideas of ʿUmar, nor love of his practices. It was out of love for the treasury, or more precisely, for its money, and fear that what was left of those lands would pass into the hands of the Muslims and the privileged or aristocratic class hostile to them [and therefore no longer be taxable]. Their preservation of this law was a good thing in itself and was useful for the welfare of the state. Therefore, there would have been no recriminations if they had collected the kharaj equally from the old landowners of the citizenry and the new Muslim landowners. However, they did not equalize these two sides for the reasons we mentioned, which caused the Arabs' rejection of the principles of equality with non-Arabs. This situation is not surprising, since many residents of the conquered lands were hostile to the Arabs and their state, and they were working covertly and overtly toward its overthrow. They resisted the Arabs with the sword and pen, perhaps more so with the pen than the sword, as is indicated by the *shuʿubiyyah* movement, in which the Persians, Nabataeans, Copts, Turks, and other people upset with the Arab Umayyad policies participated.[5]

There remains another factor in this dissatisfaction which must be mentioned, if only briefly. It derives from the administrative reforms ʿAbd al-Malik b. Marwan introduced after the unification and consolidation of the country. For example, he introduced a new system of land surveys, recording them in the vernacular, and their governmental regulation. The landowners were thus deprived of the arbitrary recording of the amount and kinds of land, and therefore the amount of kharaj or tithe owed on it. This had been the case before these reforms, when the lands were registered in the old way, dating to the Byzantine or Sasanian days. Another important reform was the withdrawal of the old coinage that had circulated in the country until the caliphate of ʿAbd al-Malik, and the casting of a new coinage inscribed with Qurʾanic verses, instead of the cross and fire altar that were on the old coins. Perhaps the most important reform in the unification of the Arab empire was the introduction of the Arabic language in the courts and official offices, replacing the Greek, Coptic, and Persian languages that were still used in Syria, Egypt, and Persia, as well as the appointment of officials from among Arabs, or those skilled in the use of the Arabic language, which, at that time were few. These were some of the important changes by which ʿAbd al-Malik tried to consolidate the land after uniting it by the sword and good administration.

All this was necessary for the life of the vast state. And it was necessary in the caliphate of ʿAbd al-Malik b. Marwan, the greatest of the Umayyad caliphs, and the farthest- and keenest-sighted of them. He saw the disorder in the land and the disintegration of the Arab caliphate after the death of his father, Marwan b. al-Hakim; it would have been destroyed if God had not given it a caliph like ʿAbd al-Malik. Nevertheless, these reforms were in clear violation of the material welfare of some of the peoples, or some of the classes of people, and their national sympathies. They did not approve of these reforms because they considered them to be intended for the welfare of the upper classes and its old traditions. Accordingly, they began to work, both publicly and in secret, for its downfall.

Nevertheless, the downfall of the first Arab empire and the establishment of the ʿAbbasid state in its place did not cause any noticeable change in the conditions of the conquered nations. The internal policies of the ʿAbbasids, in particular, those of the sons of al-Mansur and their descendants, were not significantly changed from those of the Umayyads, especially with regard to finance, land, and economics. This is not true, however, of administrative, war, and colonial policies, as is known today. For these policies had special characteristics by which they could be distinguished from those of their predecessors, the Umayyads, or the Rashidun caliphs.

I said that the financial policies of the ʿAbbasids were closer to those of the Umayyads in the days of the sons of al-Mansur and their descendants than to those of his own time. This was because al-Mansur was the most farsighted of the ʿAbbasid caliphs, and he treated the peasants and workers kindly. He was the first of the caliphs and Eastern sultans to realize this simple truth, which today even schoolboys know: that the prosperity of the state, its wealth, and its power depend on the happiness and contentment of its individual members. Whether he realized it through correct thinking and his own native intelligence, or as the result of the suggestion of his minister from the Barmakid family (not to burden his subjects with taxes and to lift some of the taxes from them or reform them in order to safeguard farmers and their wages), he did call on the farmer to take an interest in cultivating his land, and on the worker to make every effort in his work, which the reformer caliph generated in the new capital of the country and in other cities and villages. Thus the country prospered, and the people began to experience welfare and comfort, especially in the second half of that caliph's reign. Moreover, social life in the days of al-Mansur was not like that in the days of his successors, for the affluence of the days of al-Rashid and his sons had not yet appeared. The harem, with its slaves and eunuchs, had not yet gotten out of control. Nor had the other abuses that typified this time: political and familial plots; blatant manifestations of pomp and pageantry with the people's money; the accumulation of the good lands in the hands of a few; the contracting out of [the collection of] kharaj and other taxes to greedy and malicious people and state administrators even more oppressive and prone to bribery [than their predecessors]. Add to that the support of the caliph's palace, his harems, his wives, and the army; the murder of the Barmakids; and the oppression of the friends and associates of the Umayyads, to name just a few manifestations of oppression and invalid expenses that were unknown in the days of al-Mansur and the Umayyads. Then you will see the reasons for the dissatisfaction of some of the Arabs and most of the conquered nations, and understand their attempt to bring down the ʿAbbasid state.

This includes all nations except Persia, for they had expected to be happy with the ʿAbbasids and the changes they would bring, which included moving the capital of the kingdom to their region; the participation of the upper classes in the administration of the country; borrowing some aspects of their system and their ancient customs; and so on. However, as it turned out, the Persians were not pleased with their situation in the caliphate of the ʿAbbasids in general, and that of al-Rashid in particular. Their dissatisfaction became abundantly clear after the calamities of the Barmakids, when the Persians began to realize that the ʿAbbasid policies toward them had not changed much from those of their predecessors. They were not being catered to, nor reconciled, unless it was urgently needed, and then it was only for the welfare of the ʿAbbasids, and not the welfare of the Persian people. Otherwise why would they have ended the life of Abu Muslim al-Khurasani, who had assisted their ascent to the throne, as well as the lives of many other great Persians and their leaders? For these, among other reasons, it was not long before the Persians began to feel that the political change they had helped effect in the Islamic caliphate was not to their benefit and that there was no hope of improving the conditions of their economic life. They saw that the new family followed the internal political policies of the previous family, that is, the policy of "the whip and the sword," especially toward the lower classes: the farmers, laborers, and minor professionals who made up the majority of the country. Indeed, the policy of the new family toward those classes was more oppressive and pernicious than the policy of the Umayyads toward them, as history shows, and to which the books of the ʿAbbasids themselves attest.

It is well known that the true founder of the ʿAbbasid state and the greatest of their caliphs was ʿAbdullah al-Mansur. He tried to build his state, first of all, by arbitration between the two largest nations of which the Islamic state was composed in his time, the Arabs and the Persians. He thus changed the domestic policy of the Umayyads, which was purely Arab, and instituted equal deference to the great Arab allies, the Qays and the Yemeni [tribal groupings]. He also tried to bring an end to the mutual ill feelings that existed between those two peoples. It was thus that the ʿAbbasids began to reconcile the wealthy landowners and merchants, men of letters and science, and especially the old aristocratic classes, such as the Barmakid family and others, whose influence and wealth had been impeded by the democratic policies of the Umayyads. So these classes returned to their former positions. They began to play a more important role in the life of the ʿAbbasid state, but particularly in the lives of the Persians. The result was that the Persian peasant, who had begun to feel a bit of personal freedom—he was able to acquire land under the Umayyads—was now subject to two strong but conflicting influences: the state [apparatus] to the west of him, and the recently resurrected aristocratic class [in his own land]. He had two masters: the distant one in Baghdad, with whom he had little contact; and the immediate master, owner of his property and the real power over him. It was this latter master who was authorized to collect and levy taxes.

However, the dissatisfaction with the new state was not limited to the peasant and worker classes. It extended to other classes, even the upper class: that is, the great landowners and leaders of the old religion. This was due to the failure of their attempts to gain national independence, reestablish their old religion, revive their literature and language, and other hopes that they had attached to the appearance of the ʿAbbasid state. In the beginning they had been the strongest people in the state, and for their benefit lives and property had been sacrificed. But now there were increased taxes and fees and suppression of the ancient religion, as well as other factors that went against the grain of the Persian nation. These were, at that time, among the most important causes of dissatisfaction among the Persians, not to mention their neighbors, the tribes living under the influence of Persian culture and language. These were the causes of the numerous attempts to gain freedom from ʿAbbasid policy. And these attempts continued for years. In fact, they continued right up to the fall of the ʿAbbasid state (which came with the invasion by the Central Asian and Mongolian infidels).

The scope of this work does not allow for mention of all the revolutions that "the Persian people mounted against the blessed state," from the appearance of the first revolt in 755 A.D. (the Revolt of Sinbadh) to the last one, which preceded the downfall of the state. Nevertheless, it is necessary to look into a matter of which the historians of the East are now aware. These revolutions—or most of them, for example, the Ustadhsis Revolt of 767 A.D. and the ʿAta Revolt of 778 A.D.—had a religious tinge, which has led the careless reader into error with regard to their true causes. We now know that this tinge was nothing but a thin veil hiding the political and economic factors that were the true causes of these revolutions (as we indicated in the introduction). In addition, we should indicate that the number of revolutionary movements against the ruling power or its functionaries began to increase during the caliphate of al-Mutawakil (847–861 A.D.) and his sons, that is, when [gross] moral and financial decay became apparent in the ʿAbbasid state. Therefore, a large regular army was necessary to suppress these revolutions and to repel the incursions of the enemy across the northern and western borders. The caliph had to spend a great deal of money to support this army, which became larger—beginning in the reign of al-Maʾmun—than that of the Turks, Daylams, or any of the other covert enemies of the Arab state and its caliphs. Add to that the expenses of the palaces and the new cities which the ʿAbbasids began in Baghdad and Samarra, and the fact that money at that time was difficult to come by, except for those in positions of central power. For the powerful people in the distant regions began to appropriate a large portion of the taxes, owing to the weakness of the central power and its inability to punish them. Since there was no effective obstacle to their power (which was supported in the country by bribery and syco-phancy), the people were forced to redress their grievances by force. This happened, for example, in 807 A.D. in Samarqand, when they at-tacked the caliph's tyrannical and oppressive representative, brutally murdering him.

The people also rose in revolt on numerous occasions in Egypt, Iran, Armenia, and Azerbaijan, all of which were suffering under tyrants. Al-Baladhuri, al-Ya'qubi, al-Tabari, and Ibn al-Athir give full accounts of the oppression of the governors and tax collectors in the end of the eighth century and the beginning of the ninth. They report how many times the people were forced to resort to arms to relieve themselves of— or, at least, limit—the despotism of the governors. Not one year passed without "agitation" in the country, as al-Ya'qubi and al-Baladhuri say, referring to the residents of Armenia and Azerbaijan, and especially of "Sinariya," the Khazars on the western shores of the Caspian Sea, oth-ers outside the Caucasus, and the Persians.[6] They revolted against the ruling power and forced them to mobilize the armies and spend a great deal of money to restore peace. Indeed, if it had not been for the dispar-ity of those tribes in goals and means, and the difference in their posi-tions, the workers of the 'Abbasid state would not have been able to last one month in the country.

As the central power became increasingly oppressive, its authority began to approach extinction: its Arab functionaries began to join with the other dissidents and to provoke them into attack and rebellion, both for personal goals and because they realized its weakness and the immi-nence of its demise. In any event, they decided to join with them for mutual benefit when the Baghdad government fell, or when they cast it off, and to unite with the independent emirates, such as the Bani Shay-ban, the Bani Mazid, and the Kasrawani emirate, which was established later on the rubble of the 'Abbasid caliphate in the Caucasus and be-yond. This led to the appearance of a special class in Armenia and Azer-baijan known as the "triumphant" class. This consisted of none other than some of the 'Abbasid functionaries in that country, or heads of some of the tribes who broke away from their caliphs and tried to be fully or partially independent, in order to begin a new stage in Islamic history, which we call the age of feudalism in Europe in the Middle Ages.[7] It was the practice of these independent amirs to call other influ-ential people in the country and conquered nations to follow their ex-ample and to try to break away from the 'Abbasid caliphate. The first to do that and to try to hoist a banner of freedom in the hills of Qara-tagh was Babak al-Khurrami, or Papak the Persian, his real name in the language of his country.

THREE

Babak's Movement
and His Socialist Doctrine

The movement of Babak al-Khurrami and his followers differed from previous revolutionary movements in two significant respects: its organization and the goals it sought. The organization of the movement is apparent, first of all, in its success, the speed of its spread, and the perseverance of its adherents in the face of armed enemies for nearly twenty-two years. It is also apparent in the unprecedented responsiveness of the people toward it and the active participation of great numbers of people from nations neighboring Persia—the Kurds, the Armenians, those in the Byzantine territories, and others from beyond the lower Caucasus. All this indicates some prior arrangement and shared feelings of common interest among them.

As I said, Babak and his followers stood firm against the armies of the caliph of Baghdad for more than twenty years, heroically defending themselves and their principles out of love of both country and freedom. Even though they were defeated in the end, they were nevertheless able to strike the enemy a severe blow, which almost destroyed both its material and spiritual power. For it has been said by historians that the downfall [of the ʿAbbasids] began in the final days of the caliphate of al-Muʿtasim (r. 833–842 A.D.). He was indisputably one of the greatest ʿAbbasid caliphs and was venerated by poets of the age. But he was helped in his numerous wars by the great Turkish leader Haidar b. Qavus al-Afshin; without his help and that of his Turkish armies, the ʿAbbasids would surely have been defeated in their wars with Babak.

Clearly, the movement of Babak was the result of social and political factors that appeared at the end of the eighth century and the beginning of the ninth century in the ʿAbbasid kingdom generally, but particularly in Azerbaijan. Among these were a lessening in respect for the ruling power; indeed, it practically vanished among the more remote peoples such as the Persians and Turks; among non-Muslims such as the Copts, Syrians, and Armenians; and in the eyes of the Arabs themselves. Its moral standing fell to the extent that its subjects ceased to support it at all, as is evidenced by the reports of some of the Arab historians.[1] Among the goals sought in the numerous revolts was complete separation from the ʿAbbasid caliphate and union with independent kingdoms or caliphates, such as the Umayyad kingdom in Spain and the Aghlabid emirate in North Africa, or the republic that Babak tried to create in the hills of Qaratagh among the Iranian people. The ʿAbbasid caliphs were unable to join these to the Arab nation and religion, or [even] to create paths of mutual understanding between them and the victors.

We have sufficient evidence to conclude that Babak and his followers thought about attacking the caliphs of Baghdad and prepared for revolution for some time. They apparently waited for an appropriate opportunity to begin the action and announce war against their greatest adversaries, judging from secret communications between Babak and the Byzantine emperor Theophilus (r. 829–42 A.D.) and his predecessors, which probably began before the revolution.[2] Some historians mention that Babak himself went to the Byzantine capital, or at least to its southern borders, to invite the emperor to participate in a general war they would announce against their common enemies. However, this does not appear correct. It is hard to believe that Babak visited Byzantium during the war, which probably broke out in the summer of 817, and there is no proof that he visited it before the declaration of war.[3] However, we may be able to rely on reports that Babak, after he decided to attack the caliph of Baghdad, sent a messenger to the Byzantine emperor, his friend and natural ally. [This messenger is said to have informed Theophilus] of Babak's decision and the goal of his attack, and to have asked him for military assistance, or to join personally in this all-out war. For he hoped the war would benefit them both if it ended with the downfall of their mortal enemy. At any rate, there is no doubt that Babak was able to depend on Byzantine assistance in his wars with the Baghdad caliphs. We know that, when matters worsened after the twenty years of resistance, the Byzantine emperor came to his aid. Through his military maneuvers on the Arab borders, he tried to distract a large portion of the caliph's army stationed in Azerbaijan from Babak. We know also that a large group of Babak's followers waged war in the year 831 A.D. under the leadership of an Iranian man known as Theophobe, on the Byzantine side.[4] A large part of Babak's army crossed the Byzantine borders after Babak's failures, and were welcomed there and protected.

We can therefore conclude that there was a strong and well-founded friendship between Babak and the Byzantine emperor, if not a secret agreement for war. But Babak did not limit himself to this alliance. He also tried to win over his closer neighbors, such as the Kurds and Armenians, or at least to secure their neutrality (on mutually agreeable conditions) in the event of war. He did not completely succeed. However, a small group of them who lived in the region of Saywanya [Siounie, on the northern branch of the Araxes River] joined him gladly and formed a strong bond with him; the marriage of the daughter of their leader and the head of their army strengthened the bonds. The rest of the Armenians considered it more appropriate for their national welfare to take this opportunity to restore their affairs, which had suffered badly in a civil war in the year 772 A.D., and at the hands of the caliph's administrators. They decided, therefore, to remain neutral, fearing the result of a war between the communists of Qaratagh and the caliph of Baghdad if they joined with the former, despite caution or the neutrality of most Armenian generals.

The Kurds' participation in this war was almost universal. This is apparent in the statements of the historians who comment that the Maranid leaders and heads of the Kurdish tribes in Hamadan, Kirmanshah, and other eastern regions answered the call of Babak freely. Al-Yaʿqubi, expert in this area, said, "Muhammad b. al-Baʿith had followed him, and the Kurdish and Maranid princes were in his service." [5] Another historian noted that "the Kurds entered into Babak's religion in droves." [6] That indicates that they were pleased with his work and inclined toward his new principles. Similarly, it is said of the Batinis or Ismaʿilis and many of the non-Arabs and Kurds that they also were on Babak's side. They supplied him with money, advice, and men, as Abu Mansur al-Baghdadi attests in his book, *Al-Farq bain al-Firaq waʾl-Firqat al-Najiyah minha* [henceforth referred to herein as *al-Farq*]. [7]

You see, therefore, that most of the Iranian peoples conquered in Armenia and Azerbaijan, from Khurasan in the north to Arab Iraq in the south, began to conspire against the ʿAbbasid state and to work openly toward its downfall. What made the danger to the state more imminent was the collaboration of the leader of the caliphal army, Haidar b. Qavus al-Afshin, with Babak and his followers among the Persian communists. They had a secret agreement for the freedom of the Iranian and Turkish peoples to make them independent emirates or sultanates under the administration of their own men. This, then, validates the charge of treason against al-Afshin. This general rid the ʿAbbasid state of its stumbling blocks, broke up the unity of its external and internal enemies, and organized its armies. Nevertheless, judging from the public legal proceedings that were held against him after Babak's war, the accusation of treason that ensued was not devoid of truth. For it was made clear in those proceedings, which al-Muʿtasim (r. 833–42 A.D.) ordered, that al-Afshin had sympathy for Babak or for Mazyar, his ally, ruler of Tabiristan. Apparently, al-Afshin actually did

intend to detach the Turkish land, or at least a large part of it, from the
'Abbasid caliphate, in order to make of it an independent emirate or
sultanate under his administration. Mazyar said in one of the sessions
of the court-martial that Haidar al-Afshin wrote to him saying, "If you
follow me, we will be able to end Islam and return to our old Persian religion." [8]

This corroborates what al-Ya'qubi says in his history about the revolt
of Mankajur against the caliph. He writes: "The first reason al-Afshin
was arrested was that Minkajur al-Farghani, his brother-in-law and
deputy in Azerbaijan, was deposed there, and having gathered around
him the followers of Babak, marched to Warthan, where they killed
Muhammad b. 'Ubaidullah al-Warthani and a group of followers of
the sultan." [9]

Therefore, there is no doubt of the treason of the greatest leader of
the caliph's army against his benefactor, who had showered him with
favors and raised his rank. If it had not been for that, and if the caliph
had not seen proof of treason with his own eyes, he would not have
ordered the proceedings, nor dispatched his general with such ease, as
the historians mention, even though he was in greatest need of him and
his aid against the Turks.

This verifies what we mentioned regarding the eruption of the plot
against the Arab sultan and the participation of most of the conquered
nations in it. And it points to the significance of the action Babak took
against him, along with the trouble in the center of the 'Abbasid state
at that stage. In addition, there were among the conspirators some Arab
leaders who had personal or family interests at heart and who forgot,
or acted like they forgot, that the great goal of the plot was to crush the
Arab sultanate in that country and bring an end to Islam and its people.

Al-Ya'qubi mentions something even more indicative of the strained
national feelings of the Arabs at that time and of the triumph of personal or tribal concerns over the welfare of the nation. He says it was
the great administrators of the caliph in Azerbaijan who suggested to
Babak that he attack their leader and benefactor. They provoked him
into rebellion and [even] offered their assistance. Among the instigators
was Hatim b. Harthama, leader of that Arab family known for its abundant service to the 'Abbasid caliph and the Arab nation. This Ibn Harthama was the caliph's governor in Armenia and Azerbaijan, where the
Turks were traditionally favored.[10] Al-Ya'qubi says, "The power of Babak intensified and Muhammad b. al-Ba'ith followed him, as well as
the Kurdish prince, the Maranid leader." He also said, "Muhammad
b. al-Ba'ith joined Babak" ([Ta'rikh] 2:577). Hatim b. Harthama and
Muhammad b. al-Ba'ith were disloyal to the Baghdad caliphs and their
government, like others of the caliph's administrators in Armenia and
Azerbaijan and the heads of some Arab tribes there. They placed special
interests over the welfare of the nation. It was as if they had all ceased
to understand that their power and prosperity, and indeed, their very

existence in that land, were based on their compliance with the caliphs and on respect for the central government and its material and spiritual power. This was not the first time the tribal spirit and concern for its welfare had triumphed over the spirit of the nation and its welfare. History mentions that less than one hundred years after the appearance of Islam, Nasr b. Sayyar, governor for the Umayyad caliphs of Khurasan and Central Asia, urged the leaders of the Qays and Yemeni to lay down their arms and unite their authority in western lands in the face of a strong and pertinacious enemy "who intends to harm you and your state." But no one listened to him or understood that the events of the time were significant.[11]

These were the followers of Babak, his collaborators and those faithful to him and his call, upon whom he could depend in his opposition to the ʿAbbasid power. The appropriate conditions that accompanied this long war or preceded it, or perhaps helped accelerate its outbreak, were also plentiful. We confine ourselves to the mention of a few: for example, the preoccupation of the army of the caliph, al-Maʾmun, at that time with the subjugation of the revolts that broke out in Iraq, Egypt, and Arabia and with repulsing the attacks of the Byzantine army that was crossing the borders.[12] After conquering and destroying the fortress of Zibatra in the year 821 A.D., it began to penetrate into the Islamic empire, and particularly Armenia, its collaborator. It almost completely took over Armenia and began to manage it and its leaders independently, just as it had managed its own nation and population.[13] More importantly, the Byzantine army, after it occupied Armenia, became a neighbor to Babak's land, capable of supporting him with men and advice. Perhaps this is what prompted the Byzantine emperor to advance and occupy Armenia. There was another opportunity from which Babak benefited: the vicious attack of Hatim b. Harthama on the caliph's administrator in Armenia and Azerbaijan, in retaliation for the death of his father, Harthama, who was assassinated by al-Maʾmun in the year 820 A.D. We all know the prestige of Harthama among the Arabs and his influence with them and on the policies of the state. And it is only logical that Babak benefited from this revolt, as the Jewish orientalist Weil indicates in his history: "Babak benefited from this occurrence in that al-Maʾmun appeared a traitor to the interests of the Persians."[14] The revolt of Hatim b. Harthama against the caliph facilitated revolts of other Arabs stationed in Babak's region, as well as among its own citizens who were hostile to the Baghdad government and the Arabs. Among these were Babak and his followers, as al-Yaʿqubi indicates in his writings, mentioned above. We understand from him that the revolt of Hatim b. Harthama encouraged Babak's movement, but was not its cause, because Babak's preparation for the revolt against Baghdad and declaration of war on the caliph's administrator in Azerbaijan, Iran, and Armenia probably preceded Hatim's revolt.

Therefore, the followers and friends of Babak were many, and in the beginning the conditions were ripe for revolution. Most of the conquered peoples, especially the lower classes among them, inclined toward his call and followed it gladly. In hopes of good results, they waged war under his red flag of courage.[15] Abu Mansur al-Baghdadi (d. 1037 A.D.) said, "The number of Khurramis who joined Babak's army in Azerbaijan and Daylam alone exceeded 300,000."[16] Al-Tabari said, "A large group of the people in al-Jibal (Media) from Hamadhan, Isfahan, Masabadhan, and Mihrajan Qadhaq joined the Khurrami religion; they joined together and encamped in Hamadhan."[17] Other sources indicated that the number of Babak's followers was not small in the southern Iranian states and in Iraq, and that Babak's movement began to spread quickly among the peasants of these countries, that is, among the workers on rental land.[18]

Here it is appropriate for us to ask about the reasons that compelled these classes to follow the call of Babak and offer their help. We can answer that question based on the Muslim accounts of Babak's movement and doctrine. The most important factors aiding the spread of his call among those peoples and classes were not religious or political, but were social and economic. The deeds of Babak and his followers while they had power corroborate this, as do their programs, in which we find no noteworthy trace of religious or political factors.

Some of the Arab historians mention that the Babakis treated their prisoners, especially military prisoners, fairly and usually set them free on the condition that they not participate again in combat against them. They also mention that they improved the treatment of the women and children of their enemies who came into their hands during the war, even if they were from the leading or landowning class. Al-Tabari said that when Babak was captured and went with his brother to Baghdad to be tried (or, more precisely, tortured) "the women whom he had previously freed were mourning unrestrainedly before the prisoner, striking their faces and crying" in grief and compassion for him. When Haidar al-Afshin asked them the reason for their tears, they answered that Babak "was good to us."[19] As for the treatment of Babak and his followers of those who embraced the Islamic religion, and their opinion of the religion itself, we have sufficient proof of their religious tolerance and courtesy to the followers of religion. Abu Mansur al-Baghdadi, a mortal enemy of the Babakis, said that Babak and his followers, most of them Zoroastrians, did not restrain the Muslims living among them from open devotion and the practice of their religion; in fact, he helped them build their mosque "where they were called to prayer."[20]

All that leads us to believe that the goal of the Babaki movement was not opposition to Islam and its followers or opposition to the Arabs as a conquering and exploiting nation, as was the case in most rebellions in the non-Arab lands which preceded that of Babak. Rather, it was to combat that social order under which the poor classes of all nations involved in it suffered. This included the 'Abbasid state and the Arab peoples themselves, even though not all people participated openly in the rebellion. Indeed Babak and his followers sought to destroy the order that relied on the landowners and venal religious and military leaders who made a travesty of their positions. They wanted to replace it with a new, classless order, without strife and oppression, without rich or poor, master or servant, great or small, an order based on justice, brotherhood, and equality.

It is very unfortunate that the Persian and Arab historians have not preserved for us the social program of Babak in his own words. The little they have preserved neither satisfies our curiosity nor solves the difficult puzzles that researchers of the Babaki movement and its goals encounter—assuming that the historians, all of whom were enemies of the Babakis and their school, have not deliberately misconstrued their program on account of its controversial goals and their religious resentment of them.[21] Nevertheless, we can build on these reports and other noncontroversial sources. Indeed, we can prove the accuracy of what we said above—that the program of Babak and Mazyar and the other socialists of Azerbaijan and Tabiristan embraced social and economic issues only. These can be sorted into two basic issues: (1) the removal of vast territories from their owners, who had previously usurped them from the peasants or the state, and its distribution free of charge to the farmers who needed it; and (2) freeing the women of the East, or at least of Iran, from their moral bondage, and giving them the most important of the rights which men have.

Accordingly, the social program of the Khurrami Babakis was the same program as that of the communists of Iran in the sixth century A.D., known as the Mazdakis, after Mazdak, the founder of their school. Babak and his followers [must have been] students or followers of Mazdak, even though they differed, as we shall see, on some minor points necessitated by the changing times and social circumstances. The contemporaries of Babak perceived this abstract link between the communists of the sixth and ninth centuries, as did most of those later Muslims who wrote about his movement and principles, such as Abu Mansur al-Baghdadi, al-Maqdisi, al-Ghazali, and others who wrote on religious and philosophical deviations. Abu Mansur said, "The Khurramis were of the Mazdaki school." [22] This indicates that Babak and his followers acquired their teaching from the Mazdakis, their brothers in race and goals. This also holds true for the rest of the Persian and Azerbaijani communists, like the Mazyaris and Javidanis, and for others known by the names of their leaders for their agreement on the essential issues. This further indicates that the views of Mazdak did not die with his death and those of thousands of his followers whom the Sasanian state pursued throughout its subject territories. Indeed, it remained alive in the hearts of its many students who escaped death, having sought refuge in the hills of Azerbaijan and Iran. This was the heart of the

Mazdaki movement, the abode of communism and all the socialist
movements which appeared in Iran from the dawn of its history, and
indeed the sanctuary from the oppressors of their religion or their social
principles before Mazdak and Babak.[23] This was established by the author of *Mu'jam al-Buldan;* that is, that a group of Mazdakis hid, after
their well-known ordeal, in the inaccessible hills of Azerbaijan.[24] There
they continued to preserve their principles up to the days of the Seljuks
and their early successors, because they had found an environment ame-
nable to them. In that environment it did not take them long to spread
and prosper, far from the eyes of their enemy. There they jealously
guarded their socialist principles, just as they had the sacred fire of their
old ancestors, their customs and ancient morals.

The views of Mazdak continued to spread secretly among the residents of Azerbaijan and neighboring lands. They also won over other
groups displeased with their social situation such as some classes of
Persians, and some of the fringe groups of Shi'is and Batinis. These
latter despised Islam and the 'Abbasid state, and they quickly adopted
every movement from which they had reason to hope for the destruction of that state. The movement was well organized and in the hands
of experienced missionaries, who had passed the call from one to another until it reached a man called Javidan b. Sahl (d. 816 A.D.), Babak's closest friend. This facilitated the preservation and spread of these
principles among the discontented people, according to some of the
later writers. Before his death, Javidan secured for Babak the leadership
of the communist group in Azerbaijan. For he recognized in him his
natural propensity for leadership, his administrative ability, and his sincerity to the call, among other characteristics which all great leaders
need. Babak introduced into this party'sound organization and administrative procedures. This, combined with his perseverance for a period
of twenty-two years, in the face of an enemy larger and stronger than
he, proved that he was indeed that man, that mahdi, for whom the
oppressed, conquered nations and classes had been waiting to free them
from their long slavery and realize the sweet dreams of Mazdak.

There is another question we must answer as briefly as possible:
What were the factors that helped generate communism in that part of
the world and preserve it there for generations? No doubt there are
reasonable answers, as there are for every social movement in the history of Islam or elsewhere. Those factors are simply the social conditions or, more precisely, the economic conditions that had prevailed in
the area for centuries and provided sufficient nourishment for socialist
principles. At times they even produced them. The most important as-
pect of that situation, in my opinion, was the condition of the peasants
in that country and their bondage to landowners.

What we know of the land system in Azerbaijan and Iran leads us to
believe that most of their lands were assigned personally to a few people
in the landowning class (the class of landlords or khans, as we call them

today). This class of people exploited their lands, using [the labor of] the Persian peasants, the poor, and the prisoners of war. They supervised their labor themselves, from behind the walls of their palaces (which had proliferated throughout Persia, especially in the northern and western provinces). The peasants worked the lands of their masters like slaves, with no compensation to speak of. Indeed, in the days of the Sasanians they were slaves in the true sense of the word, owning nothing, and not even allowed the right to marry unless the master specifically allowed it.[25] This was the case in Russia until the year 1861 A.D., and in Europe in the age of feudalism. So we see that the conquest of this country by the Arabs did not change much of anything in the economic condition of the Persian peasants. They remained as they had been in Sasanian times. This was because the Arab authorities, in general, were unconcerned with the affairs of the peasants or other conquered peoples, except to collect taxes from them at the specified time.[26] That is what led them, in my opinion, to preserve most of the old ruling families and large tribes in their old administration. For in the view of the Arab state they were more capable than their other employees of collecting money and handing it over to the government when it was due. We also know that Azerbaijan and its neighboring lands were among the provinces that maintained, more than other Persian provinces, the former system—that is, the Sasanian system—based on the separation of the people into distinct classes, each of which had its own rights and duties.[27] That region continued to adhere to their system until the downfall of the Arab state, and beyond. This can be gathered, for instance, from the words of al-Yaʿqubi, who visited there himself and knew its conditions better than other Arab historians. He commented in his history that the poor class—the peasants who owned no land—were very numerous in that region and that their condition worsened daily. This forced them at times to attack their masters, to unite in groups, and, more important in that age, to plunder and kill. In addition, the condition of free peasants was not much better than that of their brothers, whom we just mentioned. This was especially true after the tax farmers began to collect and abuse the kharaj and other taxes, with no control whatsoever except their own personal welfare and greed. The author of *Muʿjam al-Buldan* mentioned that al-Hajjaj b. Yusuf, as administrator for ʿAbd al-Malik in the East, collected from the two provinces of Fars and Al-Ahwaz only eighteen million dinars; then, after forty or fifty years, it increased to thirty-two million.[28] Around the turn of the ninth century—that is, twenty or thirty years before the appearance of Babak and his followers—the tax farmer Fadl b. Marwan, minister of Caliph al-Mutawakkil, sent more than thirty-five million [dinars] to the treasury. This means that the taxes taken from these two provinces had doubled in one century, while the amount of land had remained the same! As for how and from whom these taxes were taken, I leave the answer up to the intelligent reader.

If we contemplate all that, we realize the reasons the communist movement took root in Azerbaijan and Iran. We also see why Iranian reformers from Mazdak to Babak pressed the demand for the removal of land from the hands of the few and for its fair distribution to the peasants. It was simply because they realized that in the freedom of the land lay the freedom of the peasant himself. Only thus could they limit the exploitation of their labors.

That was the first important point in the Babaki program. The second was the attempt to free Iranian women. And it was really no more than a result of the first. Its inclusion in the Khurrami program is irrefutable proof that no noticeable change had occurred in the condition of Iranian women since the days of Zoroaster, who began defending their rights and demanding their freedom. True, the books of the historians, most of them hostile to Mazdak, Babak, and their followers, try to explain this obviously just demand by an interpretation inconsistent with the goals of those reformers. And that indicates either ill intentions or their failure to understand the meaning of the freedom which Mazdak and Babak sought for women. Some people imagined that these reformers called for licentiousness. This, however, is not true, as we will see if we do some research and avoid the mistakes of some of the Arab writers mentioned.

Bal'ami, the Persian historian, said in his brief outline of the history of al-Tabari:

> Mazdak abolished legal marriage and the ownership of property, saying that the Creator of the World divided things among people fairly; he did not give one more than another. Therefore, the system must equalize the number of women and the amount of land which one may own. One who owns a great deal of land must not be able to say he will not give any of it to others. Similarly with one who owns a number of women, because women are public property (among people), that is, the wife of one belongs to another, and the wife of the other belongs to whomever wants to take her.[29]

Abu Mansur al-Baghdadi quoted others inaccurately and without verification: "The Babakis in their mountains celebrate at night, gathering around with wine and music; their men and women are promiscuous and when they put out the lights and fires, the men have intercourse with the women on the assumption that whoever can, will."[30] That is similar to what was reported by al-Shahristani and other historians who had no personal experience with the Mazdakis or Babakis.[31] They only repeated what other prejudiced writers before them had said, such as Abu al-Faraj al-Abri (d. 1286 A.D.), who repeated the words of Sahl b. Sunbat. He was the Armenian patriarch who seized Babak and handed him over to al-Afshin, having deceived him, humiliated him, and violated the sanctity of his wife, mother, and sister, "as that cursed Babak did if he captured someone with their wives."[32] There is another group of writers, long past the time of Babak's movement, who branded Babak's followers "thieves, brigands, highway robbers, and sowers of destruction and panic." They called them these names either intentionally to stir up public opinion and religious and national fanaticism against them, or out of sheer ignorance. In any event, they interpreted some national customs followed by the Babakis so as to equate their treatment of women with pre-Islamic barbarity and moral depravity.

Among the reasons some historians were lured into error on the moral practices of the Babakis is that they forgot (or pretended to forget) that Babak and his followers owed a debt to Zoroaster (with some modification brought about under the influence of Christianity and Islam). This religion did not prohibit marriage between brother and sister, as was the case with the Ptolemies in Egypt, for example, or among relatives forbidden to marry in Islam. Since such marriages were "filthy, the work of the devil" in the view of Muslims, they always attributed them to immorality and depravity. Some Arab writers, and the European scholars who borrowed from them, went so far as to derive the name Khurrami—the name of the followers of Babak—from the word *khurram,* the word for "agreeable" in Persian.[33] But this is not accurate. The word is taken from "Khurram," which is the name of a well-known district in Azerbaijan.

It appears to me that there is another reason for the bad reputation of the Babakis and their moral principles, and the vehemence of their defamation, especially among the writers of much later times and of different religious and national affiliations.[34] A group of thieves joined the communists of Azerbaijan while their war was going successfully, not on the basis of their principles or exalted goals, but for distinctly low purposes.[35] After Babak was defeated and his communist movement terminated in the year 834 A.D., these groups were probably dispersed in the eastern provinces. There they began to rob and murder passersby in the name of Babak and the innocent Babakis.

The Babakis probably did have a night feast during which they gathered in their hills over wine and music. And we do not deny that they permitted some marriages which Islam forbids. But we do not believe that they were promiscuous on this night. Nor do we believe that they carried out objectionable and positively forbidden acts, for this conflicts with what we already know of their moral principles. Moreover, such behavior is incompatible with their religious teaching, which they took from Zoroaster and Mazdak, and upon which they built their social views. It is known that the Mazdakis, in their daily lives and in their relationships, were closer to being abstemious ascetics than socialists. A. [E.] Christensen said in his previously mentioned book:

> The most important thing with the Mazdakis and the Manicheans (followers of Mani) was that they avoid everything which ties the spirit to material things. Therefore, they abstain from the flesh of animals and other things that ascetics do not eat.[36] The Mazdakis did not eat meat for another reason. It

would force them to slaughter these animals. Killing animals was absolutely forbidden by them, because they thought killing them prevented the release of their souls from the material prison of the body. So Mazdak forbade hostility, hatred, and strife, and called [his followers] to equality. He always said that the root of hatred and controversy among people is the disparity in social classes.[37]

It is known that Mani put limits on those of his followers from the upper classes, the "class of the faithful" or "chosen." He ordered them not to hoard provisions except what they needed for one day, and only [to gather] clothes enough for the year. Similarly, it is known that Mazdak and Babak and their followers were inclined toward abstinence and asceticism. Accordingly, we can say that they also adhered to these principles, or at least that the members of the responsible upper classes did. For it was clear to the leaders of those two schools that most people are not able to check their carnal appetites or to overcome their base inclinations to own property—which was at the time the greatest source of wealth—and women, or at least one beloved wife, unless they satisfy these inclinations and give them complete freedom.

The theory of the Mazdakis and those who came after them is firmly embedded in the communist call. From these thoughts emanate their political teaching:

> The Sublime Being grants the people all the necessities of life liberally, so that they may divide them among themselves fairly, such that no one has more than another. For the lack of equality is the result of robbery. And what is robbery if not the attempt of some people to satisfy their appetites at the expense of others? Moreover, nature and justice demand that no one have more property or land or women than another. Therefore it is necessary, where this principle is violated, to take from the thieving rich what exceeds their needs and give to the needy, in order to return people to their original equality, and that private ownership of property and women be [forbidden] like [that of] water, fire and pasture land. . . . This would please God and will be amply rewarded. But suppose that no orders of that nature come from God. Is not the spirit of cooperation among people and [concern for] their general welfare sufficient to guide them on that road which returns them to benefit and the pleasure of God?

No doubt, with regard to Iranian women and their social position, the views of Mazdak and his successor Babak—especially among the lower classes and the traditionalists—would raise doubts about the morals of the communists of Qaratagh and concern with their immodesty and "the dissolution of sacred taboos" (although we have explained that such extreme allegations were inconsistent with their moral and political principles and the witness of Muslim women among them). Indeed, these views are corroborated by those Muslim and Christian writers who were aware of their goals and recognized the truth, whether because of close contact with the Babaki movement or because they were students of truth (not propagandists and sycophants). These writers deny many of the things falsely attributed to the Babakis. For instance, the author of *Al-Bad³ wa'l-Ta³rikh* testified that he saw with his own eyes "among the Khurramis in their homes in Masabadan and Mihrajan Qadhaq . . . some who advocate the commonality of women, with their consent, and the enjoyment of everything that gratifies the soul and toward which nature inclines but does not cause harm for anyone."³⁸ He mentions, in addition, that he found them "extreme in the pursuit of cleanliness and purity, and anxious to win people's favor by spontaneous acts of kindness." Before that he had said, proving their tolerance in matters of dogma and the unusually broad range of their sources in matters of religion:

> They claim that all the prophets, regardless of their religions and codes, are inspired by one spirit and that revelation never stops. Every religious person is correct in his own view if he hopes for reward and fears punishment. They do not see him as an outcast and cross the boundaries [of their sect] to criticize him as long as he does not impose the rancor of his sect [on them]; and they strongly advocate avoiding excessive bloodshed unless it is under the banner of their religious differences [that is, in the name of religious principle.]³⁹

Thus, Babak did not call for immorality and the dissolution of injunctions against forbidden acts. Nor did he mean licentiousness by saying "People are co-owners of property and women." Instead, he intended to say that a woman has the same rights and family duties as men, that she may choose what man she loves and need not love her masters or relatives, and that she may act independently with what she owns as her heart and mind and personal welfare dictate. This is a more accurate account than those of Babak's adversaries. As for what some of the Arab and Syrian historians mentioned—that they were thieves and murdered people of different beliefs and that they "attacked people from far and near, . . . sparing neither men nor women, children nor infants, except to dismember and kill them . . . and that they killed whomever happened by of any sort, whether young or old, Muslim or dhimmi, so that people became accustomed to murder; and thieves and bandits, vicious men, malcontents, and leaders of false sects flocked to him (to Babak)"⁴⁰—this is either fabricated about them, a reference to wartime, or to the atrocities of those "highwaymen, thieves and leaders of false sects" who threw in their lot with the Babakis but never shared their moral and social principles. Otherwise we cannot reconcile these statements, whatever their motivation, with those of al-Maqdisi and with what we know about the Babaki and Mazdaki principles.

From these few reliable testimonies regarding the followers of Babak, we can conclude that their program included nothing but simple social principles and just demands. These were aimed at obliterating those conditions that separated people into hostile and antagonistic classes, and called for equality in rights and duties. In particular, they advocated the right of ownership among all people, regardless of religion; they worked to kill the sources of enmity and hatred, and to strengthen the bonds of true brotherly love. Moreover, their program included only the sort of measures that would be useful for the attainment of their great goals and the very heart of social organization at that time, built on new foundations.

We indicated above that Babak gathered both material and spiritual power in the hills of Qaratagh before he declared war on the capital of Baghdad—or more accurately, on the ʿAbbasid social order. We also mentioned something of the factors that helped the Babakis stand up to their powerful enemies for more than twenty years. And we showed the reader—if you allow our written sources—how much time the communist leader (*andarzgar*) spent in Azerbaijan preparing what was necessary for war and his great feats, perfecting methods of offense and defense, and so on. Yet what we know of the characteristics of this war are virtually reducible to one factor: The followers of Babak fought a heroic battle, a battle fought by those defending principles and a faith deeply rooted in their souls, not by unwilling employees. Nor was there any disloyalty or treachery among Babak's warriors throughout this whole long period, but there was, during the same period, among the armies and leaders of their enemies.

The movement of Babak began in the summer of the year 816 or 817 on the borders of the republic of Azerbaijan—now belonging to the U.S.S.R. (or, more accurately, situated inside it)—and Arran and old Balkan, where the city of Badhdh or Badhdhin (located near the Araxes or Ras River, as the Arabs call it) was the headquarters of the general staff.[41] This movement began to strengthen and to spread with remarkable speed until it became almost universal in the non-Arab lands.[42] Three hundred thousand warriors joined under their red banner from Azerbaijan and Daylam alone.[43] When they realized how strong they were, they went down from the hills and began to advance to the neighboring countries, and all the dissatisfied people joined them. The government of Baghdad was oblivious to them, or powerless to stop them at the borders, because they were busy at the time suppressing revolts in Egypt, Iraq, and the Arab countries, and repulsing the attacks of the Byzantines from the north (as we mentioned above). Therefore, they paid no attention to them until 204 A.H./819 A.D., that is, three years after the movement began. Then they devastated them, capturing some of them and killing their leaders, up until the beginning of 205/820.

Al-Tabari says on the events of 820 A.D.: "Babak afflicted ʿAisa b. Muhammad."[44] On the events of 209/824: "Al-Maʾmun Sidqa b. ʿAli, known as Zardiq, was ruling Armenia and Azerbaijan, and fought Babak. But he captured him. Then Ibrahim b. al-Laith b. al-Fadl al-Tajibi of Azerbaijan came to power." He said on the events of the years 212–14/827–29, "Al-Maʾmun Muhammad b. Hamid al-Tusi turned his attention and strength to Babak to fight him on the road to Mosul . . .

and he killed Muhammad b. Hamid al-Tusi at Hashtadsar on the Sab-
bath. . . . He scattered his soldiers and killed all the many who were
with him." This defeat was a severe blow to al-Ma'mun and his government. Some of the leaders of the caliphal army began to waver in their
devotion to the caliph from that day on and to consider joining Babak.
For instance, the disloyalty of ʿAli b. Hashim was known to ʿAmira b.
ʿAtba, and so he seized him and handed him over to the caliph. If it
had not been for that he would have reached Babak, who was then in
complete control in most regions of Persia, such that the people began
to fear his strength and seek his favor even in Iraq; and in Baghdad
itself they began to fear for the state and the religion. Al-Masʿudi said,
describing the situation of the country in the [final] critical days, "Then
the head (of Babak) was carried to the City of Peace [Baghdad] and to
Khurasan after that, and all the cities and villages, because of the horror
in the hearts of the people stemming from his terrible power, his great
prestige, his huge armies and the fact that he was almost able to destroy
a kingdom and alter a religion" ([*Muruj al-Dhahab wa Maʿadin al-
Jawhar*] 2:352, 1346 edition).

One of the results of Babak's brilliant victories in those two years
was despair among the caliph's soldiers and their leaders; they could no
longer believe in themselves, and the caliph could no longer depend on
them. He was left with only two alternatives: either leave the country
to his enemies or mobilize a new army under the leadership of his most
famous general, the one most experienced in mountain warfare, who
could infuse the army with a new spirit and teach them to fight the
enemies of the state and their social order in their own rugged hills. The
latter was his choice. He began to work toward realizing it, even though
he died before he could finish it.

Al-Ma'mun, who died grieving over his failures in his wars with Babak, and fearing the extinction of the state, was among the greatest of
its caliphs. When he realized he was near death, he called his brother,
al-Muʿtasim, and beseeched him to persevere against the Babakis "reso-
lutely, rigorously, and steadfastly." Then he advised him to support the
governor of Azerbaijan with "money, weapons, cavalry, and infantry,"
and that he be deprived of helpers and leaders for some time.[45]

When al-Muʿtasim took over the reins of government, he saw that it
would be wise to conclude a truce with the Byzantine emperor. Thus he
recalled Haidar b. al-Afshin from a diplomatic mission in Africa and
put him in charge of training the army in the new methods demanded
by mountain warfare. He ordered him to prepare to attack the enemy,
and Haidar set out to obey. Meanwhile, he received news that Ishaq b.
Ibrahim b. Musʿab, one of the caliph's most loyal and determined leaders, had splintered the Babaki army.[46] He forced the remnants of his
defeated army to flee to Byzantine lands where they sought support,
and entered into the service of the Byzantine emperor. However, this
was not a death blow to Babak and his army because the largest contin-

gent of his soldiers was stationed in Azerbaijan or, more precisely, in Arran, which was the headquarters of the army and its war columns. Therefore, it was possible for Babak to recover and collect his forces before al-Afshin attacked him with his new armies. However, the Turkish leader did not give him time to do that. He marched against him on 29 Jumada al-Ula [220 A.H.] (1 July 835) at the head of a great army made up of Turks and Berbers and volunteers from Basra and Iraq. They began to draw near Babak's capital, army after army of horsemen and infantrymen.

Haidar al-Afshin's campaign against Babak lasted more than two years. During this time he kept an eye on them, tracked them, and tried to comprehend their strategies in order to discover the secrets of their success and pinpoint their areas of strength and weakness. Only then did they begin their attack on him with hopes of annihilating him. Haidar nearly succeeded in the Battle of Arshaq in the year 836 A.D.[47] However, Babak escaped from him and retreated into the Muqan swamp-plain and from there to Hashtadsar, whence he attacked in the following year al-Afshin's vanguard, headed by Bugha al-Kabir, one of the best-known leaders, and utterly defeated it. When this news reached al-Afshin, he himself marched against Babak and pursued him until he caught up with him. There was a battle between them in which Babak was defeated. Then Haidar overtook one of his leaders by the name of Tarkhan, killing him and destroying his army. This latter blow was devastating to Babak and his followers, for he had lost in the two last battles both the right and left wings of his army. Nothing remained of his soldiers except what was directly under his leadership. So he was forced to retreat from the battlefield to his fortress at Badhdhin. He spent a number of months there, defending himself and his followers heroically until his provisions ran out. But [soon] his forces lost strength. He was forced to leave his capital by night and seek secret entry into the Byzantine empire to ask help from his friend Emperor Theophilus. But the fates betrayed him; actually, one of the Armenian patriarchs, Sahl b. Sunbat, from whom Babak asked protection, betrayed him. He apprehended him and his brother ʿAbdullah, and those who were with them—family, friends—and, having gained their trust, turned them all over to a representative of the caliph.

Some of the historians[48] mention that when the news spread of the fall of Babak and his capital into Muslim hands, "the people raised a great cry of praise to God and they were overcome with joy and happiness."[49] The residents of Baghdad and Samarra began shaking hands in the streets. "That was one of the greatest victories in Islam and the day he was captured was a feast-day for the Muslims." Al-Muʿtasim raised the rank of al-Afshin, and ordered poems of praise to be presented to him. This is not surprising if it was true that Babak wanted, as al-Masʿudi said, "to abolish private property and completely transform the nation."

The historians say that when Babak arrived at Baghdad, al-Muʿtasim ordered that he be brought to the palace of al-Afshin, known as al-Matira. There the caliph visited in disguise (see al-Tabari's history, 10:332) and asked him some questions. I think this is among the lies of al-Masʿudi—who was more like a compiler of anecdotes and fiction than a true historian interested only in establishing the truth. I think when al-Muʿtasim visited Babak, he wanted to see with his own eyes the man who nearly destroyed his state and established on its rubble a new state, based on justice, brotherhood, and equality.

Al-Muʿtasim visited his greatest enemy and then returned to his palace, where his ministers and generals awaited him, to ponder with them the injustice of killing their weakened prisoner, who had set free their prisoners by the thousands and sympathized with their women and children. But when morning came, the people crowded around the head of the bridge [near the prison, demanding] to see "the prisoner of the state and religion" crucified. When night fell, they brought him down from the cross, then cut him limb from limb and sent his head to the rest of the lands. Then they went to his brother and some of his close associates and killed them in captivity, after having brutally killed tens of thousands in Badhdhin. Then it was not long until they apprehended Haidar al-Afshin and threw him in jail where he died, poisoned, perhaps, for the treason we mentioned above.

When Babak died, his socialist movement in Azerbaijan and neighboring countries died with him, although the ideas that he tried to spread and implement among his people did not die. They remained, growing in secret, as before, to the end of the eleventh century. Al-Maqdisi, in the tenth century, mentioned that he visited them in their country and saw with his own eyes "that there were no mosques in their country, nor did they follow Islam." Abu Mansur al-Baghdadi, in the eleventh century, mentioned that the Babakis "had built mosques in their hills for the Muslims where they taught their children the Qurʾan, but they did not pray in private,[50] nor did they fast during the month of Ramadan or practice jihad against the infidels."[51]

It now remains for us to ask about the reasons for the destruction of this socialist movement, for it had been thought that they would overcome all obstacles placed in their way.

The reasons for the destruction are many. Some of them are external and some are internal, from the Babakis themselves. The most important of them, in my view, is that the Babakis restricted their call to the Iranian nation and did not share it with the Arabs or Turks, who at the time were the greatest Islamic nations. There is another reason, of no less significance than the first. Many of those who gathered around the flag of Babak and battled in the first years with him were not interested in this intellectual movement, except insofar as it would harm the ruling government and benefit them personally. They were the ones who obeyed the call of Babak out of greed, to get material benefits which they could only get through revolution and internecine wars. Most of this group were Kurds.

These are some of the factors that helped kill the Babaki movement. Yet some of the seeds that Babak and his followers sowed fell on good, fertile ground, and germinated well in time, as we shall see in the following chapter.

FOUR

The Isma°ilis

We have said that the Babakis were defeated and died as a socialist party, although they lived on as a group until the days of the Seljuks. Since the legacy they left to the rulers of Khwarazm was a religious sect of only minor importance, the Baghdad government paid no attention to them. They [simply] put in charge of them religious leaders and writers of religious tracts who challenged their school and order, alleged lies against them, and at times incited ignorant and fanatical people against them. In this way they forced the Babakis to go into hiding, to conceal their call, and to spread it secretly, as every religion or social idea which is prohibited is suppressed. Accordingly, they became more of a threat to the government and to Islam than when they had openly called people to their principles. Far from becoming futile, their movement became a source of great benefit: many people learned from it and from their mistakes. Most important among these were the Isma°ilis, or Batinis, the people closest to the Babakis in dogma and goals, and most dependent upon socialist principles. This will be clear to all intelligent thinkers from the following discussion regarding the Isma°ili movement and its doctrine, the works of writers of the East and West on the Batinis and Isma°ilis, and the ideological relationship between these two groups.

As we have seen, among the reasons for the downfall of Babak and his followers was that most of the residents of the °Abbasid state were not prepared to accept the socialist system that Babak wanted to intro-

duce, and the Babakis were thus limited to spreading their socialist call
to a small group of people, mostly confined to the hills of Aran and
Azerbaijan; that is, only among Iranian tribes. As for the Arabs—who
were the majority and held power throughout the land—Babak lacked
either the wisdom or the courage to draw them into his school, and did
not bother spreading his thoughts among them. The same was true of
the Turks and Berbers, who were at the time "members of Islam and
their regular army," as al-Jahiz called them.[1] Indeed, a large part of the
Persian nation did not enter Babak's religion because he did not concern
himself with converting them. Nor did he seek their help by force.
Moreover, Babak and his group never even considered destroying the
Islamic religion, as the ʿAbbasid state accused them of doing, and
thereby gain real power. Babak seems to have considered it sufficient to
destroy the system based on the interests of wealthy landowners and to
establish a new system. But his aim was to spread his ideas among only
one people, or class of people.

What he did not realize was that whatever the beneficial effects of his
ideas on his listeners, this alone was not sufficient to attain the desired
goal. It was necessary to universalize the call and adopt stronger measures, means offering a better guarantee of success. This is what ʿAbdullah b. Maimum al-Qaddah's group, or the Ismaʿilis in general, realized for the first time in the history of Islam. After careful study of the
affairs of the ʿAbbasid state, they saw that in order to eliminate the
ʿAbbasids and their social order it was necessary to spread the new
socialist call among all peoples, classes, and religions in the state of
Mansur. It was also necessary to incorporate all those dissatisfied with
the Baghdad caliphs, and then destroy the bases on which the ʿAbbasid
state had rested. The most important of these were its religion, its morals, and national feeling, or what took its place at that time. But how
to accomplish that and avoid the obvious difficulties? Is it possible to
balance the incompatible interests of the different classes of people? Is
it possible to bring together under one banner differing or even antagonistic parties, religions, and nationalities and to reconcile in one program several opposing political and social positions? This, the most important question and the greatest problem in history, is one with which
the Ismaʿilis dealt accordingly. After a number of tries, they succeeded
in achieving a solution unique in the East and the West. All human
history witnesses that there had not been until then (and probably
would never be in the future) a party, religion, school, organization, or
association that joined together under its flag

> the conquerers, the conquered, free thinkers who considered religion a bridle
> necessary for the lower classes of people only, religious enthusiasts of all
> groups; to make the moderate believers transfer power to the skeptics, using
> the conquerors as an instrument for the destruction of the power they had
> built, and hand it over to others; and then build a large, coherent party useful
> as a basis for placing the crown of power, when the opportunity presented

itself, if not on the head of the actual founder of that school, then on the head of one of his successors.[2]

This was the fundamental goal of 'Abdullah b. Maimun, and these were his ideas. As you can see, they were strange, amazing, bold ideas, which his uncommon shrewdness, his amazing skill, and his deep knowledge of the hearts of men helped him realize.

If you look into the various factions of the Isma'ilis, you will truly find among them representatives of all people subject at that time to the caliphs of Baghdad—Arabs, Persians, Kurds, Turks, etc.—and all political and social parties, from the left and the right. And you will see among them anarchists and communists, regardless of their sect or principles, and representatives of all religions and schools, from Sunnis and moderate Shi'is to apostates and atheists "who believe in nothing."

We conclude, then, that the term "Isma'ilis," which in the beginning referred to one of the moderate Shi'i sects, began in time to refer to the adherents of various religious sects, numerous social and political sects, and [those who held various] philosophical, scientific, and ideological opinions. Yet this vast difference in principles and opinions, and the apparent discrepancy between the parties and sects within the Isma'ili school, did not prevent its adherents from seeking one goal and achieving success as no one before them had done. This is one of the most important things which anyone who knows anything about Isma'ili history, their internal order, and their political principles must realize.

These Isma'ilis were basically a secret association whose few leaders (and the intellectuals close to them) were the only ones familiar with its goals and methods. Only those who passed through the various required steps or stages of inauguration, and swore a secret oath that they would not reveal to anyone the secrets of their association, understood its innermost secrets.[3] The majority knew only what little about the organization was entrusted to them by the missionaries. It was up to them to choose the members, their trials, and their preparation to ascend the six or seven ranks which the Isma'ilis had at that time.[4] It is well known that these initiates were not allowed to break into the association until after the missionary tested them and established that they were trustworthy, neither to be feared nor dreaded, and that they were able to spread the call of the Isma'ilis and defend the organization from anything, whatever the cost or danger. Thus the missionaries only accepted into the organization those with will power and sound intelligence, and those proficient in reading and writing. And when they accepted someone into their organization, they educated him and trained him. They informed him of some of the secrets of their school so that if the initiate made the grade, they allowed him to swear the oath. This was its form, as related by Abu Mansur al-Baghdadi:

> As for their belief, their missionary said: "You took upon yourself a promise to God, an agreement with Him and a covenant with Him and His messen-

gers. And the covenant and agreement God requires of the prophets is to hide what you hear from me and what you know of my affairs and the affairs of the Imam who is the master of your age and controls his followers in this land and in all lands and commands the obedient, both male and female, not to reveal anything which may lead to him, whether in writing or symbols, except what the Imam, Master of the Age, allows you or what he allows you through his authorized intermediary. Always take care in that with whatever you are allowed. Now that you have done that, persevere in situations of good will and anger, desire or fear." Then the member must swear, "So be it." Then the missionary says to him, "Take upon yourself to protect me and all named to you as you protect yourself by an oath to God and His covenant and the covenant of His messengers. Be loyal to them outwardly and inwardly. Do not betray the Imam, his helpers, or those who follow his call, either their person or their property. Do not reinterpret these oaths nor believe anything that abrogates them. If you do any of that, you will be cut off from God, His messengers, His angels, and all of the writings that God has revealed. If you diverge in any way from what we have mentioned to you, then you must make a pilgrimage to His house and march around it one hundred times, making the required vow. And everything you own at that time you must give as alms to the poor and needy. All the slaves you own the day of your error or afterward must be set free, and you must divorce three times all your wives now or at the time of your disavowal or that you marry after that. God the exalted is witness of your intention and the agreement in your heart to what you swear." Then the initiate says, "So be it." (*Al-Farq*, 289)

He does not say "So be it" unless his belief in his new religion is true, and his will is firm to live by it, whatever the cost. It is of no consequence when Abu Mansur accuses: "Their faith has no scope nor respect and they do not see in it or in its dissolution sin or atonement, nor shame nor punishment in the afterlife" ([*Al-Farq*], 290). For, despite what is attributed to them by their adversaries, it is known that their leaders were devoted to the ideology and principles of the education they received from their missionaries.[1]

There is no doubt that the means adopted by the missionaries to affect the will and daily conduct of these simple members were intended to form strong bonds, both to their great leader and to each other. They sought to make them instruments in the hands of experienced missionaries; indeed, to make them [like] lifeless bodies (*perinde ac cadaver*), acting in accordance with their wishes and intentions. Who among us is not familiar with the organization of the Fedayyin or Hashashin, famous Isma'ilis in the days of the Crusaders and Seljuks? They undertook the most dangerous deeds and showed great love for the commonweal and obedience to their spiritual leaders. And why, if not because they were utterly sincere to their leaders and faith, and believed that they walked the path of righteousness. This faith, firmly established in their hearts, worked miracles and caused alarm in the hearts of its enemies. Of course, [the initiates] did not reach this degree of faith and blind obedience to their leaders until after long intellectual practice. They advanced gradually from one step to the next, as is the situation today in communist and Masonic organizations, and other secret organizations which probably appeared under the influence of the Isma'ili organization, as we shall see in the last chapter of this book.[5]

The keen observer of Isma'ili methods and the details of the psychological means which they used, whether to draw people to their school or to gain domination over their wills and keep them in total obedience, is astounded at their skill and complete knowledge of the human soul. At the risk of boredom, I will mention a good deal of these methods. We assume these accounts are accurate, even though they are only mentioned in the books of the Isma'ilis' enemies, such as Abu Mansur al-Baghdadi and al-Ghazali, among others. In any event, we can say that the ultimate goal of these methods was that the missionary arouse doubt in the soul of the initiate regarding his basic beliefs, his political, moral, and social principles. They aimed at convincing him to join their secret organization [in order to gain access to true knowledge] and correct understanding of their call. What we know of the deeds of those missionaries is that, with few exceptions, their methods led to the desired goal. "Their seeds" fell, as they put it, almost always "on fertile soil."[6] It did not bother them if the seeds did fall on "bad soil" because they were always on guard. They watched what they said and did and those they addressed. And if they suspected rejection of their teaching or treachery or lack of sincerity, they stopped teaching or they changed the subject and addressed a new subject totally unrelated to their message, and therefore unlikely to put them in jeopardy. This was not difficult for the experienced missionary because he did not reveal important matters or divulge all his secrets when there was danger to him. The missionaries only treated general subjects in their first conversations with the initiates, in order to get acquainted with their personalities and mentalities and the strength of their desire to enter the new religion. Even if an initiate joined them and remained for two years, they informed him only by degrees of the social and moral teachings and goals of their organization, until the initiate reached the seventh step—which few did. Then he alone was informed of the highest social goal and the means of achieving it. The missionaries themselves only reached the fifth step, at which they acquired some of the social secrets after swearing the above-mentioned oath of faith in the fourth step. Those who did not reach this step remained simple obedient members, bound to the will of others, in particular, the *imam al-zaman* (master of the age). It was he who informed the people of the social goals and secrets and gave them mastery over the service of those simple members.

It can be concluded from the statements of some of the preceding writers that those Isma'ilis who only achieved the fourth degree and did not swear the required oath were not informed of the social program. They received only its religious and moral principles. They did not re-

ceive political and social education until after they passed the fourth
stage and swore the prescribed oath. There is no doubt that this sort of
secrecy caused suspicion in Islamic society concerning the Isma'ilis and
led to accusations which, with rare exceptions, did not accord with the
truth. What is surprising is that most of the lies about the Isma'ilis, and
the widely diverse ideas about their doctrines, came not only in the
books of the historians but also in the books of their contemporaries,
both Muslim and Christian. Some of them called the Isma'ilis material-
ists; others considered them atheists who claim the eternity of the world
and blaspheme the laws of the prophets. There were also those who
claimed they were Zoroastrians and Mazdis, still dreaming of reviving
the ancient religion of Persia. And finally, there were those who considered them Sabians, or followers of ancient Greek philosophy of whichever school.

Accordingly, they attributed to the Isma'ilis words and deeds of
which they were, in fact, innocent. Take, for instance, the report erron-
eously attributing to some of the Isma'ilis grievous charges and disgusting statements; if these were even partly true, the Isma'ilis would
have been among the most immoral people in the world, and much
worse than what we already know of them through other historical
sources.[7] This report claims that they were "heretics, atheists, and anarchists who approved of forbidden acts and perpetrated the worst of
them" and that they used any means to achieve their desired goal. Abu
Mansur al-Baghdadi said that the writer of that report said [of Isma'ili
views]:

> "What is more remarkable than a man who claims to be rational yet, having
> a beautiful sister or daughter and no wife as beautiful, abstains from [the
> sister or daughter] and gives her in marriage to an outsider? If the fool were
> sensible, he would know that he is more entitled to his sister and his daughter
> than the outsider" (*Al-Farq*, 281). "And what is the reason for that if not
> because their master (the Prophet) forbade them pleasures and frightened
> them with the unseen and irrational; he is the God whom they claim and
> who told them about things they will never see, such as the resurrection from
> the grave, the last judgment, and heaven and hell. Thus he quickly subjugated
> them and made them slaves for himself and his progeny. And thus he made
> their property his by saying, 'I ask of you no reward for it except love for
> my kin' " (Surah 42:23). So his dealings with them were on a cash basis and
> their position with him was on credit; he wanted to hurry them in spending
> their lives and their property in the expectation of something which does not
> exist. What is paradise if not this world and its comfort, and what is hell and
> its suffering if not the trouble and deception involved in following the laws
> of prayer, fast, jihad and the Hajj?[8]

This report also mentions, for the first time in history, the three im-
posters whose sayings fill the reports of the Middle Ages, as well as
other statements attributed to the Isma'ilis, such as allowing impermissible acts and the abrogation of the morals of that age. In addition, it

claims "that they permitted their followers to marry their daughters and sisters, and permitted the drinking of wine and all such sensual pleasures. Corroborating that is the story of the youth who appeared among [the Ismaʿilis] in Bahrain and al-Ahsa . . . and prescribed sodomy and ordered the murder of the boy who refused those who wanted him to fornicate" ([*Al-Farq*], 270). So if we add to that the [other] lies, hypocrisy, and deceptive ways attributed to the Ismaʿilis, we can understand what their adversaries said about their principles, morals, and religion.

It will be clear to all who examine the works of Abu Mansur, among others, that the Ismaʿilis' enemies had far less information regarding their political and social principles. In sum, what we can gather from the scattered and often contradictory reports of these various writers is that the leaders of the Ismaʿilis and their policy chiefs, or at least most of those who were from Persia, were either nationalist zealots working to resurrect their past kingdom or internationalists whose goal was to destroy the pillars of the ʿAbbasid state—tribal solidarity, nationalism and Islam—and build a communistic international state on its ruins. This new state would be founded on the equal rights of all peoples and on a rational religion. They were also called anarchists, who intended nothing but the destruction of the state, so hateful to them, and its loathesome order. Regarding the goals of the Ismaʿilis, the Muslim writers say that they tried to take power from the ʿAbbasid caliphs and hand it over to the ʿAlids, from whom they expected to receive benefits themselves.

This is the gist of what the Muslim writers said about the Ismaʿilis' teachings and their political and social goals. If we compare it with what the rare Ismaʿili books said and with what has been preserved of the books and reports of the religious and social organizations that grew out of the Ismaiʿlis, such as the Qaramatis, Fatimids, Hashashin, Druze, the Zaidis in the Yemen, and the Ismaiʿilis of today, and so on, we find that much of what was attributed to them by the writers of the preceding age does not accord with the truth, especially what was said about their morals and ethics. Rather, the opposite of what was attributed to them is nearer the truth. It was known, for instance, that some of the Fatimid caliphs were inclined toward monogamy and that they exhorted their subjects to adopt this type of family organization. They mention that the caliph al-Muʿizz (953–75) exhorted the chiefs of the North African tribes to single marriage "because thus would be increased the happiness of life and preserved the strength of the soul, and because we need all your power and understanding."[9] The same was true of the Qaramatis, who (as we shall see in the next chapter) were the people most akin to the Ismaʿilis, and indeed, a large branch of them. It was reported in the diary of the Persian traveler and writer Nasr Khusrow, who visited their capital in the year 442 A.H./1050 A.D., that "they do not drink wine," not because it is forbidden, but because they are mindful of good reputation and their public morals, contrary to what one of their adversaries said in a *qasida* [ode], claiming to speak for them:

What is wine, if not the water of the heavens,
Permitted, and so blessed by this sect.[10]

Thus you see that the Isma'ili ethics in general were not as degenerate as their adversaries imagined, and that they did not advocate amorality as some thought. The same was generally true of their social and political teaching. Caution is necessary, then, as well as discretion in judging them and correcting the errors and excesses their enemies attributed to them. Indeed, it is difficult sometimes to determine the extent of these exaggerations, because of the secrecy of the Isma'ilis and the distinctions between the followers and the leaders. Then, too, it is necessary to bear in mind that most of the Isma'ili political teachings developed with time, and that their missionaries attuned their sayings to the intellectual and moral level of their listeners, to their religious devotion in general, and to Islam in particular, as well as to their nationalities and their political and social inclinations. For they addressed each listener in his own language and in terms of his inclinations, sympathies, and the degree of his intellectual development.[11] Perhaps they addressed the Persians differently from the way they addressed the Arabs, the Muslims differently from non-Muslims, the philosophers and educated people differently from the lower classes, and so on. From this it can be concluded that the Isma'ilis had two programs (higher and lower). If so, it is easy to understand the obvious disparity in the statements of some of the Muslim writers about the Isma'ilis and their education. It does not follow that the Isma'ilis did not have a specific program on which most of them agreed, which we may call the "minor program," a program that mentioned the basic principles which did not change significantly and which distinguished them from the followers of the other numerous sects and parties in that time.

There is no doubt of the existence of this minor program, because we can gather bits of it today from the testimonies of the enemies of the Isma'ilis themselves, or from those organizations (mentioned in the foregoing) that were ideologically related to them. If we compare all these reports and examine them on purely scientific grounds, free of prejudice, we can extract the following picture of the Isma'ilis.

It is known that the origin of the Isma'ili movement, and most of the social, political, and moral movements that severely shook the Islamic world, was 'Alid Shi'ism. We know that this moderate Shi'ism broke into two branches: one branch was known as the Twelvers, and the other as the Seveners. The followers of this latter branch were called by this name because they were devoted to the seventh imam, Isma'il b. Ja'far al-Siddiq (al-Sadiq) al-Akbar, the sixth imam of this branch. It is also known that Ja'far refused to appoint his son, Isma'il, as successor and imam after him because of his bad behavior and his addiction to wine. However, the party of Isma'il—and they were the majority of the branch mentioned—objected and supported Isma'il and recognized him as imam; they are known by his name to this day.

Isma'il died in the year 143 A.H., that is, before his father. He was buried in the city where his family remained living until the end of the eighth century. At that time they were forced to leave their land due to their active participation in the political events of the day; [at least] it seemed to those in power at the time that they participated in them. Therefore, Isma'il's sons and grandsons were dispersed throughout the land, settling in the north of Persia, Iraq, and Syria, and later in India and North Africa, etc.[12] However, the 'Abbasid scouts followed them wherever they went because they feared their influence and considered them the most dangerous of all their enemies. As a result, the Isma'ilis were forced to keep out of sight and to live in faraway places and small towns, whence they began to send their call to all parts of the 'Abbasid caliphate. Thus they spread their political and religious teachings. But under the influences to which they were subject in remote garrison towns, [especially] philosophical views, their beliefs gradually began to diverge from the Islamic religion—indeed, from any religion. In fact, within a short time, it became a school [of thought] rather than an established religion, whose tenets we can summarize as follows.

As above, the Isma'ilis were a secret organization headed by a leader, known as the imam or *sahib al-zaman* [lord or master of the age], who had absolute power over all members of the organization, that is, over their lives and what they owned. His word was obeyed by them as if it were law—in fact, it was more binding than law. For the imam was, in their opinion, infallible. He was the deputy of God on earth, and his will was not to be refused, since one could not be the servant of God without executing his will and being sincere to him. Whoever recognized the imam al-zaman swore by his name and depended upon him in everything, acknowledged his orders, adhered to them, gave to everyone his due, and did not turn away from the truth.[13] One also had to accept that the imam al-zaman was a prophet of the highest order. For the ordinances that [lower] prophets set in place had relative importance; that is, they did not outlive their own time. But the ordinances of the imam al-zaman (or his interpretations thereof) had absolute importance and were not limited by time or place. Because the Isma'ilis interpreted religious laws and their rites esoterically (*batiniyyan*), they were known as the Batinis. Their outward manifestations changed, but not their overall understanding. In addition, they borrowed in their interpretations from Greek philosophy, especially Neoplatonism. As a result of this, among other influences, they came out against revealed law, further raising the importance of the imam al-zaman and putting all authority in his hands.

We do not deny that the Isma'ilis outwardly rejected revealed law in general, and the Qur'an in particular. For they saw in it no benefit for the lower [intellectual] classes, the class of "the blind and foolish," as the Isma'ilis called them. As for the upper [intellectual] classes, "whom God infused with understanding and insight," they understood the truth. In the view of the Isma'ilis, therefore, they were not in need of these laws and external practices. Accordingly, it can be concluded indisputably that the leaders of the Isma'ilis did not believe in the revealed religions and their basic doctrines, just as some Muslim writers say. Abu Mansur al-Baghdadi said that al-Qairawani wrote in his report (which he gave to Sulayman b. al-Hasan al-Qaramati): "I enjoin you to instill doubt in the people about the Qur'an, the Torah, the psalms, and the gospels, and call upon them to relinquish the laws and [belief in] the hereafter and the resurrection, the angels in the heavens, and the Jinn on earth" (Al-Farq, 280). He said in another place that "they are atheists and unbelievers who advocate the eternity of the world and deny the messengers and all laws because of their tendency to consider permissible everything to which their nature inclines" (Al-Farq, 278). The following, in effect, was reported in one of their letters, whose import has been preserved to the present day:

> The doctrine of the resurrection is ridiculous because the purport of "everlasting life" or "infinity of the soul" is the return of the soul to its original source.[14] In this way they interpret the final judgment on the last day and other basic religious ideas. And they say that the true believer is he who interprets divine revelation in this way; as for those who follow revealed law in its external form, they are no more than infidels and asses.[15]

You can see, therefore, that the Isma'ilis spurned literal interpretation. They sought to interpret the law according to its internal sense, based on reason alone. Thus they were the first sect [bid'a] in Islam to which we can apply the name "rationalists" in the contemporary meaning of the word. The difference between them and the Mu'tazilis is that the Isma'ilis interpreted religion and its laws in a way that led to their denial, whereas the Mu'tazilis tried to reconcile religion and reason without sacrificing one for the other.

This new doctrine, which the Isma'ilis wanted to spread among Muslims and non-Muslims alike, was simply a result of their basic teaching on religion and its position in their philosophical system. And true religion, in their view, consisted of the following: the individual attains, by continued practice and elevation from degree to degree, knowledge of the levels of being into which the world (the inhabited world) was divided after it was separated from God; that is, from "the absolute idea" (immaterial) or "the first intelligence" or "highest light," which radiates from itself the second level, the universal intellect and soul of the world.[16] These produce—after they differentiate—human intellects, the intellects of the prophets and imams and the best people. The rest of the people do not have intellects, but "likenesses of non-being," unless they move to the second level by means of illumination and education.[17]

This education had several stages, which correlate with the degrees of consecration (mentioned above). Through these the individual sets out to reach the highest degree of intellectual and moral perfection, the greatest goal in the life of the individual on earth. The means of achieving this goal was, in their view, the development of intellectual power. Then proper conduct and a moral life [will follow], in accordance with the demands of sound reason. This is entirely in keeping with what was said above regarding the high moral standards of the Isma'ilis, and refutes what some of their enemies said.

This is a summary of Isma'ili doctrine on morals and education. As far as their political and social principles are concerned, we can say that they were closely tied to their philosophical and moral views. Indeed, they were a logical result of them. It is nonetheless necessary to study their political principles and the social issues around which their ideas turned. For they did not appear [fully developed] at the outset [of the Isma'ili movement] and did not remain the same for long. Rather, they developed naturally, according to the exigencies of time and circumstance, and according to the intellectual and moral development of the leaders of the Isma'ili movement. Thus they passed through a number of periods and [only gradually] developed for themselves a definitive form, the form by which most later historians would recognize them.

We do not deny that it is difficult for the social historian to track the course of the Isma'ili movements and their developmental stages to determine what changes occurred in their basic program. But it is necessary for anyone who studies the history of intellectual movements in the Islamic East to try, [at least] to the extent the available texts allow.

It appears that the political goal of the Isma'ilis in the first stage did not differ significantly from the goals of other Shi'is. That is, they intended to take power from the 'Abbasids and hand it over to the descendants of 'Ali, from whom it had been seized, according to their claims. It is known that these demands were openly supported in the beginning by some members of the usurping family, as well as by their followers, both among Arabs and Persians. In some cases, these movements led to Shi'i rebellions, endangering the 'Abbasid state and forcing it to severely punish the rebels, both innocent and guilty. This did not deter them, however. They were convinced they were right and that it was inevitable they would attain their goals. Their belief changed, under the influence of ideas foreign to Islam, to a strong faith in the imminent appearance of a man—a mahdi—who would triumph over the 'Abbasid state and reclaim their power, and hand it over to their followers. Thus, and under the combined influence of the defeats and hardships the 'Alids had endured, as well as new social and political elements which had entered the 'Abbasid state, they began to attach new hope to the appearance of the mahdi, or imam al-zaman—above and beyond political hope. They began to expect that he would spread justice and cure the earth of its social diseases, and so on. In short, they began to expect the imam to realize many of the principles and ideals which were then infiltrating the movement from outside, that is, from Greek philosophy, from communistic groups, from religious sects, and from foreign nationals who hated the ʿAbbasid state.

In any event, there is no doubt that social goals soon entered the Ismaʿili program. This was due to a number of causes, but the most important was [the need] to attract people to their party. However, this was not simply to strengthen it numerically, as their opponents claimed. These [social] goals were directly related to their basic beliefs; they were a natural supplement to them.

The most important social goals which the Ismaʿilis introduced into their program were (1) equality between the sexes and (2) the abolition of private property and its distribution to the needy free of charge.[18] That, as we saw, is what [certain] communistic groups before the Ismaʿilis had tried to effect. However, the difference was that the Ismaʿilis based their demands on scientific, philosophic principles, not on specific moral principles, as their communist predecessors had done. There is another difference between the two schools. The Batinis did not just set a new foundation under old communist principles; they also included a social program and were successful at implementing it in some regions, as we will see in the next chapter. Furthermore, the Ismaʿilis were the first to create internationalist sentiment in Islam and to defend the idea of a true brotherhood (internationalism). This was a desire for fraternity, not among Muslims alone but among all peoples, regardless of nationality, class, or religion; that is, brotherhood based not on one religion, as was the case in Islam and Catholicism in the Middle Ages, but on the demands of sound reason. So they did not restrict their efforts to a specific group of people, as the Mazyaris, Babakis, and other Iranian communists had done. Rather, they turned to all lands and peoples. Therefore, we must assume that the reports of some writers on the Ismaʿilis—that they were Iranian communists and fanatical nationalists for that country—originated either in the desire to impress the Arab view on the leaders of this movement, or in ignorance of Ismaʿili principles. The source of such reports could also be that in the beginning, the movement was directed by a group from Persia. Also, because it was a brotherhood comprising all nations and sects, there may well have been among the Ismaʿilis a small group of Persians working secretly for the revival of the Persian kingdom and the restoration of Sasanian splendor. However, this fact—if it is true—does not reflect negatively on the Ismaʿili school in general; it was international, based on specific philosophical tenets. The skeptics need only scrutinize the [various] national groups of which the Ismaʿili brotherhood was composed; there were Persians, Arabs, Kurds, Nabataeans, Indians, Turks, Berbers, etc. Abu Mansur al-Baghdadi said (and his words on this subject are trustworthy):

Those among whom the Batinis are popular are of several types, one of which is the people whose understanding has been deadened by the principles of science and philosophical speculation, like the Copts, Kurds, and Mazdis; the second type are the Shu'ubiyya who prefer Persians over Arabs. . . . And the third type are the sheeplike members of the Bani Rabi'a because of their jealousy over the fact that the Prophet came from Mudar and not from them. (*Al-Farq*, 285–86)

We see from this comment (and others which we need not mention) that the Isma'ilis were truly the first in Islam to rise above the nationalist zeal against which both the Umayyads and 'Abbasids had been powerless. For the Isma'ili declared at the outset that nationalist issues did not interest them; their goal was not a nationalist goal, and nationalist prejudices, which were tearing the body of the 'Abbasid state apart, were not in keeping with their philosophic principles. They and the Shu'ubiyya in this sense were on opposite sides—perhaps they appeared in reaction to the Shu'ubiyya. If it is possible for us to call the Shu'ubiyya the party of extreme nationalist zeal (chauvinists), then the Isma'ilis were the party of "no-nationalism" (international). However, this certainly does not imply that the Isma'ilis were merely enemies of the Shu'ubiyya or emerged to resist them alone. These two groups were interdependent, [although] they sought different goals and used different means to achieve them. But it can be said that their paths intersected and indeed coincided for a distinct period; [during that time] they were side by side, without clashing or battling, even though their principles were at variance. For there was a point of commonality between them: their hatred of the ruling government and Arab nationalism. That is what Abu Mansur noticed. He indicated it when he said, "The Shu'ubiyya entered the Isma'ili religion and supported it" (*Al-Farq*, 285).

Here it is appropriate for us to remind the reader that the Isma'ili missionaries spread their call among all nations subject to the 'Abbasid state and among all parties and religious sects, for their highest goal was to bring intelligent people into their society. Therefore, you see among them representatives of all peoples, classes, religions, and various opposing views, to the extent that their brotherhood became something of a Pandora's box, from which they could take what they wanted.

The Isma'ilis proceeded with this unusual course of action and evinced this boldness, so outstanding in human history, only because they felt their strength to be ideological and spiritual, the result of the principles they advocated. They were self-confident. They believed that with a bit of time and effort, they could unite their members, so mixed in goals and attitudes. They believed they could forge them into a single worldview, a single goal, with a single method of achieving it. And that is what they did.

There is no denying that unifying the hearts and minds of these various organizations was not an easy matter. The attempt caused un-matched troubles for the Isma'ili leaders and missionaries. It would have been far better had the members been of a single party and ideol-ogy before joining, or had they been prepared to accept its principles and policies. This was an unusual thing in the history of social groups and political parties, as is known. For every party that wants to realize its political or social dreams in this worldly life must struggle to join forces with all who support them, their doctrine, and their practice, or their effort will be in vain.

This is what the Isma'ili leaders realized, once their political party had become a social school or communistic philosophical brotherhood. That is why 'Ubaid b. al-Hasan al-Qairawani, one of the Isma'ili writ-ers, said (in his letter to one of the most effective missionaries of the school, Sulayman b. al-Hasan Abi Sa'id al-Jannabi): "When you gain mastery over a philosopher, hold on to him through our subversive phi-losophy. We agree with them that the laws of the prophets are against teaching the eternity of the world, if not on what some of them disagree with us about, for example, that the world has a master who does not know it." [19] He had said shortly before that, "You gain access to the people through what they like and make each of them think that you are one of them; whichever ones you discern are rational, raise the veil for them" (*Al-Farq*, 278–79).

This is an example of the means the Isma'ilis used to snare people and mold them into one strong and unified block. It was through these methods that they succeeded in uniting hundreds of thousands, indeed, thousands of thousands in their school. They imbued them with their new principles and made them a willing instrument in the hands of the sahib al-zaman and his helpers, They discharged them whenever they wanted and made them subservient for the purpose of realizing their goals. For we know that those members obeyed the call of their leader happily and sincerely, as if their lives depended on it. This their history testifies—that they defied hardships, even death, alone and together. They manifested courage and sacrificed personal welfare, indeed life, like no other political party or social group in that time. It is no wonder that such courage led, for the most part, to great results. Nor is it any wonder their movement spread socialism for three centuries and led, in the end, to the establishment of great states in Egypt and North Africa, leaving among its traces things that immortalized its name, and was succeeded by societies such as the Hashashin, Qaramatis, Druze, and others (most of which are still active today).

It would take several books to trace in detail the history of the move-ments which the Isma'ilis spawned and which remained under their in-fluence. The same would be true if we wanted to detail the influence of Isma'ili ideas on Islamic ethics, philosophy, and social life throughout the centuries. Therefore, we must be content with indicating that the ideas which the Isma'ili missionaries spread among the Muslim and non-Muslim groups were such as to turn their lives around and produce changes whose effects still remain today. Philosophy is indebted to them for the epistles of the Brethren of Sincerity, the first official society of sciences and learning to appear in the world. This group tried to spread their scientific principles and special view of nature and humanity. They also spread their opinions of the Greek philosophers, who were in their view on a level with prophets, or even higher, and thus prepared the way for the philosophers of Islam, such as al-Farabi, Ibn Sina, and others. There is no doubt that many of the theories of those philosophers and their exalted ideas were taken from the books of the Isma'ilis. Of those, we mention their theory of the prophetic disposition—in other words, on the "perfect imam." There is no doubt that that was among the ideas of the Isma'ilis; the same is true of other original theories that we find in the story of "Hayy Ibn Yaqzan" of Ibn Tufayl.[20] They also clearly had a strong influence on the science of Qur'anic commentary, where they helped to spread the idea of interpretation, and in Sufi philosophy, where their influence was felt in the books of Ibn 'Arabi, al-Ghazali, al-Hallaj, and so on, to say nothing of the Persian Sufis who were (and still are) more inclined toward Isma'ili principles than their Arab brothers. More important than that, in my opinion, the Isma'ili movement prepared the way for the spread of liberal ideas in the Islamic world and encouraged people to be frank about them, while previously they had been afraid to pursue things much less dangerous. If that is not the case, then how could Ibn 'Arabi venture to say:

I used to, before today, disavow my friend
Because my religion was not like his.

In the same way, we see dozens of writers and poets launching large-scale attacks on suspicious, religious fables, and on those who participate in nationalist antagonisms. They protested without fear and without the threat of suppression of personal freedom by those with civil and religious power. This is what Abu al-'Ala' al-Ma'arri [d. 1057], imam of those hostile to tyranny and a leading free-thinker, was able to say:

The laws set forth among us feuds
And deposited among us all sorts of enmities.[2]

Or:

Religion has diminished in value to the extent that
At best, it is like a falcon for the falconer or a dog to the hunter.
What is the Black Stone in the opinion of people I won't mention
But a remnant of idols and graven images?

All creation has become so corrupt
That religions are equally misguided.

I do not say that the stars were made into mortars [protecting heaven
    from would-be intruders; see Surah 72:9]
At the commission of Muhammad [to prophecy].

The eternity of the stars is not my belief,
Nor is the co-eternity of the world my school [of thought].

The mind wonders if all religious laws are mere tradition, blindly fol-
    lowed.
No one has actually deduced them by analogy.
The Mazdis and Muslims,
the Christians and Jews are all groundless.

They visit temples of fire in worship,
And mosques and churches are in constant use.
The Sabians glorify the planets.
But beneath the surface of these practices is evil.

If they ask about my school [of thought], it is clear;
Am I not simple like everyone else?
I was created from the world and live like its family;
I strive as they strive, and play as they play.
Yet I bear witness that I came to it by [mere] fate;
I shall depart fearing God and pronouncing His name.

Or finally:

As for bodies, their end is in the earth;
But I am puzzled about the destiny of souls.

Reason does not teach one religion;
He is taught religiosity by his relatives.
They obey the deceiver and trust him.
But how often the wise advise but are rejected.
The religious laws of all nations came
As a result of something they had already devised.
Some of them changed the teaching of others;
The intelligent nullify what they affirm.
Do not be happy if you are honored by them;
They have exalted the inferior and honored them.

Could Abu al-ʿAlaʾ and others have spread such negative ideas publicly, called the people to their notion of religion and to revolt against
the sinful, domineering ruling family, if the Ismaʿilis had not paved the
way before them? Similarly, Ibn al-Hani (d. 973), the Spanish natural
poet, did not fear to adopt Ismaʿilism and enter their school openly.
There were many others like him and Abu al-ʿAlaʾ among the Arab and

Persian writers and poets. How nice it would be if someone would go to the trouble of studying them, collecting their poems and statements, and analyzing them from the standpoint of what we are discussing. And how nice if our scholars would take an interest in the influence of Isma'ili thought on the Christian writers of the Middle Ages and on the Jesuit order (which contrasts with other monastic orders in objectives, in the absolute power of the head of the order, the existence of the degrees through which the sojourner on the spiritual path passes before reaching the highest order, and other characteristics which we only find in the organization of that brotherhood). It was these characteristics that inspired some European writers to attribute the appearance of the Jesuits to the influence of the Isma'ilis, or the followers of Sufi orders influenced by their doctrine and their internal order. And how nice if some of our scholars would take the trouble to research the influence of the Isma'ilis and their doctrine on the organization and doctrine of the Masons and the rest of the secret societies, monastic brotherhoods, professional guilds, dervish orders, and so on. True, some research on these topics has appeared which attempts to shed light on some of these uncertain issues. Yet such attempts have fallen short of the mark, not having been pursued by scholars or people knowledgeable in Eastern languages and philosophy. Therefore, this research is still in the beginning stages. We have plentiful materials related to these questions and the influence of the Isma'ilis on the social organizations in that time and after, and on the effects of their beliefs. Unfortunately, we are not able to pursue them here and can only mention the history of the organizations directly descended from the Isma'ilis: the Fatimids, Hashashin, Qaramatis, and Isma'ilis that today are scattered in many lands. In fact, we limit ourselves here to just one organization in which the Isma'ili spirit is revealed most completely, one which implemented their social beliefs and order. This is the Qaramati society, or Bahraini Isma'ilis, as some historians have called them. But before we discuss this group, I would like to discuss the accusations frequently made against the Isma'ilis by their opponents.

The opponents of the Isma'ilis said that the leaders of this school displayed violent cruelty in their wars and in all dealings with their enemies from the beginning; that they went to extremes, killing individuals and groups, [especially] the influential and powerful; and that they employed every means to annihilate their enemies and attain their goals, whatever they were. As proof, these commentators cite the activity of the Qaramatis, Hashashin, and other Isma'ili groups who later entered into the service of sultans and princes and became willing tools in their hands, so that they could avenge their personal enemies.[21]

All that is true and no one denies it, but the explanation is not accurate. No doubt the Isma'ilis were a courageous party, particularly warlike, whose guiding principle was more offensive than defensive. It was a party that tried from the very beginning to bring an end to the 'Abbasid state and to build on its ruins a new state with a socialist system. In the beginning, this party only used peaceful means, argument, and entreaty. However, their opponents forced them into armed attack, as in the year 909, when circumstances demanded it for their own welfare. As for the murder of individuals unawares—that is not known for certain except in a small group of the Hashashin, a group only distantly related to the Isma'ilis and known for their excesses. Their organization and goals differed from those of other Isma'ili groups. And the antagonistic means they used to attain their goals, as well as their independent system, were unfamiliar to their opponents. Thus, people began to associate with all the Isma'ilis those things that were specific to only one group of them. It was for that reason that they began to hate the Isma'ilis in general. In fact, their hatred of the members of this school reached such an extent that they campaigned for their expulsion from the Islamic nation. They called their murders and [other] activities acts of blasphemy. Yet they knew that the Isma'ilis forbade murder except in the battlefield and in self-defense under specific conditions. Their enemies created [those conditions] in order to condemn them, not for the offenses they committed but because they were of a different viewpoint. How many of the Isma'ilis fell victim to this blind zeal and atrocious hatred!

Al-Hamadhani mentioned that one of the princes of Khurasan killed in a short period "more than 100,000 Batinis and built from their heads a minaret from where the muezzins called people to pray." [22] The following appeared in the book of Abu Mansur al-Baghdadi: "In the city of Multan in India Mahmud b. Subuktekin, the famous sultan of Ghazna, killed thousands and cut off the arms of one thousand of them" (Al-Farq, 277).

It was as if the Isma'ilis' opponents had decided to wipe them off the face of the earth. For they were convinced

> that the danger of the Isma'ilis to Islam was greater than the danger of the Jews and Christians and Mazdis, indeed, greater than the danger of the materialists and the rest of the groups of blasphemers, and greater than the danger of the antichrist who will appear at the end of time . . . and because the vices of the Batinis are more numerous than the grains of sand and drops of rain. (Al-Farq, 265–66)

There is no doubt, then, that the position of the Isma'ilis in that popular war was critical indeed. When they were at a numerical disadvantage, they had to defend themselves; they were offensive only when they were the majority or when conditions were on their side and they could exploit them for revenge against their enemies. This is like [all] family and class wars resulting from conflicts over welfare and principles. In such wars, both sides apply means which no one uses in ordinary wars, and both sides are more barbaric than animals. There is no doubt that family wars are more barbaric than others. The victory of one of the sides quarreling over principles or a new order costs more in terms of personal sacrifice than political or other wars.

Nevertheless, with all the persecutions and hardships that the Isma'ilis bore and the difficulties that obstructed their path, their call spread through the country with uncanny speed. There did not remain any area in the 'Abbasid domain in which the Batinis had not established numerous cells to work, secretly spreading socialist principles and preparing the way for the new social order and the destruction of the old, outmoded order.

The adherents of these new principles would have reached their goal and demolished the 'Abbasid state if powerful help from a new nation—filled with zeal, ardor, and barbarism incredible in those days—had not arrived. This nation was that of the Turks, who became, from the middle of the ninth century, the sole power in Baghdad. They had the power to defend the state and its religious and civil order, and they did, opposing the enemies of the state and religion with their famous energy, severity, and zeal. There is no need to mention here what befell the Isma'ilis at their hands; suffice it to say that they were forced to withdraw from many troubled areas and to retreat to the hills and distant cities where they were able to preserve their ideals, their socialist school, and many of their social systems to this day. In addition, no sooner had they finished their battle with the Turks than a new enemy invaded from the West, no less zealous and savage than their Turanian opponents who came from the deserts of Mongolia and Central Asia. This new enemy was the Christians, who came to our country carrying hatred in their hearts and old and timeworn ideas in their minds. It was inevitable that they would be drawn into battle with those who held new ideas. In the end, they were defeated and left the country they had ravaged. They returned to their country filled with hatred and nationalist zeal, but carrying the germ of new ideas and a new world. This germ continued to ripen and mature until, after two centuries or more, it manifested itself in various forms—from the ideas that their ancestors had taken from the East in general and from the Isma'ilis in particular.

FIVE

The Qaramatis

The Qaramatis were the greatest of the Isma'ilis. They differed from other divisions of this brotherhood scattered throughout the 'Abbasid domain only in that they worked among the Arabs and their brothers, the Nabataeans of Iraq, Syria, and the Arabian peninsula; and that they worked in matters of secondary importance, concerning the methods of proselytizing only, and not on fundamental political issues. The reason for those differences was that the Qaramatis operated in a different land that had a different level of civilization. Most of its inhabitants, as we know, were Bedouins. Therefore, it seems to me that the Arab Qaramatis were less radical in religious and moral issues than the Persian Isma'ilis. Thus, some of the Persian customs, such as marrying sisters and other relatives forbidden by the Qur'an, were unknown among them, and there was no "night of the imam" or other such moral depravity rumored untruthfully about them. The same is true of the false statements in the book of the historian Ibn al-Jawzi, who said of them, "It is not permitted for any of them to seclude his wife from his son." It appears to me that their antagonists interpreted the word "seclude" (*hajaba*) as "bar" or "prohibit" (*mana'a*) or the like. It also appears to me that the Qaramati leaders who established that branch among the Arabs and Syrians did not know the major goals of their secret movement.[1] Either they had not reached the last stage of consecration or they were not allowed to know them, since only a few did. Yet it is true that today the Qaramatis of Bahrain and Arab Iraq do not differ from the rest of the Isma'ilis in the political issues on which their program is based, and that they follow in every situation the orders given by the imam [or sahib] al-zaman. Therefore, we may consider the Qaramatis to be a branch of the great Isma'ili tree which spread the communistic message among the Arabs, and especially the Nabataeans.

The center of this branch—where their missionary lived at the outset of the movement—was the city of Wasit located between Kufa, Basra, and their neighboring villages. Most of the residents of this area were a mixture of Arabs, Nabataeans, and Negroes. The latter had been imported from Africa by the large landowners to work the lands. They were exploited, as we have mentioned, under conditions similar to those in the southern United States before the abolition of slavery. It is no wonder, under such circumstances, that most of the residents of this area were dissatisfied with their social situation and were receptive to calls for relief from their heavy burdens, for compassion and mercy. This is the reason for the success of the Qaramatis in that land. It is why people flocked to them, believing that the sahib al-zaman and his missionaries would free them from the yoke of slavery and the oppression of the state and landowners.

We do not know exactly who founded that center or when, or the laws operant there. It is reported that it was established before Hamdan al-Qaramati, by whose name the call is known, that is, that some Isma'ili missionaries visited this land before Hamdan arrived. However, they did not leave any noticeable influence to indicate that they stayed any length of time. Therefore, nothing prevents us from assuming that Hamdan was the first missionary to this area, and the first to organize the affairs of the new Isma'ili order.

The historians mention that Hamdan—who had been a simple plowman working the land of others—came to this land as a delegate of a missionary greater than he. He built a new center for the Isma'ili cell, called the *dar al-hijra* (near Kufa), where all the villagers who had followed his call gathered to hear spiritual counsel, to speculate on conditions before the economic and social call, and to glean what they could about the imam al-zaman and his assistants. They also performed symbolic poetry unknown among the Isma'ilis except in these villages, whose residents were Nabataeans, Arabs, and those who had been arabized. When Hamdan saw that the people were receptive to the call and entered into the new school in large groups, he organized them in such a way as to assure the success of the movement and its quick spread. They also had a constitution to which they turned when in need. Among the conditions of the organization was that every member contribute money each year for the "hidden imam," leader of the Isma'ilis. There was also a tax known as *al-fitr*, a dirhem which all Isma'ilis without exception contributed, and another tax known as *bi'l-hijra*, a dinar paid by all adults to be spent especially for the needs of dar al-hijra. They contributed it gladly, to the extent that if one of them was unable to pay, someone else paid his share.

One of the minor historians mentioned that Hamdan, after building the dar al-hijra and organizing its affairs, suggested that the most cherished of those who followed his call would pay another tax, called the *bulgha*.[2] This was a special tax to be paid by everyone who wanted to participate in the *'isha' al-muhibba* (*agape*), that is, to eat the bread of paradise, or, as Hamdan himself called it, the food of the people of paradise, which would arrive from the imam al-zaman presently. Some writers added that Hamdan, after levying the bulgha on his followers, called on them to pay to the dar al-hijra one fifth of what they owned. They responded to his call gladly. They evaluated their property and then paid one fifth of it. A woman would present the missionary one fifth of her spinning, the laborer one fifth of his fees. This tax was fair; each person, as a member of the brotherhood, paid it to the brotherhood's treasury. However, Hamdan was not content with these taxes, but ordered the villagers who had entered his religion to carry everything they owned to a certain place. When they had gathered there, he announced to them that one of their number, a trustworthy man, would be in charge of distributing it. He gathered the furniture, jewelry, robes, food, and so on, which they had produced, and distributed it to the needy in their group, so that not one poor person remained among them. Thus, the men worked happily and enthusiastically, and the women carried to the *bayt* [dar] al-hijra what money they earned from their spinning. Even small children presented to the director of the [dar] the allowance they earned from the garden owners by "guarding during the day, and shooing the birds from the trees and vegetables." Thus, one owned nothing personally except "his sword and weapons."

This is a summary of what the above-mentioned writer [Nasr Khusrow] said about the new organization that Hamdan al-Qaramati introduced to his followers in Iraq. We have neglected the immoral practices attributed to the Qaramatis because we have not ascertained their truth. When the missionary to Iraq finished his duties in Wasit, he moved to a place known as Kalwaza, near Baghdad. He lived there a long time, working to spread the Isma'ili call and corresponding with the Khurasani branch, which had sent him to Kufa, and the sahib al-zaman, who lived in 'Askar Mukarram. During all this time, Hamdan kept an eye on the course of political events in the 'Abbasid capital, in order to benefit from their mistakes. In general, he surrounded them with the Isma'ili movement and the operations of the center which he established, in particular. His brother-in-law, 'Abdan, author of some of the sacred books of the Qaramatis, helped Hamdan in the administration of the Iraqi branch and carried on all his correspondence with the sahib al-zaman and the other Batini cells. It was he who designated Zikrawaih missionary to Arab Iraq, and Abu Sa'id al-Jannabi to southern Persia and Bahrain.

The Qaramati call began to spread from Wasit to the rest of the Arab countries near and far, until it reached the southern Arabian peninsula where a strong Ismaʿili cell was created. After a short while, this cell became antagonistic to the administrators of the central government and gained the attention of the caliphs of Baghdad. Then, through the efforts of Abu Saʿid al-Jannabi, a second cell was formed in Al-Ahsa in Bahrain, which gained considerable importance. Within a short period it became one of the most important Ismaʿili cells, because Abu Saʿid knew how to approach the Arabs of Bahrain and attract them to his call; its seeds had been sown in fertile soil, and so matured quickly and bore fruit.

These calls began to flourish and spread throughout most Arab lands, Syria, and Iraq. They were all striving for the same goal, working under the supervision of skilled, experienced missionaries like Abu Saʿid al-Jannabi, Zikrawaih al-Dindani, and others who derived their spiritual power from missionaries greater than they, such as the *sahib al-naqa,* Abu ʿAbdullah Muhammad, and his brother, the *sahib al-khal* (Abu ʿAbdullah Ahmad). It was not surprising, then, that this mission grew stronger and the people were receptive to it all around; even in the caliph's capital a large group of upper-class people joined it. The Qaramatis depended on them in times of misfortune. They also kept an eye on the Baghdad government, which was not aware of the power of these dissenters. As a result, Baghdad did not perceive the danger beginning to surround and threaten it until the year 278/891, when the Ismaʿilis emerged from their secrecy and prepared to attack their greatest enemy. Thus in the year 284/897, a group of Qaramatis tried for the first time to realize their socialist program actively, although unsuccessfully. They were forced to put off their operation until another opportunity. Yet they continued to watch their enemy closely and to attack them whenever an opportunity presented itself (287/900; 288/900; 289/901). They also withstood their operations in regions far from the capital, but they were not successful in the battlefield because their enemy was still stronger than they, and was led by one of the best leaders in the ʿAbbasid family. He was the caliph al-Muʿtadid, who resisted the Ismaʿili movement and warded off evil from the state of his ancestors. However, he died in the year 289/902 and was followed by a man weak in both determination and will, and unsuccessful in his operations. And the leaders of the communistic movement did not hesitate to benefit from his weakness. They turned against their adversary once more and wore them down by attacking them on all sides. Soon the central power was no longer able to control Ismaʿili activities or extinguish their revolts in more remote regions. Accordingly, these regions began to separate from the caliphs of Baghdad and to develop into independent groups.

It is not necessary here to mention the numerous revolts launched by the Qaramatis, nor to delve further into the history of the states that were stripped from the ʿAbbasid caliphate and became independent principalities or kingdoms. It is necessary, however, for the reasons elu-

cidated above, to mention something of the history of one of these principalities: that founded on the shores of the Persian Gulf and known as
the Qaramati republic.

We have mentioned that among the missionaries who worked in Iraq
under the supervision of Hamdan al-Qaramati was Abu Saʿid al-
Jannabi, from near Jannab in southern Persia, and that Hamdan sent
him as a missionary to Bahrain.[3] Abu Saʿid had hardly begun his work
in Bahrain when the residents of this region, irrespective of class or
ethnic background, began to gather around him. These were people of
the cities who were hostile to the ʿAbbasid political and social order,
which they had not created and which had not been created for them.
There were also Bedouin who had always hated the ʿAbbasids' state
and regulations. They had especially hated—ever since the early days of
Islam—the zakah and tithe. These were novelties to which they could
not accustom themselves.[4] It is no wonder, then, that they followed the
call of Abu Saʿid and supported him in their land. He had called on
them to abandon religious laws and most of the religious restrictions
that were not in tune with that time, and called them to a brotherhood
of people, regardless of race or religion. And he promised them happiness on this earth and in this life, not in a world to come, which they
could not describe and of which they knew nothing. Thus, he became
more powerful and his principles spread, with the help of Hasan b.
Sanbar.[5] When this highly respected and influential man entered Abu
Saʿid's religion and Abu Saʿid married his daughter, Abu Saʿid's position in Bahrain was further strengthened and even more people accepted
him. It was not long before the entire region was in his hands; only the
capital and some of its neighboring villages remained faithful to the
caliph. Within a short time, Abu Saʿid was able to take control of them
(287/899), too, and join them to his communist republic. Then he began
to advance to Basra.

When this news reached the caliph al-Muʿtadid, it troubled him. He
therefore ordered that his governor there, ʿAbbas al-Ghanawi, be supplied with money and ten thousand men. He advanced at their head to
meet the Qaramatis, who were being led by Abu Saʿid himself. When
the two groups met near Basra, the army of the caliph was defeated and
its leader captured. The soldiers dispersed, seeking safety in the open
country, and only a few were rescued. Those taken prisoner were killed
by order of Abu Saʿid in revenge for the Qaramatis who had been killed
in Baghdad by order of the caliph.[6] Abu Saʿid spared no one but the
leader of the caliph's army, ʿAbbas al-Ghanawi. He then set him free
and sent him to the caliph to report what had happened to his army, to
tell him of the courage of the Qaramatis, and to give him the following:[7]

What is this? Will you compromise your dignity, kill your men, and make
your enemies covetous by sending out armies against me? I am but a man in

the wilderness, without seeds, grain, crops, livestock, and land. I have no town or country. I have become content with the coarseness of life and with defending my life and honor at the end of a spear. Notice that I have not overtaken your land nor removed your authority on any great issue. Yet I swear that even if you send your whole army, they could not overcome me because my men and I were bred in this austerity and have become accustomed to it. There is no hardship for us here in our domain. We are comfortable. But you sent your soldiers from the [comfort of their] silks, ice[d drinks], flowers and incense, from a long distance and on an arduous road. They reached us but the trip had decimated them before our battle. Therefore, they decided to make a show of facing us in battle only for a moment, and then flee. Had they attacked me, then that would have been my greatest aid against them. The best they could do would be to come and rest. Then their numbers would still be great and their perception clear. And I would not be able to challenge them and would flee. Still, your army would be unable to follow me except at some distance, more than 20 or 30 parasangs [ancient Persian measure equal to about 3 1/2 miles]. I would wander the desert a month or more, then launch a surprise attack and kill all of them. And if this proved impossible, that is, had they fortified themselves and been on their guard, still they would be able neither to surround me in the open country nor follow me in the prairies. Neither their provisions nor the land would be sufficient to support them. So the majority would leave, and the few of them remaining would be killed by my sword the first day we met. And this could happen [only] if they were [able] to escape the ailments of this district and its awful water and climate, which they would be unable to bear. They have come from a place opposite it and their bodies are not accustomed to it. They could not endure it. Think about this and its ramifications. Is pursuing me worth the trouble and danger to your troops, your financial expenditures, your equipment, [and all] the dangers and difficulties? I am immune to it and my companions and I are out of harm's way. Your dignity will be degraded; the borders will rebel; your enemy kings will gain courage against you, just as whenever something like this happens. So you will not conquer my domain or take anything from me. If you choose to fight anyway, then seek counsel of God, advance deliberately, send whomever you will, and more, as you wish. But if you [choose to] refrain, that is up to you.

When the caliph read Abu Saʿid's letter, he was very angry and wanted to march on him himself. But the condition of the caliphate at that time, especially the condition of the caliphal army and the treasury, forced him to accept the advice of his opponent and leave him alone. As that was what Abu Saʿid had hoped for, he seized the opportunity and took over the city of Hajar, the capital of Bahrain, after a long siege. Then he took over the other lands that were still under the power of the caliph or his sheikhs or princes, until all Bahrain was indisputably in his hands (290/903). Yet he was not content with that, and began to prepare to take over the lands neighboring Bahrain, spreading his call. He advanced to al-Yamama and incorporated it into his nation. Next came Oman. He took over a large part of it, including a number of the islands subordinate to it. If he had not died (he was killed at al-

Hammam in 914), he would have made all of them a part of his republic, but he did join other Arab countries and Iraq, and made them into a great republic based on new socialistic foundations.

Abu Sa'id left many sons undistinguished for their zeal, farsightedness or endurance in battle, except Abu Tahir Sulayman. It was he who succeeded his father and worked toward realizing his goals. No sooner had he taken over control of the government and leadership of the army than he marched by turns on Basra and Baghdad and to the west, that is, to the Hijaz and the two holy cities. He was successful in all his military expeditions to the extent that the caliph began to fear him. His capital and its residents came to tremble at the mention of him or of the Qaramatis. Thus, the name "Qaramati" became synonymous with that of a dreadful soldier. The spread of this fear was helped by a number of calamities that befell the 'Abbasid caliphate in the first quarter of the tenth century, endangering their [very] center and hastening the approach of their defeat: the appearance of the Qaramatis in Syria, their cutting off the roads to the people, robbing passersby, and so on. The greatest catastrophe that befell the 'Abbasids at that time, and which nearly put an end to their prestige and moral influence in the country, was undoubtedly when Abu Tahir entered Mecca by force (on 12 January 930), plundered the holy city, and killed its residents and the pilgrims. These are among the abominations Abu Tahir and his army committed in Mecca and in Medina; we must mention some of these in pursuit of the part of the Qaramati program related to religion and morals.

It appears that the goal of the Meccan siege was, first of all, to avenge one of the great Qaramati missionaries, Zikrawaih, and his army, whom the commander-in-chief had captured in the year 929 and whom the caliph had ordered killed. Second, it was to reduce the power and prestige of the caliph of Baghdad in the eyes of the Muslims. And third, it was to distract the caliph and his army from the important events that were taking place at that time in North Africa, where the imam al-zaman and the great Isma'ili leader 'Ubaidullah had begun to pave the way to take control of this region from the caliph's governors or his allies and to establish the well-known independent state of the Fatimids. Accordingly, the incentive for that raid was not mere love of plundering and killing. Rather, there were important political and military reasons that mitigate, albeit slightly, the atrocities Abu Tahir and his followers committed at the Ka'bah. Nevertheless, whatever the real reasons for this attack, Abu Tahir did not permit an opportunity to offer itself or a year to go by without benefiting from it. Thus he risked dispute on the road to and from the two holy cities in an effort to prevent the performance of the Hajj and its related rituals. For he considered them holdovers from the pre-Islamic days of ignorance, and similar to idol worship. In the final event he practically terminated the Hajj and its rituals completely, and, with but a few exceptions, caused the Muslims to ne-

glect their trips to Mecca and Medina.[8] He limited these raids to robbing the pilgrims and preventing them from visiting the Ka'bah until
the year 312/924. That was the year of the greatest calamity the pilgrims had experienced since the day Arabs and Muslims began making
pilgrimages to the Ka'bah.

The Arab historians mention that the number of Muslim pilgrims the
Qaramatis killed that year in the house of God and in the streets of
Mecca and its outskirts exceeded three thousand (not counting those
who died of starvation in the desert and those captured by the enemy).
Among them was a large group of the educated people, as well as those
with high positions, such as al-Azhari (d. 370 [A.H.]) and 'Abdullah b.
Hamdan Abi al-Amir Sayf al-Dawlah, and others. They also mention
that the money alone seized by the Qaramatis in that raid exceeded
several million dinars, of which a part was sent to the imam and the
rest of which was spent on the needs of "the faithful," that is, the Qaramatis.

When the news of this great calamity and its disgusting details
reached the caliph's capital and the rest of the Islamic regions, the people cried out against it. They began to leave the capital, to move to the
farther shores, and to seek shelter inside the walls of their houses while
the enemy was still a great distance from them.

Ibn al-Farat, one of the caliph's ministers at that time, tried to allevi-
ate the suffering of the injured, ease the fear of the residents of the
capital, and mitigate the mounting threat to Islam and its capital. He
tried the old, diplomatic means, that is, alternately offering threats,
promises, and gifts. He was not successful, however, because these
things were of no use to Abu Tahir, nor was he deceived by them. For
he had been apprised, through his aides in Baghdad, of the true conditions of the Arab state and of the material and moral strength of the
caliphs of Baghdad. He therefore wanted to expand his holdings and
incorporate all the Arab lands into his small republic. Accordingly, he
demanded of the minister that he surrender Basra and al-Ahwaz to him
in the name of the caliph. When Ibn al-Farat did not meet his demand,
Abu Tahir marched on Kufa, seized it, killed most of its residents, and
desecrated its chief mosque (making it into a stable for his horses). He
then began to think about attacking the capital itself, but did not accomplish that for unknown reasons. Still, the people feared him, and he
did stop the pilgrimage for several seasons.

The government of Baghdad was not able to resist the Qaramatis by
armed strength. It had to be content with taking some of the people
related to them (or considered to be) and punishing them. They also
destroyed one of the Baghdad mosques where some of the Qaramatis
met in secret.[9] Ibn al-Jawzi mentions that the Qaramatis had signet
rings of white clay given them by al-Ka'ki,[10] with the inscription "Muhammad b. Isma'il, the expected imam and friend of God." [11] The government of Baghdad recognized them by these rings, seized them, and

punished them, since they were unable to fight their brethren outside the walls of the capital. True, they tried to unleash against them the armies of Azerbaijan under the leadership of Amir Yusuf b. al-Saj, the caliph's governor there. But this operation was ill-fated, or, more accurately, nearly disastrous, because Amir Yusuf was sympathetic with the Qaramatis. He had informed them of the Baghdad government's plans and the movements of its army. For he was awaiting the imminent demise of the ʿAbbasid state and working with others toward it in hopes of establishing on its ruins an independent state in Azerbaijan and leaving it to his son. This is what another man in his family before him, called Muhammad, had contemplated. If the accusations of the secretary of Amir Yusuf are true, that man was Muhammad Khalq al-Niramani. In a message to Nasr, the caliph's lieutenant, he said:

> Yusuf concealed from him (from his secretary) his religious sect. When he went to Wasit he was on good terms with him and was delighted with him. He disclosed to him that he professed obedience neither to (the caliph) al-Muqtadir over him, nor to the ʿAbbasids, and that the expected imam was the ʿAlid who was in Qayrawan and that Abu Tahir al-Hajari was a follower of that religion . . . and that he (that is, Yusuf) saw the weakening of al-Muqtadir and the rest of the usurping ʿAbbasids as a God-given duty and that his obedience to the Byzantine tyrant was better than obedience to the caliph.[12]

If this accusation is true, we can conclude that the ʿAbbasids were left without sincere men on whom they could rely in times of need. The people closest to them—their ministers, lieutenants, governors, and soldiers—had begun to lean toward their opponents, gathering information for them and instigating intrigues against the state. At the very least, their devotion to their benefactors and to the state to which they had sworn devotion became suspect. Further indication of the straightened circumstance in which the state found itself is that the malady was not confined to the upper classes. It included all classes, families, and individuals, to the extent that in one family one could see different political and social positions among husbands, wives, fathers and sons, brothers and sisters, and friends. "Thus the people were of two positions on them (the Qaramatis): those who openly declared hostility and opposition, and those who advocated reconciliation and tolerance. Those who were antagonistic toward them feared their strength, and those who were tolerant were of a similar idolatry. Such people were in great danger on two sides."[13] Here let us relate a story from the history of Ibn al-Athir which demonstrates the spirit of the age, the degree of disintegration of the social and moral fabric, and the effects of the Ismaʿili movement on the minds and lives of the people. The gist of this event is that a young man who had joined the Ismaʿilis and participated in Abu Tahir's attack, which ended, as we said, in the murder of some of the pilgrims and in the capture of the rest, saw among the female captives the Qaramatis had taken a woman he recognized to be his mother. He asked her about her health and her religion. When he learned she was still a Sunni Muslim, he turned away from her and refused to help her. Then, when he learned she had obtained permission from the leader of the Qaramatis to return to her daughters, who remained by themselves in Baghdad, he overtook her and beat her with his sword. She said, "He wounded me and the people held him back. Then they led me to the people who called him their friend and left me, and I went up to them. When the leader had the Qaramatis and the prisoners come forward I saw my son among them, cloaked, on a camel, and he was crying. I said to him, 'May God neither relieve nor free you.' "[14]

Is there any greater hatred than that? Has there ever been any greater hostility? Indeed, has the history of Islam passed through a stage of greater social disintegration or disparity among the classes? The nation was divided into two parts, each of which swore to defeat its enemy or die—such that one side must annihilate or at least greatly restrict the other. Woe to the vanquished in this merciless war of principles!

The two sides began to prepare themselves for battle. When the time came and each side considered itself the stronger and assured of victory, they became embroiled in a number of wars in which each was alternately successful until 312/924. Then fate began to forsake the armies of the caliph and smile on the Qaramatis. In 315/927 they again captured Basra and plundered it. Then they shattered the armies of Yusuf b. al-Saj, governor of that city. They did the same thing to the rest of the armies the caliph sent against the Qaramatis, until the people were thoroughly alarmed. They began to invent wild stories about Abu Tahir's army and its numbers. They believed his success in the battlefield was a result of miracles and magic performed in the thick of the battle, that superhuman strength aided him, and other such foolish fantasies. In reality, the Qaramatis triumphed in most of their battles only because of their unity, their complete obedience to their leader, and their total trust in him. Their steadfastness in battle depended on their deep-rooted belief in the correctness of what they were fighting for. Moreover, they were more courageous and brave, and more tolerant of the hardships of war, than the caliph's soldiers, most of whom were residents of cities and accustomed to comfort, and "the ice[d drinks], perfumes and incense" of which the Qaramati chief spoke. Ibn al-Jawzi relates: "One day one of them asked the Qaramati the reasons for the victories of his followers with such a small number of soldiers.[15] The Qaramati answered him, 'Because we seek our salvation in courage while they seek theirs in flight.' "[16] Perhaps there is another reason, of which we spoke before: the possibility of treason on the part of the head of the caliph's army, Yusuf b. al-Saj (if what his secretary wrote is true).

The ultimate victory of the Qaramatis and the fall of Basra into their hands had a powerful effect on Baghdad's residents. They began to flee to neighboring lands because the road was open.[17] There was no longer

an army the caliph could depend on to repel the attacks of the Qaramatis [even] if they had wanted to take over the capital. For unknown
reasons, however, Abu Tahir did not think of attacking the capital with
such a small army. He returned to his land content with the spoils he
had gotten and the blows he had struck the tribes on the road to his
Bahrain capital. When he left Basra, he wrote to Mu'nis, leader of the
caliph's army, a sarcastic qasida, in which he said:

> Tell your Mu'nis to relax with some wine,
> And follow the wine with the zither and the flute.
> In my eagerness
> I recall an exemplary verse which has become proverbial:
> "We visit you but we do not blame you for your rudeness.
> For a gentleman visits even if he is not invited.
> We are not like you in your negligence;
> For he who burns with eagerness never finds the home of his hope
>   too distant."

Abu Tahir Sulayman had scarcely returned to his capital when, apparently on the order of the sahib al-zaman, he began to prepare a
distant foray, the likes of which no one of the religion of the Prophet
had attempted before. He did not tell anyone of his decision or plan
until he had prepared the equipment for the trip. Then he left the capital
of his country and set out for the sacred Ka'bah, in order to strike Islam
at its very heart and in its homeland, if possible. Undoubtedly his intent
was also to put an end to the prestige and political and moral influence
of the caliphs of Baghdad in the Islamic world.

As the year 317/930 began without unrest, thousands of pilgrims set
out once more for the Ka'bah. They did so peacefully, with no concern
except to perform the rites of the pilgrimage and return to their home-
lands. However, they had scarcely finished these rites—and some of
them had not yet even begun—when they heard that Abu Tahir was
marching toward Mecca with an army of six hundred horses and nine
hundred men. This news had only spread among the public for a few
days when Abu Tahir and his men were at the gates of Mecca. Mecca's
leader, along with a large group of his officials, tried to conciliate Abu
Tahir and persuade him to return to his land compensated with money
and precious gifts.[18] But Abu Tahir did not cooperate; he and his followers entered Mecca and began killing its citizens, as well as whatever
pilgrims were there, both men and women: "They were hanged from
the Ka'bah; [the well of] Zamzam was filled with them; the mosque
and its surrounding area was paved with them. People from Khurasan,
the Maghrib, etc., were killed in the side streets and ravines of Mecca,
some thirty thousand; a similar number of women and children was
captured. He stayed in Mecca six days and no one continued the ceremonies of the Hajj or the nusuk ["sacrifice," a related ritual] that year."
The most merciless and least compassionate person was Abu Tahir him-

self. He moved through the Ka'bah and the city, from one group to another, calling his followers. They were intoxicated with the force of [their] victory, and the money and jewels they had taken as booty. They had put an end to "idolatry and the worship of graven images," leveled the pillars [of the Ka'bah] until no trace of it remained.[19]

One of those who had been in the Ka'bah the day Abu Tahir entered it described the condition of Mecca and the shrines and what happened to the pilgrims that year:

I saw a man who had climbed the Ka'bah to tear off the roof gutter, but he did not succeed. Then the hostility subsided after a day or two.[20] I had walked around the Ka'bah. All of a sudden a drunken Qaramati entered the shrine with his horse. By whistling he signaled to the horse to urinate as he performed the *tawaf* [rite of circumambulation of the Ka'bah]. Then he drew his sword to strike whomever came along. I was near him and ran. Then he caught up with a man who was near me; he struck him and killed him. Then he stopped and shouted, "Asses. Did you not say from outside this house that in it was safety? How is it safe when I killed him just now in your presence?"[21]

Another one whom the Qaramati captured reported,

One of them grabbed me, inflicting pain on me and forcing me into his service and mistreating me whenever he was drunk. One night when he had again drunk too much, he placed me opposite him and said, "What do you say about Muhammad, your master?" I said, "I don't know but what you teach me, O Believer, I will say." He said, "He was a leader. What do you say about Abu Bakr?" I said, "I don't know." He said, "He was a contemptuous weakling. What do you say about 'Umar?" I said, "I don't know." He said, "By God, a brutal lout. What do you say about 'Uthman?" I said, "I don't know." He said, "He was an ignorant fool. What do you say about 'Ali?" I said, "I don't know." He said, "He was duped. . . . These men are heretics who don't appreciate any of the companions of the Prophet."[22]

Ibn al-Jizzar (d. 395 [A.H.]) reported from a trustworthy man:

One of the followers of Abu Tahir entered the shrine and I was among the casualties and wounded lying on the floor. I didn't move until the hoofs of his horse trampled me. When he saw me move, he came up to me and asked me if I knew the [Qur'anic chapter entitled] Surat al-Fil. I said that I did. He said, "Where are the swarms [to save Muslims under attack, as described in the Surat al-Fil]?" I said, "Wherever your lord wishes." He shouted at me, "You are such fools that you should be added to the stones around which people wander and dance in honor and touch with their faces. Your legists devote their studies to them and don't understand anything better than this. Nothing remains of these superstitions except these swords and that's all."[23]

Abu Tahir and his followers stayed in Mecca twelve days, using their swords on its residents and pilgrims in the Ka'bah, plundering and carrying out ghastly deeds. They also took everything they could get their hands on: costly jewels, the ancient robes that hung on the walls of the

Ka'bah, and [others] stored there, the valuable 14-*mithqal* [unit of
weight currently just under 5 grams] pearls and earrings of Maryam,
the horn of Ibrahim, the rod of Moses inlaid with gold. These Abu
Tahir took to his capital or destroyed and threw to the wind, until not
a trace of them remained. One of those who carried the booty exagger-
ated the amount he took with him to the capital of Bahrain, saying that
he used fifty camels to transport what he took from the Ka'bah alone,
and one hundred thousand camels for the booty from Medina and its
surrounding areas. He also transported female prisoners in great numbers. However, most of them returned to Mecca or their distant lands
with the help of the Bani Hadil, who ambushed the Qaramatis on the
road and forced them to free most of the prisoners.

Among the booty the Qaramatis took from Mecca was the famous
Black Stone, which the pilgrims used to circumambulate and bless (and
still do). This stone remained in Al-Ahsa, discarded in one of the cor-
ners of the city and abandoned until the year 339/950. Then the Qaramatis returned it on the order of al-Mansur, one of the Fatimid caliphs
(r. 946–953) whose orders the Qaramatis carried out in the beginning,
as we shall see.

> Abu Tahir and his group marched out of Mecca reciting:
> If this is the House of God, our Lord,
> Then fire would be pouring over us from above,
> Because we performed a pilgrimage of the Jahiliyya [pre-Islamic igno-
>   rance].
> Utterly shameful.
> We left among Zamzam and Al-Safa
> Corpses wishing for no lord but the lord.

It is only to be expected that this incredible disaster had an enormous
impact on all Muslims and on the caliph in Baghdad.[24] It was, in addition, a strong incentive to gather both the material and spiritual resources of the Muslims and put an end to the raids of the Qaramatis,
along with their vile deeds and scorn for religion. But how was it that
"nothing was left to the 'Abbasids then except their name," and nothing remained of their former power except great, long titles?

> The caliph died and no one grieved.
> Another was established and no one rejoiced.
> That one passed, as did the misfortune which followed:
> He rose up and then rose up calamity and disaster.

> Another said:

> A caliph in a cage, between servant and whore.
> He says what they say to him, just as a parrot does.

Real power during this time was actually in the hands of the leaders
of the army, most of whom were Turks, and those who held administra-

tive offices and high positions, most of whom were Persians and other non-Arabs who were only concerned with the interests of their own offices or personal benefit.[25] And no one outside this virtually universal framework, such as ʿAli b. ʿIsa, the head of the government and an outstanding and intelligent minister, was capable of spreading a new spirit in the corpus of the ailing state or of saving it from rapid decay. It was as if he, too, sensed the approach of the end of the state of al-Mansur and could do nothing about its outcome. Therefore, the battle in Mecca was not reported in Baghdad for fear of an uproar. But the matter was not concealed from the Qaramatis. They knew the true situation in the ʿAbbasid capital, through their aides there who sent the news by carrier pigeon.[26]

Nearly a year after the calamities of the Meccan pilgrims, the government of Baghdad [still] had not taken action. This implies that they intended to retaliate against the Qaramatis or limit their raids [sometime] in the future. But the Qaramatis saw their weakness, determined that they were incapable of fighting them, and decided to take advantage of the situation. They marched on Oman and occupied it in the year 318/930. This amounted to the occupation of the entire Arabian peninsula, considering Oman's economic and military importance; it secured the Qaramati army from the rear. Thus Abu Tahir was able to take over Kufa the following year. Kufa, as the reader knows, was the key to Baghdad and its stronghold. If Abu Tahir had wanted to enter Baghdad in that year and finish off the power of the ʿAbbasids, he could have. However, he was content with taking Kufa and plundering it in his usual way. Then he left and returned to his capital, reciting:

If my return to Al-Hajar misled you,
Then shortly the news will come to you.
When Mars rises up from the land of Babylon
And two stars accompany it, beware!
Am I not mentioned in all the scriptures?
Am I not described in the Surah of the Companions?
I will rule the people of the earth, east and west,
To Qairawan of Rum, Turkey, and the land of the Khazars.[27]

His return [to his capital] could have been due to a variety of causes: personal matters, order of the Fatimid caliph of Egypt, or astrological considerations (on which the Qaramatis based important decisions in their lives, both personal and social).[28] At any rate, it appears that Abu Tahir's failure to conquer the capital of his greatest opponent was not due to weakness or indecision with regard to its necessity, but rather to extraneous reasons that forced him to put off his final strike on the ʿAbbasid state until another opportunity. However, circumstances did not permit Abu Tahir to carry out his plan immediately. Those circumstances were the internal trials caused among the Qaramatis by one of the Mashudis of Khurasan. He distracted them from continuing their

wars with the caliph's army, and weakened them materially and spiritually. Thus they were forced to wait until the year 325/937, when Abu
Tahir once again marched on Kufa and occupied it. He forced the caliph to conclude a truce with him and to pay him 120,000 dinars annu-
ally, as well as a specified tax on every pilgrimage. Still not satisfied,
from that year on he began to participate in Baghdad's politics and to
influence the running of its internal operations.

Matters remained as such for half a century. The death of Abu Tahir
(332/943) did not affect them since his successors, most of them his
sons or near relatives, inherited many of his essential qualities: courage,
good administrative skills, a proclivity for sacrificing personal welfare
for the sake of the common good, an interest in what was beneficial for
the peasants and laborers, and devotion to the new system that made
him the founder of the Qaramati school in Bahrain, and which Abu
Tahir preserved until the last day of his life.[29] Moreover, the successors
of Abu Tahir were content with the conquests he had made and did not
seek new conquests. The 'Abbasid state had collapsed a year after the
death of Abu Tahir and a new state had been established in its place,
known as the state of the Shi'i Bedouin. And Abu Tahir's successors
began to court them. The Qaramatis were close to the Shi'is because
there was, after [an initial period of] strain, an ideological relationship
between the two groups. Therefore, we do not hear anything about the
Qaramati raids and activities until the year 343/954. The Qaramitis
seem to have occupied themselves with trading with their neighbors,
repairing their internal situation, strengthening their new social order,
and adapting their lives to it. Indeed, what we know of the republic of
Bahrain at that time leaves no doubt that they made progress in their
economy, their equipment for war, and their morals. In fact, most of the
Islamic countries envied them and wished that they had been destined to
achieve such progress, progress that the Qaramatis achieved only because of their new order, which was introduced for the first time in the
history of Islam.

The internal order of the Qaramatis can be summarized, based on the
ancient sources, as follows. We have mentioned above that the founders
of the Qaramati or Isma'ili republic in Bahrain were common people.
They called upon people to join the new school in the name of the
hidden imam al-zaman, and then in the name of the Fatimid caliphs,
once that state appeared. This indicates that the Qaramatis acknowledged the spiritual and political leadership of those caliphs in the beginning. They collected taxes and the zakah in their name and gave a large
part of [these revenues] to them. They supported them both financially
and with manpower in their wars with the Baghdad caliphs, and obeyed
them in everything. They even returned the Black Stone to Mecca when
the [Fatimid] caliph al-Mansur ordered it (339/950) in order to satisfy
his Sunni subjects in Egypt and to curry their favor. We can conclude,
therefore, that Abu Tahir, Abu Sa'id, and their successors were simply

the imam al-zaman's administrators in Bahrain, ruling the land in his name and obedient to him. However, some of the [later] operations of the Qaramatis (as well as other factors we will mention later) indicate that the distance between them and their imam weakened the bond between the Qaramatis and the Fatimids and led to a kind of internal independence. For the government in Bahrain was more like a republic or government by consultation than government by a [single] individual.

We do not deny that the Qaramati government was headed by individuals from the family of Abu Tahir al-Jannabi and those nearest them. This has led some to think that the government of Bahrain was by the tyrannical few (oligarchy), rather than a true republic. However, those individuals were not distinguished from other ministers and members of the consultative council [*majlis*], known to them as "those who bind" [*al-ʿaqdaniyya*], except with regard to specific matters, such as leadership of the army and the leadership of the council of distinguished ministers over some of the secondary administrators. Thus, they were more like the leaders of the South American republics of this century than Arab and Persian princes at that time.[30] In other words, they were first among equals (*primum inter pares,* as the Latin expression has it). The real power, that is, legislative and executive power, was in the hands of the members of the majlis, composed of six people (ministers) chosen by the people from the family of Abu Tahir, those nearest him or others trusted by them, and those who had achieved high rank in the group. These six ministers had deputies who sat behind them on a high dais or in the seats of the ministers, if for some reason they were unable to attend the meeting. What we know of the operation of this council is that it governed the country and determined by consensus what issues were presented, and that its leadership took precedence over that of Abu Tahir or his brother-in-law (the brother of his wife), Abu Muhammad Sanbar, one of the men of Bahrain known for their generosity and justice and the people's devotion to them.

The *Safar Name* of Nasr Khusrow, who visited the land of the Qaramatis in 1052 (that is, a number of years after Ibn Muʾqil), confirmed what this writer had said and substantiated the bonds of affection and harmony among "the faithful" as still strong until this year. He mentions in his diary:

The descendants of Abu Saʿid are now living in a large palace known as "dar al-hijra." This palace is also the seat of the government, where the dais on which sit the six ministers, who make judgments after discussing and agreeing on one view, is found. These six ministers have assistants who sit on another dais behind them. The council only decides on matters by consultation.[31] The credit for this harmony lies not with the police or some other military power of which we know nothing, but with the new socialistic system and the people's trust in it and its leaders.

The strange thing about the words of Nasr Khusrow is that he did not mention a thing about the president of the council. We may conclude, therefore, either that it did not have a president at that time or that they had agreed not to have a president after Abu Saʿid and Abu Tahir and their sons, out of respect for the founders of the communistic republic or out of fear of the autocracy of their successors and rejection of the socialistic principles on which their state was founded (or other reasons not mentioned by that writer or on which we disagree with other writers). It is true that the descendants of Abu Tahir and his relatives preserved their influence and some of their advantages until the days of Khusrow and perhaps after. However, they did not choose the president of the majlis, except in rare cases. For power was concentrated in the hands of the ministers and their assistants, most of whom, as we saw, were from the family of the founders of the Qaramati republic or those closest to them. Accordingly, the organization of the government in Bahrain was closer to that of the Russian republic in modern times, that is, a consultative government (soviet), headed by the founder as long as he lived, and by his closest assistants after his death. Thus, we can say that every social system has its own administrative order as its product, as is apparent in each case one encounters between the Qaramati system in the tenth century and that of the communist Russians today. Although space does not allow us to mention the numerous similarities between the two systems, there is no doubt of the accuracy of the comparison. For the source of strength for both groups was the same—the lower classes, or the class of laborers and peasants—and they were the overwhelming majority of the Qaramatis, as may be gathered from the words of Ibn al-Athir on the people of Iraq (the Sawad).[32]

Bahrain and the neighboring lands which the Qaramatis conquered in the days of Abu Tahir and his sons were independent of the ʿAbbasid state. Their daily affairs, both internal and external, were conducted according to a new order which it formed for itself and adapted to without opposition. The first step the council took toward reforming the country and assisting its people was the abolition of the land taxes. Then they abolished or decreased some of the taxes under which the farmers and laborers suffered and began to examine other resources in order to fill the requirements of the state but not burden its residents. Among these new taxes was one on the ships that passed through the Persian Gulf, as well as taxes on Oman, on the pilgrims who visited the two holy cities every year, and on the fishermen in the waters of Bahrain and the Persian Gulf. If we add to these taxes the annual compensation paid by some of the cities and villages of Iraq like Kufa (among others), we have approximately one million dinars per year. This amounts to around fifty or sixty thousand Egyptian pounds, only thirty thousand of which was taken from the land in the form of tithe or kharaj. Considering that the land of Bahrain and Oman was (and still is) among the most fertile in the Arabian peninsula, and was known for the excellence of its fruit, this is a relatively insignificant amount. Bahrain's fruit was among the goods that the Qaramati government traded with her near neighbors, like Persia, Iraq, Syria, and so on. In fact, the wealth of Bahrain in the age of the Qaramatis reached a degree unprecedented in its history. If we discount from that budget the part the Qaramatis sent yearly to the treasury of the imam, or the "exchequer of the imam" as it was called in those days, and another, larger portion which was paid to the dar al-hijra, or the house of the government and the sons of Abu Tahir, there still remains a large sum that the government spent on operations and for the general welfare, that is, for the betterment of the position of the farmers and laborers, and to buy land to distribute to those who needed it.

Unfortunately, we do not have sufficient information on the new system in Bahrain to explain the most important issue connected with the system, that is, the ownership of land or lack thereof. Did land remain in the hands of individuals who had the right to act independently with regard to it, or was it made public, in the control of the government, who gave it to whomever wanted it and was able to work it with his hands? It appears, from some of the statements of the Persian writers, that the government did not remove land from the hands of its owners, either because most of it was jointly owned by the farmers (as is the case with the Bedouin) or because land was not an issue there (that is, there was not a land crisis in Bahrain) because the peasants did not own land (as is the case today in most European countries), or because the government itself bought what land it needed to distribute to the peasants who had no land they could work with their own hands. The communistic character [of this community] was apparent in other bases of social life and its expressions, and in individual life and its characteristics. And the Qaramati government worked toward spreading and supporting it in every way it could. The Persian writer [Nasr Khusrow] cited above mentions that when he was in Al-Ahsa, he saw

> thirty thousand black slaves working in the fields and gardens at the expense of the council. Those were fields bought with common funds. The people there did not pay taxes to the government, nor did they tithe. If one of the poor suffered a loss or was burdened with debts he had no way of paying, the council loaned him the money he needed to correct the situation. And if someone incurred debts, when they were due he paid only what he owed, i.e., without interest.[33]

He said elsewhere in his diary, "To every foreigner who enters Al-Ahsa and has a profession, the government will advance—if he wants it—a sum of money to spend on the needs of his profession. It remains at this disposal until he collects money enough for himself and his family. Then he works and earns money and returns the exact amount borrowed to the government without interest."[34] He also said that if the owner of a house or mill experienced some kind of calamity and was unable to repair it, the council would supply him with a specified number of slaves to repair the damaged portions of the house or mill, without compensation. He added, "There are mills in Al-Ahsa owned by the government which grind the people's wheat for them free of charge because the government itself pays the workers their wages and all the expenses of the mills." [35]

If we compare these reports with what some of the Arab writers said about the Qaramatis, such as the statement by one of them that "everything was jointly owned by them except swords and weapons," we can conclude that the social and personal lives of the Qaramatis were based on communistic principles. Those were the principles that the leader of the Isma'ili movement and his governors in Bahrain spread and tried to implement.

We do not deny that some variations occurred in the life of the Qaramatis and their internal order in the days of Nasr Khusrow. However, the communist character in general was still apparent in the life of the country and its residents until the fifteenth century or later. Among the most important manifestations of it was that "no poor person remained in the country, and the majlis coined new money which was only circulated in the country.[36] They coined it from lead so it was very cheap, to the extent that if someone wanted to buy something in the market, he had to fill baskets with this money, putting into each of them six thousand dirhems." [37]

Among the manifestations of the communistic system in Bahrain was that trade, especially with the outside, was in the hands of the government, and its proprietors provided for common operations and improvement of the conditions of the farmers and laborers. No wonder, then, that the residents of this country were happy with their government and its system and supported it in times of need, just as it is no wonder that we hear nothing to indicate the existence of a group trying to destroy the new system or bring down the government that created and implemented it.

This is the gist of the Arab and Persian reports on the social and economic portion of the Qaramati program. Now we will elaborate on what we have found regarding their moral and religious principles (those not already mentioned in connection with the Isma'ilis or in the brief general outline).

The existence of the socialistic Arab republic in Bahrain for more than five centuries, its preservation, effectiveness, and economic success despite difficulties and adversaries who longed to take over its wealth, is convincing proof that the republic of Bahrain was based on strong economic and social foundations and authoritative moral and ethical principles, both on the social and individual levels. We have seen that the members of the majlis al-'aqdaniyya agreed among themselves in word and deed. There are other manifestations, which we shall mention below.

Ibn Hawqal, the well-known writer and traveler, lived among the

Qaramati for several months and studied their system and their daily lives. He mentions several factors at variance with the immoral acts and base principles of which they were accused, and expresses respect for their culture, morals, and good conduct. Later, al-Maqdisi visited them and mentioned them in his travelogue. He did not mention anything that would impugn their moral character or malign their reputation. The Persian poet and writer Nasr Khusrow came after him and lived among them for several months, observing their social and individual lives.[38] He became familiar with young and old, great and small, and frequented their gatherings in order to understand their ideas and morals and to inform his readers about them. If he had seen anything among them at odds with general moral principles, he would have indicated it in his *Safar Name*. Yet he did not censure them or describe them other than as we saw: Abu Sa'id "ordered his successors and followers to treat the people with justice and generosity." Elsewhere, "If someone called upon a member of the council and greeted him or asked him a question, that member answered him with graciousness and modesty." He said of the residents of Al-Ahsa: "They do not drink wine, not because it is forbidden but for the preservation of order."[39] We may conclude from the words of Khusrow and others that adultery was not known or widespread among the Qaramatis. Indeed, polygamy was also probably not widespread, since all the sons of Abu Sa'id were from one mother. This was not surprising, considering that the prohibition of drunkenness and moral depravity is the logical result of the Qaramati convictions regarding the purpose of human existence and the highest goals of this world.

Among the accusations leveled at the Qaramatis by their opponents was hypocrisy and lack of sincerity of purpose. They cited as proof that the Qaramatis acted as if they were devoted to 'Ali and his line. They seemed to follow him and his family, not out of love for them but to satisfy their own needs and personal or party welfare and to achieve their political ends. The Qaramatis' accusers claimed, in support of this allegation, that Abu Tahir never visited the tomb of 'Ali or his son Hasan, even though he was near them several times. They also cite the fact that the Qaramatis probably fought on the side of the Fatimids several times, but later deserted them and even rebelled against them in the year 360/971, joining their greatest enemy, the 'Abbasid caliphs.

We do not deny these occurrences. However, we explain them differently from the way the adversaries of the Qaramatis did. Abu Tahir's failure to visit the tombs of 'Ali and Hasan does not indicate his scorn or lack of devotion to those two individuals whom the Isma'ilis, in general, revered. Rather, it indicates that the Qaramatis prohibited visiting tombs and kissing them, as is the case with the Wahhabis today. As for their second proof, it is based either on ignorance of the history of the Qaramatis in Bahrain or on the desire, not unprecedented in history, to conceal historical truths or misrepresent them.

It is known that the early relationship between the Qaramatis and the

Fatimids was friendly, marked by sincerity, devotion, and obedience. They supported the Fatimid movement with money and men. This was not because they feared their strength, but because they believed that the founder of the Fatimid state, ʿUbaidallah, was really the imam al-zaman and the expected mahdi, the last person in whom the highest intelligence was incarnated. He was that person for whom the Qaramatis and the rest of the Ismaʿilis had been waiting, and upon whom they depended to destroy the oppressive states and establish a fair and just state, the kingdom of "peace and love." This was among the hopes the followers of the hidden imam used to (and still do) cherish. However, after observing the operations of the Fatimids in Syria and Egypt, Abu Tahir and his followers began to realize that the founder of this state was a liar and a deceitful trickster, between whom and the seventh imam, Ismaʿil b. Jaʿfar, there was no relation. This false imam had deceived them and used them as an instrument to attain his own personal goals. Realizing this had a powerful impact on the Qaramatis, Bedouins who had always been known for their naïveté and purity of heart. Their anger was stirred against the founder of the Fatimid state and his sons, and they broke off relations with them. They also drew closer to their enemies, who began to appear better than their previous deceitful caliphs. Wars resulted that cost the Fatimids innumerable victims and inestimable material losses since the advantage was generally on the side of the Qaramatis. The caliphs of Cairo were forced to abandon their offensive strategies and to resort to policies of defense. Perhaps this is what forced them (between 371 and 385 [A.H.]) to build the fortress of Cairo, the present capital of Egypt, to defend their old capital, formerly known as Al-Fustat.[40] The Qaramatis did not stop with that, but drew nearer to the government of Baghdad, concluding political and trade agreements with them, corresponding with the ʿAbbasid caliphs, and offering them gifts. Thus they preserved their rights, their welfare, and their socialist system. Is that the revocation of principles, or anything like hypocrisy? If so, then the consultative government of Russia is treacherous, hypocritical, and deceitful, because it, as the reader knows, concluded commercial and political treaties with its enemies in the beginning.

Based on that, there is no truth to the accusations of the enemies of the Qaramatis. Indeed, I believe that anyone who studies the history of the Qaramatis in Bahrain and looks at what has been preserved of their reports without prejudice, and unconcerned with personal considerations, will perceive the sincerity and truthfulness of this brotherhood and the purity of heart of its members. M. deGoeje, the famous Dutch orientalist, collected their scattered reports and gave them careful consideration, seeking nothing but facts. He then put [his observations] in his book (which we have cited in this chapter). He said, "Despite what I know of the devilish practices which Hassan b. al-Qaddah introduced to the Ismaʿilis, I firmly believe that the Qaramatis, and especially those of Bahrain, were working from a firmly rooted belief that they were performing good works."[41] Of course, strong faith in the truth of that to which an individual or group dedicates its life overcomes all obstacles and performs miracles; I would be the first to admit that. I perceive such belief in the words and deeds of the Qaramatis, even though it is sometimes mixed with something of the severity and harshness of the Bedouin. Ibn al-Athir reported in his *Al-Kamil [fi'l-Ta'rikh]* about a Qaramati man who was living in Baghdad:

> A man came to ʿAli b. ʿIsa (a minister of the caliph, al-Muqtadir) and told him that there was a man among his neighbors from Shiraz, a member of the Qaramati school, who was corresponding with Abu Tahir for news. He sent for him and questioned him, and he confessed. He told him, "Do not be friendly with Abu Tahir except when I confirm that it is permissible. You and your friend are infidels, taking upon yourselves what is not for you." . . . ʿAli b. ʿIsa said to him, "You have mixed with our army and you know them. Who among them is of your sect?" [The Qaramati] said, "You, with this information, have designs on the government. How do you expect me to hand over the faithful to the idolaters who will murder them? I will not do that."[42]

As for the religious beliefs and practices of the Qaramatis, we shall not prolong the presentation lest we bore the reader, and because we have mentioned parts of them in the foregoing chapter. We shall here content ourselves with what follows.

If we mean by religion and its practices what is understood by those terms today or what simple people understand by them, we can say that the Qaramatis did not have religion or religious practices to speak of. Their leaders and writers did sometimes use expressions and terms used by followers of [organized] religion. This led [some] of their adversaries to believe that they had a religion and religious practices, like other Muslims and non-Muslims among their contemporaries. However, the Qaramatis, like the Bedouin on the one hand and the Ismaʿilis on the other, did not believe in religion and its outward practices. Like most communists of this age, their real religion was the great social goal which they served and firmly believed the need to realize. We do not deny that the Qaramatis had some religious beliefs in the accepted sense of this term, like their belief in the periodic incarnation of God or the incarnation of the first intelligence in their imams or mahdis or great men and philosophers, all of whom had the power to realize their great social goal or ideal. The above-mentioned Qaramati from Shiraz said, "God must make the pilgrimage to his earth and the mahdi is before us, Muhammad, descendant of Muhammad b. Ismaʿil b. Jaʿfar al-Sadiq." Nevertheless, this belief is closer to political or philosophical thought than to purely religious thought.

Thus, there is no doubt that the Qaramatis based their socialistic ideal on one of the descendants of ʿAli, and on no other house. Yet their love of the house of ʿAli was really [part of] a political plan. It was a strong link between them and other Shiᶜis, and it inclined the hearts of the hostile ᶜAbbasids toward them. But it did not matter to them if the imam, the savior of this world and its mahdi, were from the sons of ᶜAli. For the Qaramatis [truly believed] only their basic principle: the possibility of realizing their socialistic ideal in this life. The question of who would realize this ideal was, in their view, secondary. It was unimportant; they believed that the realization of their hopes and political dreams was a matter entrusted to anyone who embodied the highest power and the first intelligence, and that was God.

Thus, the Qaramatis' religion was really only an expression of worship of sound intelligence [al-ᶜaql al-ᶜala al-salim] or the highest intelligence [al-ᶜaql al-ᶜala]. Therefore, they did not have religious practices or rites, nor any need of them. This is what the Muslim writers observed and indicated several times, saying that the Qaramatis "denied all the messengers and laws" and that they "interpreted all the pillars of the law with the effect of heresy; and claim the meaning of the salat is friendship of their imam, and the Hajj is visiting him and zeal in his service; and the meaning of the fast is the abstinence from divulging their secret to the uninitiated."[43] They claim further that those who know the meaning of devotion are released from its obligation, and they are convinced of the certitude of the knowledge of interpretation.[44] Nevertheless, they did not prohibit the Muslims living among them from building mosques and performing the salat and the rest of their religious practices. Nasr Khusrow said, "There is no mosque in Al-Ahsa where the Friday prayers are performed and they do not preach and do not pray, although they allowed the building of a mosque at the expense of one of the Persian Sunnis."[45] Later he said, "No one here is prevented from performing the salat, but they do not do it."[46]

Indeed, they rejected all conventional historical religions. It only remained for them to reject all the statutes and practices pertaining to food, drink, dress, and so on, which were based on those religions, and to advocate the dissolution of those not necessary for truth or conducive to fulfillment of needs and the attainment of happiness in this world, not in the next. This is what Khusrow described of them: "In Al-Ahsa they sold the meat of all animals, like cats, dogs, donkeys, oxen, lambs, etc., on the condition that the seller put the head and hide of the animal near its meat. And they raised dogs like sheep in the pasture until, when they became fat and unable to run, they slaughtered and ate them."[47] Thus, they condemned the practices of the ancient religions and their many restrictions, and declared that they were above obeying these ordinances. They considered them suitable only for the feeble and small-minded, or "asses," as they called the lowest, uneducated classes. Among the restrictions abolished was the prohibition of drinking wine, and some of them began to drink it in public, as some writers have testified.[48] Yet its use was not widespread among them, for the reason we mentioned above. Indeed, Nasr Khusrow did not see anyone among them who drank wine publicly or privately. As he wrote in his diary, "The residents of Al-Ahsa do not drink wine." Perhaps the opinion of the Qaramatis with regard to wine had changed in the days of Khusrow or, for some unknown reason, they had relinquished wine. At any rate, there is no doubt that the drinking of wine or lack thereof, in the view of the Qaramatis, was absolutely unimportant. For it did not pertain to religious issues, as it had before, but came from social or moral issues. Its use was not prohibited, and there was no merit from God or society in abstaining.

The paucity of information on the Qaramatis of Bahrain after the second half of the eleventh century—owing to the distance of their lands from the centers of Islamic, Arab civilization and the trials that befell the Arab lands and Islamic caliphate during the days of the Turks and Mongols—is very unfortunate. It prevents us from following the progress of the communistic republic in the eastern Arabian peninsula and from tracking the changes in their social order before it became a thing of the past. All we can derive from the statements of some historians on the Qaramatis after the eleventh century is that they were involved in external wars with Baghdad and its neighboring tribes. There were also conflicts with the house of Abu Tahir and his relatives; his son Sabur was killed in the year 361/972, and the council of old "gentlemen" died out. All of that, no doubt, led to a weakening of the power of the Qaramatis and inspired the greed of their neighbors and enemies, who had been awaiting an opportunity to bring an end to them and their loathesome system. However, this period was not long. Ja'far, one of the descendants of Abu Sa'id al-Jannabi, encountered the Fatimid army in the year 368/978 and slaughtered them and forced them to flee. In addition, Abu Bahr b. Shakhwaih, one of the Qaramati leaders, marched to Kufa and occupied it in the name of the sultan, 'Adud al-Dawlat al-Buwaihi (r. 949–983). We gather, then, that circumstances for the Qaramatis at that time were favorable, their status high, and their organization intact, to the extent that the sultans of Baghdad sought their favor and assistance.

Then, in the year 374/984, their star began to set and their situation worsened. The first indication was their war with Sultan Samsam al-Dawlah (989–998), which ended with their defeat and the return of the remnants of their vanquished army to Bahrain. This news had scarcely spread among her neighbors when the residents of the central Arabian peninsula revolted and broke away from them. The residents of Oman followed in 375/985, as well as other Bedouin tribes. They attacked the Qaramatis in 378/988 and utterly defeated them. Then they followed the Qaramatis to their capital, where they had taken refuge, and besieged them there. But the tribal warriors were unable to defeat the Qaramatis, so they turned away and went to Qatif and defeated it, taking a great deal of booty back to their country. Therefore, the failure had a negative impact on the economic and domestic situation of the Qaramatis.

The result was that power was removed from Abu Saʿid's descendants and was handed over to others, who tried to follow a new policy. They began to court the Fatimids, their brothers of old, for assistance in their wars with the Bedouin and the sultans of Baghdad, or [at least] to secure their neutrality. However, this new policy did not benefit them; indeed, it was more damaging than the first policy. The sultans of Baghdad began to watch all their activities, fearing their closeness to the Fatimids. And when the Baghdad authorities learned of the Qaramatis' correspondence with the rulers of Egypt, they advised the Bedouin to rebel against the Qaramatis. The Bedouin obliged and, although not quite successful in securing their independence, they did force the Qaramatis to remain in their own area and refrain from spreading their call beyond the seas.

Ibn al-Nadim, author of *Al-Fihrist,* said, "For some twenty years the power of the sect (the Qaramati school) gradually decreased and the missionaries became so scarce that I do not see anything in the works of those who wrote about it, although in the earlier days of its power there was widespread evidence. The missionaries had spread their doctrine in every region and area."[49]

The Qaramatis expected their situation to improve under [the Fatimid Abu ʿAli Mahsur] al-Hakim (r. 996–1021), who was known for his inclination toward an extremist sect of Ismaʿilis, or under [al-Hakim's successor al-Zahir (r. 1021–1036)], when the Fatimids expected the fall of the ʿAbbasid state.[50] But this hope was based on false assumptions. When it was not fulfilled, the Qaramatis decided to remain peaceful and to concentrate on preserving their independence and strengthening the internal framework which they had so long preserved (as can be seen from the words of Nasr Khusrow, who visited them in mid-443/1052).

We can determine from the words of Khusrow that the socialistic order was still in effect among the Qaramatis in the middle of the eleventh century and that the Qaramatis in those days were called "Abu Saʿidis" in reference to Abu Saʿid, the founder of their republic. Their leader at the time was one of Abu Saʿid's descendants, known as "the master," which indicates that some change had occurred in the Qaramati administration. We can also discern from the words of Khusrow that the country was in good [economic] condition and that trade was widespread, thanks to the state monopoly. Furthermore, its policies appeared just, and the people perfectly happy. For Khusrow heard no one complain of their treatment or about the new system. He mentions things which indicate that food supplies were plentiful and that the people lived in comfort, lacking no necessities: "In Al-Ahsa, dates were so plentiful that people fed them to the sheep" and "they sold a thousand of them for one dinar."[51] Therefore, Bahrain was an object of envy for her neighbors. They watched her with desire, wishing to take possession of her riches. The people most envious of the wealth of the Qaramatis were those closest to them, the idle and hungry Bedouin Arabs who used to (and still to this day) live at the expense of others, robbing and plundering. They had been awaiting an opportunity to rebel against the rich republic and destroy it, if possible.

The Persian traveler mentions that he encountered a leader of one of the Arab tribes marching toward Al-Ahsa, "and after besieging it for a whole year, he took over one of its four fields" and gained many riches. But he was not able to take Al-Ahsa and did not overcome its people. "When he saw me, he began to ask me about the positions of the stars and then told me, 'My goal is to take possession of Al-Ahsa because its people are infidels without religion. Will I be successful in my quest?' "

We do not know how Nasr Khusrow answered the Arab prince. However, it is probable that the prince was unsuccessful because we have reports indicating that the republic of Bahrain was still, in the beginning of the seventh century A.H., independent and progressing. Its affairs were run by a council chosen from her people according to the old system, which remained current in the country until the beginning of the twelfth century, when Ibn Battuta visited there, and when none of the descendants of Abu Sa'id remained. Neither the Arab nor Persian writers (who were closest to them, both geographically and ideologically) have told us what was left of the power of the republic after Ibn -Battuta. However, it appears from some scattered reports that remnants of the Qaramati system remained in Bahrain or Oman until the beginning of the twelfth century, and perhaps some of them remain until today.[52] How nice if there lived among us a traveler such as Nasr Khusrow or Ibn Battuta who could visit this Arab republic and its neighboring countries that were influenced by its socialistic system and doctrine, research its history during the "dark ages," [examine] what is preserved of its old books, and inform us of its current circumstances. However, all we know today of this country—in fact, all we know of the rest of the Isma'ili groups and their movements in India, Africa, and so on—does not quench the thirst for accurate information.

According to our newspapers and magazines, the Isma'ilis are still numerous in Oman, especially in Musqat, Al-Matrah, and other cities. The Isma'ili school apparently moved with the emigrations from those cities to Zanzibar and East Africa. Before the German colonial wars, this is where we saw intellectual movement and activity spreading the Qaramati principles among the original residents of the country. However, we are ignorant, unfortunately, of the nature of this movement and how much of the old Qaramati principles were included in it. Are Abu Sa'id and Abu Tahir and their descendants still mentioned among the Isma'ilis of Bahrain and Oman and their African colonies? Still, we doubt that the Qaramatis of today—if we determine that they still remain—are the same as the Qaramatis of yesterday, "whom the people in the cities and deserts feared" and at the mention of whose name the caliphs of Baghdad and Cairo trembled.[53] What are they today—having lost or forgotten most of their social and political principles and neglected their socialistic system—but a peaceful religious sect, stagnating and petrified for ages? They are, doubtless with few exceptions, scarcely a movement that directs inner life.

This is the situation of the Qaramatis' descendants today in Bahrain, Oman, India, Persia, Central Asia, Africa, and Syria (the Druze). There are exceptions in a few groups, like the Druze in Syria and the Zaidis in Yemen, who still preserve their old Arab zeal, the glory of their souls, and the nobility of their morals, even if they have not preserved all the Isma'ili social and philosophical principles.

Conclusion

Numerous factors prevented the complete realization of al-Sabbah's program, especially the socialistic portion. They include the appearance of the Turks and Mongols in the theater of history; their invasion of Islamic countries from the ninth century through the middle of the fifteenth century; the ensuing wars, horrors, and inestimable material and indescribable spiritual losses; the coming of the Crusaders to the Arab East; their zealous attempt to take over lands more beautiful and more advanced than their own; the disagreements between the Fatimids and the Qaramatis resulting from differences on some principles and goals; other disagreements that occurred among the Qaramatis themselves, and so on. Still, we must affirm that a large part of that program was realized. It became a living foundation for many people. The success attained by Isma'ili missionaries among 'Abbasid citizens, regardless of nationality or class, was also great, even more so than the party of the democratic republic in Islam—that is, the Kharijis. No other call or intellectual movement left such a deep impression on the history of Islam or had such potent results as the Isma'ili movement.

For years, Isma'ili ideas and programs continued to make their influence felt in the Islamic world and beyond, as a single party or school. The seeds which the Isma'ilis had spread among the Islamic peoples in particular, and Eastern peoples in general, were so potent and full of life that even the hoofs of the horses of the Turks, Mongols, and Crusaders, and the terror of their attacks, were not able to kill them. I do not want to imply that all the seeds the Isma'ilis sowed germinated and flourished, or overcame the trials of the age and survived until today. Yet many did, although some were deformed and corrupted, as I mentioned above. This was also the case with some other groups, such as the Hurufis, some varieties of Sufis, and other groups based on cooperation in material things, justice, social equality, the unity of moral principles, and so on.

Among the most important features of the guilds, brotherhoods, and Sufi or *darwish* [mendicant] orders (which the East can boast of because it first paved the way for their appearance) are the idea of mutual support among the classes, defense of the economic and social rights of all their members; and the unanimous consolidation of the goals of their members. There is no need to explain that guilds in the East were not mere trade or professional societies seeking only material gains. This is the case now in Europe, just as in some Eastern countries during the Ottoman period. Their meager understanding, weak hearts, and affinity for autocracy and the monopoly of power served to keep them out of politics and social affairs, and settle for material goals only. In the preceding age, however, they had been concerned not just with improving material conditions but with strengthening their social rights, their morals, and their minds as well, as was the case with the Isma'ilis and the Qaramatis. In fact, we know that the members of the [original] guilds were not concerned primarily with material issues. Their greatest concern was with spreading their principles and giving their members sound moral education in conformity with their political principles. Accordingly, we can conclude that the Eastern guilds were, when they first appeared, more like charitable religious groups than labor or trade unions today. They included diverse pursuits and professions under the supervision of experienced elected leaders from the upper classes, known as sheikhs, imams, pirs, and so on. It is known that the members of these groups were equal in rights and responsibilities and treated each other like brothers. Thus they were called "brotherhoods."[1] That was the name which was then (and is still today) used by most members of guilds and orders. Based on the testimony of some contemporary writers, the first brotherhood to appear among the Qaramatis was the Brotherhood or Brethren of Sincerity [Ikhwan al-Safa']. It was established in the second half of the tenth century, as can be gathered from some of their epistles—which comprise the first scientific encyclopedia of its kind—as well as the testimony of writers from later ages.[2]

The Brethren of Sincerity was a group operating in secret, whose members did not want anyone to know their names, goals, or gathering places. Therefore, we see the above-mentioned Arab writers and most scholars of this age were very careless and uninformed although not deliberately. However, it appears from some of the lines in these epistles that the Brethren of Sincerity was a Qaramati group, founded in Basra to spread Isma'ili principles and attempt to realize them in peaceful, intelligent ways. Professor T. deBoer, writing on Islamic philosophy, said:

> As a matter of fact, it was a religion and social league with extremist tendencies, or more precisely, Isma'ili tendencies and principles. The members of this group, which had Basra as one of its most important centers, were called "the Brethren of Sincerity" because their goal was to make the people work toward the purity of their souls through [the spirit of] cooperation and other means, especially "pure knowledge." We know of no other group in the Islamic East that depended on knowledge and wisdom (philosophy) in preparing the way for personal happiness in this life as did the Brethren of Sincerity.[3]

Accordingly, the Brethren of Sincerity was the first to advocate using knowledge and work" for personal happiness. That is what was advocated, after hundreds of years, by LaSalle and Marx, and what has become today the motto of the Bolshevists in Russia, where it can be found written on the walls of cities and doors of houses wherever you look.

Unfortunately, we lack information which would enable us to determine [absolutely] that this group had branches outside of Basra, and, if so, to determine what their relations were with these branches, and so on. Nevertheless, we can assume the existence of such branches in the cities and capitals of Iran, Central Asia, Russia, Egypt, and other countries to which Isma'ili principles had spread with obvious effect. It is likely that the reaction that began to manifest itself in the second half of the tenth century—the retreat of the Qaramatis in Bahrain and the important political developments in the 'Abbasid caliphate in the beginning of the eleventh century—all influenced the Brethren of Sincerity and its activity. Among the results of this activity was that those who held civil and religious power began to persecute the Brethren and force them into hiding—working "underground"—that is, to postpone their work or change its character. Therefore, it is probable that the Isma'ili cells which had spread throughout the land were also forced, under the same pressure, to avoid politics and to devote themselves to social and economic or moral and religious issues only. Some concentrated on the former issues, and some on the latter. This assumption is based on what we know of the activities of the groups descended from the Brethren and influenced by their principles: those which appeared in the Ottoman era among the Arabs, Persians, and Turks, that is, the guilds, brotherhoods (*baradaran, akhilar*), and some of the Sufi and darwish tariqas, like the Naqshbandis, Rifa'is, Yekichar, and others who were spiritually linked to the Brethren of Sincerity or Isma'ili groups. Today the idea that there was among those groups a spiritual link is quite credible and agreed upon by scholars.[4] The Russian orientalist Gordlevsky, professor of Turkish at the School of Oriental Studies in Moscow, said, "It can be inferred from the works of the brotherhoods (akhilar) of Asia Minor—generally confined to hospitality, guests, and attention to travelers and foreigners—that they were foreign at first, or more precisely, that they were of Iranian origin." Furthermore, the following factors lead us to believe that these groups, and others of their type, were descended from the Qaramati organization and its legitimate inheritors: the [use of the fraternal] term *ba akhi* or *akhi* (which was common among the Brethren of Sincerity); communistic tendencies; the apparent partiality to 'Ali b. Abi Talib, or "the Patron," as they called him, and to his sons; the kind of activities of those brotherhoods; their internal and external organization, and so on.[5] It is known today that these groups still preserve something of the spiritual bond that links them to the Qaramatis or Isma'ilis in general. Similarly, the *asnaf* (Turkish professional guilds [sing.: *sinf*]); still preserve, in some cities, religious rites and strange customs not found in other [such] Western or Eastern associations. This is what was indicated in the above-cited Russian book: "The Turkish sinf is closer to the spiritual moral brotherhood on the principle of recognition of leadership and ranks of blind obedience to the sheikh or leader, than to professional societies. From that it can be concluded that the old order of the Turkish guilds still manifests a spirit other than that of mere professional guilds."

If we scrutinize this order, we find it very similar to the *darawish* [mendicants, plural of darwish]. The latter were more concerned with spiritual, contemplative life and the religious and moral education of those who seek spiritual enlightenment through their orders than were the asnaf. In addition, at times they entered into political affairs, as did their Isma'ili predecessors, defending the rights of oppressed people and demanding social welfare from the Ottoman rulers.

Those who study the history of darwish orders like the Mevlevis, Bektashis, and Naqshbandis, and the books of the sheikh of the Mevlevi order or the social works of some of its members, will no doubt come across radical Shi'i tendencies and a Persian or Isma'ili spirit.[6] Thus we may assume that all these groups—regardless of their names, tendencies, or internal and external order—are traceable to the one from which they were born and took many elements, still preserved (perhaps unconsciously) to this day. The most important of these elements is the social spirit that Hasan-i Sabbah stirred in the hearts of his followers, urging them to [perform] good works. The asnaf, then, and some of the darwish orders in whose principles we still see extremist tendencies, were the sanctuary in which was preserved the rebellious, active Isma'ili spirit, and the shelter from which we can sometimes hear bold voices calling absolute despots (the Ottoman sultans, Persian and Turkish shahs and khans) to reform, and reminding them of their duties toward people whose rights have been oppressed.

If it were not for lack of space, I would give many examples from the history of the asnaf and Sufi and darwish orders corroborating this idea, since it appears strange to some people. But I must be content with only two examples: the darwish rebellion in Turkey in 1415–1418, and the Babi or Bahai movement in Persia.

Those familiar with Ottoman history know that the leader of the darwish rebellion, the darwish scholar Badr al-Din Samawna, came from Persia, that is, from the Isma'ili home and source of social and moral movements in all the East. There he imbibed the radical socialistic principles that he and his two students, Bürklüdje Mustafa and Al-Yehuda al-Muhtadi Torlaq Kemal, tried to spread among the residents of Asia Minor. They were at the time the most susceptible to socialism, as a result of the trials and tribulations which had been their lot shortly before that: the conquest of the Mongols, Timur Lang, and the ensuing internecine wars that turned most of the fertile land into desert where the few remaining residents roamed without shelter or food.

The sultans and princes of the country owned vast properties. They were concerned only with themselves and the wealth they had amassed [on the burdens of] the poor and enslaved. Badr al-Din and his followers, comparing this situation with that of the poor, protested sharply in the mosques and streets. Their words had a powerful impact on the poor and oppressed. They began to gather around them and espouse his position. They called out publicly "for justice and equality among all classes, regardless of religion or nationality, and for distribution of wealth equally among the people." His call echoed widely throughout the country, causing many of those dissatisfied with the economic and social situation at that time to support Badr al-Din and his followers with armed strength. Several wars broke out between them and the government, lasting some three years, in which the socialist party heroically defended itself and its principles. But their forces gave out; they lost their provisions and were defeated near the city of Izmir by the armies of Sultan Mehmed the First, known as Chelebi. They seized one of their leaders, Mustafa Bürklüdje, and crucified him near the city of Magnesia. Then they pursued the greatest leader of the movement and its great hero, Badr al-Din Samawna. They seized him in the hills of Macedonia, killed him, and dispersed his followers. The movement died without attaining its goal.[7]

The Babis or Baha'i movement, filled with extremist Shi'i ideas, is known to most readers since it is recent and our journals and newspapers publish numerous articles about it. Moreover, its greatest leader and some of its followers live among us in Acre and in other cities in Palestine, Syria, and Egypt. There is no need, then, to elaborate on this information. Suffice it to say that this movement also appeared in Persia and among the extremist Shi'is (the Hurufis), maintaining the old Isma'ili spirit. It is certain that 'Ali Muhammad (1821–1850 A.D.), known as Al-Bab, was a Twelver Shi'a. Furthermore, the [use of the] term *bab* ["door" or "gate": precursor], the language of his *bayan* [manifestation], his methods of interpretation, some of his activities, and his symbolic systems, lead us at once to the Isma'ili school. That is where the use of the word bab in the modern sense appeared for the first time in Islam.[8]

I am certain that the foregoing arguments could benefit from further proof and support. However, space does not allow for it; I only hope that other works on the history of social thought in the East will appear to fill the gap, discovering the conduits that link the Isma'ilis with the Babis and other extremist groups of Shi'is, as well as the reasons Persians rebel against civil and religious order. They should also point out how the Babis, who began their work by seeking moderate religious and social reforms, lost no time changing into socialist groups of their own kind (sui generis), but still varying from the socialist groups of Europe in their methods and some of their principles.

In the beginning of this chapter, we tried to elucidate the influence of the Qaramati Isma'ilis on professional guilds or asnaf, charitable societies, darwish societies, and so on. One should not derive from our arguments, however, that those societies were always the source of free social movements in Islam or that the ideas and principles of Hasan-i Sabbah and his followers were always manifested in the education and behavior of these societies. On the contrary! We know that many of the darwish fraternities were the cause of reactionary and religious or blind nationalist movements. They were often instruments of exploitation of the good religious sentiments of the masses. We are referring only to some of the Sufi orders, especially those that flourished in Iran and that imbibed Shi'i ideas. How many movements began in the name of God and ended in the name of the devil! This movement of Bab and Baha'ullah was, at first, a free and good movement, from which the Persian people expected to benefit. But following the death of its founders, it changed to a religious heresy or [at best] a simple moral brotherhood with a reactionary character and weak social program. We are all reminded of how the Baha'is, who from 1905 to 1909 strongly supported the liberal party and political programs advocating a constitution (similar to the English constitution), soon became a party of landowners. They began to oppose the Shi'i leaders who joined the liberals and became leaders of the nationalist movement hostile to the Shah and his reactionary government.

All that is well known to us. So is the fact that the doctrine of Bab and Baha'ullah regarding religious tolerance, the unity of religion, and justice and equality for all contains an obvious contradiction. And their successors have preserved it in their books and "epistles" and discussions with English and American women. The educated reader need only remember the conflict that occurred in the beginning of the Babi movement, the hostility between Baha'ullah and his brother Subh-i Azal, and the schism of the Babis into two hostile groups, each of which has tried to eradicate the other with arms, slander, and other means.

Some say that the Baha'is forbade killing in the name of religion or over religious issues. However, Professor Browne (known for his affinity for them) notes that he heard from one of them in Shiraz: "It is up to the prophet (head of the group) to get rid of anyone he considers an enemy of the religion or in whom he sees danger for mankind, as the doctor removes the part of a diseased patient." In addition, the Baha'is themselves agreed that they could not seek civil power in their country until after religious wars in which blood flowed like rivers. And after that, the situation of the Jews and Christians improved, but not that of the Muslims or the followers of Subh-i Azal and the "sheikhs." Their situation, no doubt, worsened; perhaps they died out.

All that is true. Yet it does not affect the truth of what we tried to establish: the existence of a historical or ideological link between the Isma'ilis and the Babis.[9] The enormous number of points of similarity between those two groups makes it difficult to argue for coincidence. Moreover, I do not maintain the absolute agreement between Isma'ili principles and organization and those of the guilds, Bektashis, Babis, and so on. But I do think it is likely that some of the Isma'ili ideas and systems infiltrated that milieu in various ways. There they remained latent until economic and political conditions were appropriate. Awakening from their sleep, they then emerged from the subconscious world to the conscious, and became a driving, motivating force, [albeit] in a different form.

Nor is the influence of the esoteric Isma'ili principles limited to Islamic society, or to the East in general. Rather, it went beyond, to some of the Christian nations of Europe, where it had an obvious ideological effect on the lives of the people, their social organizations, their constitutions and social groups, etc. It is no exaggeration to say that the Qaramatis had some effect on the regulations of the Jesuit order, for instance, and some of the monastic orders, or on the regulations of the guilds, the Knights Templars, the Maltese knights, and so on. For the guilds in Europe were not, in the beginning, simply professional guilds, established to defend the material welfare of their members. They were a kind of brotherhood or charitable organization whose goal was to strengthen religious and moral principles, as was the case in the East:

> Every guild had a patron and sometimes an altar in one of the city churches where contributions were collected to be distributed to the sick and needy among them. . . .[10] And when one of them died, his associates took part in his funeral and looked after his children. Furthermore, the guilds had the right to supervise the lives of their members, their behavior, and their education, among other responsibilities we find mentioned [also] in the laws of the darwish orders and all the guilds and Islamic organizations we know of.[11]

The character of these organizations changed; just as in the East, they gradually became mere unions with no relation to religion or morality. It is not our intention to research the factors that led to this result.[12] However, we would like to direct the reader to another matter of greater interest—the ways in which Qaramati principles entered Europe and were able to affect its organizations and bring forth among them similar movements and systems. Among those routes were the wars of the Crusaders and the resulting contact between the Islamic world and the Christian Western world. These two drew together, despite their differences. No doubt the Westerners who had lived a long time in the East, and especially in Syria and Palestine, were influenced by the Isma'ilis there, and carried a great deal of information about their order back home with them. There they began to apply it to their own needs and goals, producing both religious and nonreligious groups. Those intellectual movements led to the age of renewal [Renaissance] in Italy and its neighbors, then to the age of explorations and inventions. In addition, the tendency toward intellectualism entered Europe by way of Spain and southern Italy, which remained under Arab rule and its cultural influence and social practices for hundreds of years. Furthermore, we must not forget the commercial, political, and cultural ties between the Islamic East and Christian West in the Middle Ages (which were stronger than some historians think).

In any event, there is no doubt that the ideas and practices of the Islamic East penetrated Europe in numerous ways, most of which we still do not know, and influenced the life of her people socially and intellectually. Perhaps among the influences was, for example, that the German people assimilated the word *sinf* [guild] (plural of *asnaf*) and changed it to *"Zunft."*[13]

The effect of Isma'ili ideas and systems on the character and development of some of the Latin monastic orders, such as the Jesuits,[14] is a recurring theme among Western writers.[15] It has supporters and detractors who still battle, with alternating success. Among the indications cited by the supporters of this idea is that the regulations of some of these monastic orders, and especially the Jesuits, have certain characteristics in common with the Brethren of Sincerity: the existence of several levels or steps that the initiate must ascend in order to achieve moral fulfillment; the restriction of authority to the hands of an autocratic leader; the inclination toward use of intellectual means; the goals and peculiar means used; and other characteristics that differentiate the regulations of this brotherhood from those of other Christian brotherhoods. How nice it would be if some of our scholars who devote their lives to oriental studies, or some of the European orientalists, would take the trouble to study these questions, illuminate them, and help solve them scientifically, without prejudice.

It seems to me that what I have mentioned regarding the social and socialist movements in Islam—only a small part of the whole—is sufficient to satisfy the unprejudiced reader that the Eastern nations in general, and the Arab Islamic ones in particular, have passed through the same social stages as the nations of the Christian West. We are therefore convinced that our Arab people must pass in the near future through the same social stage now being experienced by Western nations, our brothers in humanity who have preceded us due to their good fortune and historical role. And we hope, based on the cultural reawakening and heightened consciousness we see today in the East, that it will be short.

Notes

PART I

Introduction

1. For biographical details, see al-Sayyid and ʿAllush's introduction to Bandali Saliba al-Jawzi, *Dirasat fiʾl-Lughah waʾl-Taʾrikh al-Iqtisadi waʾl-Ijtimaʿi ʿind al-ʿarab,* ed. Jalal al-Sayyid and Naji ʿAllush (Beirut: Dar al-Taliʿa, 1977), 8–9, and Shawki Abu Khalil, "The History of Islam in the Eastern Regions of the Caliphate as Described in the Work of Panteleymon Zhuze [Bandali Jawzi]" (Ph.D. dissertation, Institute of Oriental Studies, Academy of Sciences, Azerbaijan, 24 April 1992), from both of which this summary is compiled. Al-Sayyid and ʿAllush relate various reports that Jawzi was from Bethlehem; however, his nephew Spiro Jawzi of Bir Zeit University confirms that Jawzi was from Jerusalem. His birth and death dates are also in dispute; those listed here are the opinion of the majority of sources.

2. Abu Khalil, "History of Islam in the Eastern Regions of the Caliphate," Introduction.

3. Muhammad Kurd ʿAli, in *Majallat al-Majmaʿ al-ʿIlmi alʿArabi bi-Dimashq* 9 (1929):125. Quoted by C. Ernest Dawn, "Pan-Arab Ideology in the Interwar Years," *International Journal of Middle East Studies* 20(1): 73 (1988).

4. Personal interview with Dr. Spiro Jawzi, emeritus professor of history at Bir Zeit University, Ramallah, July 1992.

5. Darwish Miqdadi, *Taʾrikh al-Ummat al-ʿArabiyya*. First edition, Baghdad: Matbaʿat al-Maʿarif, 1350/1931; second edition, 1351/1932; third edition, 1353/1934; fourth edition, Baghdad: Dar al-Hadithah, 1355/1936; revised edition, Baghdad: Government Press, 1939.

6. Al-Jawzi, *Dirasat fiʾl-Lughah waʾl-Taʾrikh al-Iqtisadi waʾl-Ijtimaʿi ʿind al-ʿarab*. Note that al-Sayyid and ʿAllush use al-Jawzi rather than Jawzi; I have retained the name as it appeared in Jawzi's original publications (without the definite article).

7. Maxime Rodinson, *Islam and Capitalism,* trans. by Brian Pearce (Austin: University of Texas Press, 1973), 267.

8. Personal correspondence, dated 22 February 1983. See also Tamara Sonn, "Bandali al-Jawzi: Progressive Palestinian Politics?" *Muslim World* 79(3–4): 188–89 (1989), from which this summary is taken.

9. See Werner Ende, *Arabische Nation und islamische Geschichte: Die Umayyaden im Urteil arabischer Autoren des 20. Jahrhunderts* (Beirut: Orient-Institut der Deutschen Morgenlandischen Gesellschaft, 1977), 188–91. Ende is concerned only with Jawzi's treatment of the Umayyads, which he describes as very positive. In *Min Ta'rikh*, Jawzi levels harsh criticism at the Damascus-based caliphate. The positive attitude referred to by Ende is, however, expressed in his essay "Arab Nostalgia for the Umayyads," in *Al-Muqtatif* 78/6 (June 1931); also in *Dirasat*, 59–69, 70–79. There, like some of his contemporaries, Jawzi valorized the Umayyads for their administrative and political skill.

10. C. Ernest Dawn, "The Formation of Pan-Arab Ideology in the Interwar Years," *International Journal of Middle East Studies* 20(1): 67–91 (1988).

11. See Philip K. Hitti, *History of the Arabs* (New York: St. Martin's, 1970), 722, n. 1.

12. The agreement is contained in the McMahon-Hussein correspondence. See George Antonius, *The Arab Awakening* (New York: Capricorn Books, 1965), 168. For a discussion of various interpretations of this correspondence, see C. Ernest Dawn, *From Ottomanism to Arabism: Essays on the Origins of Arab Nationalism* (Urbana: University of Illinois Press, 1973), 151ff.

13. For a discussion of the Sykes-Picot Treaty, see A. L. Tibawi, *Anglo-Arab Relations and the Question of Palestine, 1914–1921* (London: Luzac, 1978), 114–15; J. C. Hurewitz, *The Middle East and North Africa, A Documentary Record: European Expansion, 1535–1914*, vol. 1 (New Haven: Yale University Press, 1975), 62–64; and Elie Kedouri, *England and the Middle East: The Destruction of the Ottoman Empire, 1914–1921* (London: Bowes and Bowes, 1956), 40–43. Assessing the agreements among the Europeans and Arabs following World War I, Drysdale and Blake state: "The European powers had, thus, imposed their own arbitrary boundaries on the central Middle East without reference to the people of the region. These bore no relationship to physical or cultural features. The Jews and the Turks had reason to be satisfied. The Arabs felt betrayed and frustrated, whereas the Kurds and Armenians remained stateless." Alasdair Drysdale and Gerald Blake, *The Middlle East and North Africa: A Political Geography* (New York and Oxford: Oxford University Press, 1985), 66.

14. The classic treatment of this period is Albert Hourani's *Arabic Thought in the Liberal Age: 1789–1939* (Oxford: Oxford University Press, 1970).

15. See Paul Rabinow, ed., *The Foucault Reader* (New York: Pantheon, 1984), 46; see also Foucault's *The Archaeology of Knowledge,* trans. A. M. Sheridan (New York: Harper & Row, 1976); John McGowan, *Postmodernism and Its Critics* (Ithaca: Cornell University Press, 1991).

16. Power "forms knowledge, produces discourse." Michel Foucault, *Power/Knowledge,* ed. Colin Gordon (New York: Pantheon, 1980), 119. "[T]here is no power relation without the correlative constitution of a field of knowledge, nor any knowledge that does not presuppose and constitute at the same time power relations." Michel Foucault, *Discipline and Punish,* trans. Alan Sheridan (New York: Vintage, 1979), 17.

17. This entire issue, the relationship of the individual to the power structure and the question of intellectuals' autonomy, is hotly debated. See Fredric

Jameson, *The Political Unconscious* (Ithaca: Cornell University Press, 1981); Frank Lentricchia, *Criticism and Social Change* (Chicago: University of Chicago Press, 1983); Terry Eagleton, *The Function of Criticism* (London: Verso, 1984); Edward Said, *The World, the Text, and the Critic* (Cambridge: Harvard University Press, 1983); and John McGowan's discussion of the issue in *Postmodernism and Its Critics*, 145–80.

18. Michel Foucault, "The Ethic of Care for the Self as a Practice of Freedom," *Philosophy and Social Criticism* 12 (1987): 129; McGowan, *Postmodernism and Its Critics*, 133.

19. See in particular Foucault's discussions in "What Is Enlightenment" and "Polemics, Politics and Problemizations," both in *The Foucault Reader*, 32–50, 381–90.

20. See Edward Said, *Beginnings: Intention and Method* (New York: Basic Books, 1975) and *The World, The Text, and the Critic*.

21. See Edward Said, *Orientalism* (New York: Pantheon, 1978), 12.

22. Edward Said, "Interpreting Palestine," *Harper's* 274 (1987): 22; see also McGowan, *Postmodernism and Its Critics*, 167–68.

23. Said, *Orientalism*, 12.

Chapter 1

1. According to the Ba'th party's constitution (promulgated in 1947), "The Arabs are one nation which has a natural right to live in one state and be free in directing its destinies. . . . The Arab homeland is an indivisible political and economic unity." For the text of the Ba'th party's constitution, see Tareq Y. Ismael, *The Arab Left* (Syracuse: Syracuse University Press, 1976), 126–37.

2. See Shibli Shumayyil, *Falsafat al-Nushu' wa'l-Irtiqa'* (Cairo: n.p., 1910).

3. See discussion by Tareq Y. Ismael and Jacqueline S. Ismael, *Government and Politics in Islam* (New York: St. Martin's, 1985), 47.

4. Quoted in Albert Hourani, *Arabic Thought in the Liberal Age: 1789–1939* (London: Oxford University Press, 1970), 304, from an article on Bolshevism in *al-Manar* 23 (1920): 254.

5. See Maxime Rodinson, *Marxism and the Muslim World*, trans. Jean Matthews (New York: Monthly Review Press, 1981); Olivier Carré, *La legitimation islamique des socialismes arabes* (Paris: Presses de le Fondation nationale des sciences politiques, 1979); Tareq Y. Ismael, *The Arab Left* (Syracuse: Syracuse University Press, 1976); and Issa J. Boullata, *Trends and Issues in Contemporary Arab Thought* (Albany: SUNY Press, 1990). See also Sami A. Hanna and George H. Gardner, *Arab Socialism: A Documentary Survey* (Salt Lake City: University of Utah Press, 1969).

6. See Tamara Sonn, "Bandali al-Jawzi's *Min Tarikh al-Harakat al-Fikriyyat fi'l-Islam:* The First Marxist Interpretation of Islam," *International Journal of Middle East Studies* 17 (1985): 89–107.

7. See Alexandre Bennigsen and Chantal Lemercier-Quelquejay, *Islam in the Soviet Union* (New York: Praeger, 1967), 35–37, 238, n. 3. For a full treatment of the development of modern Islamic thought in the Soviet Union, see ibid., pp. 3–122, and Alexandre Bennigsen and S. Enders Wimbush, *Muslim National Communism in the Soviet Union* (Chicago: University of Chicago Press, 1979), from which this summary is taken.

8. This modernizing trend was mirrored in movements that called for cul-

tural reform, particularly in language and education, such as that of Ismail Gas-
prinski. See Bennigsen and Lemercier-Quelquejay, *Islam in the Soviet Union*,
38–39.

9. Quoted in Bennigsen and Lemercier-Quelquejay, *Islam in the Soviet
Union*, 67.

10. Ibid., 67–68.

11. Ibid., 82.

12. See Bennigsen and Wimbush, *Muslim National Communism*, 8. The
same is true on the individual level. The exigencies of revolution had necessitated the acceptance of members of the bourgeoisie into the Bolshevist ranks,
since the Muslim lands were as yet preindustrial and had not yet developed an
indigenous proletariat. These members would be "re-educated" through a process of assimilation and would thus lose their bourgeois character, which was
the source of nationalism. See Bennigsen and Lemercier-Quelquejay, *Islam in
the Soviet Union*, 125.

13. Bennigsen and Lemercier-Quelquejay, *Islam in the Soviet Union*, 125.

14. Alexandre Bennigsen, "Sultan Galiev," *The Middle East in Transition*,
ed. W. Z. Laqueur (New York: Praeger, 1958), 406–9.

15. Alexandre Bennigsen says of Sultan Galiev: "Among the communist
command, his was the voice most listened to on matters affecting the nationalities. It is no surprise therefore that his theories on the communist revolution in
a Muslim context should have been copied or adapted by those of his coreli-
gionists who, with him, had consented to collaborate with the Soviet regime.
His ideas, with local variations, were the model for all national communists in
the areas named and even, after his first fall from grace, until 1928." Bennigsen
and Lemercier-Quelquejay, *Islam in the Soviet Union*, 110.

16. Max Weber, *Die protestantische Ethik und der Geist des Kapitalismus*,
vol. 1(Tübingen: Mohr, 1920), 4. English translation by Talcott Parsons, *The
Protestant Ethic and the Spirit of Capitalism* (New York: Scribner, 1958), 17–
18.

17. Translated by Bennigsen in "Sultan Galiev," *The Middle East in Transition*, 402.

18. Ibid., 401.

19. Ibid., 404. Sultan Galiev's comments on the implications of these actions
for the future of Russian communism indicate that he was a visionary as well.
As Bennigsen and Wimbush summarize it: "In early 1920, Sultan Galiev concluded that the socialist experiment in Russia was doomed to failure, leaving
only two possible outcomes: (1) The gradual transformation of the Communist
Party of the Soviet Union into a state capitalist system and into a bourgeois
democracy; (2) the destruction of Soviet power as a consequence of an armed
struggle with the Western European bourgeoisie. In the event of the transformation of Soviet power into a state capitalist system, right-wing Great-Russian
elements, who at the present time are hostile to the general line of the Communist party, will assume power and put an end to the revolutionary experience."

20. Bennigsen and Lemercier-Quelquejay, *Islam in the Soviet Union*, 91.

21. Ibid., 107.

Chapter 2

1. Yvonne Yazbeck Haddad, John Obert Voll, and John L. Esposito with
Kathleen Moore and David Sawan, *The Contemporary Islamic Revival: A Criti-*

cal Survey and Bibliography (New York: Greenwood, 1991). See also John L. Esposito's *Voices of Resurgent Islam* (London: Oxford University Press, 1983) and *Islam in Transition: Muslim Perspectives* (London: Oxford University Press, 1982); Yvonne Y. Haddad (with Byron Haines and Ellison Findly), *The Islamic Impact* (Syracuse: Syracuse University Press, 1984); and John O. Voll, *Islam: Continuity and Change in the Modern World* (Boulder, Colo.: Westview, 1982).

2. As John Voll characterizes: "In the early centuries of Islamic history it became clear that Muslims had not succeeded in creating and maintaining a truly Islamic society following the death of the Prophet Muhammad. As a result, there were periodic calls for a renewal (*tajdid*) of the commitment to the fundamental principles of Islam and the related reconstruction of society in accord with the Qur'an and the Traditions of the Prophet.

"These efforts were often seen in the perspective of a well-known Tradition of the Prophet that 'God will send to His community at the head of each century those who will renew its faith for it'. Over the centuries Muslims have looked back at important reforming leaders of the faith and identified them as mujaddids or 'renewers.' " Voll, "The Revivalist Heritage," *Contemporary Islamic Revival*, 24.

3. See Andrew Rippin, ed., *Approaches to the History of the Interpretation of the Qur'an* (Oxford: Clarendon, 1988), especially Jane Dammen McAuliffe's "Quranic Hermeneutics: The Views of al-Tabari and Ibn Kathir," 46–62, and Fred Leemhuis' "Origins and Early Development of the *tafsir* Tradition," 13–30.

4. Muhammad Iqbal, e.g., claims he is working in the tradition established by the Prophet's interpretive efforts. See Leemhuis, "Origins and Early Development of the *tafsir* Tradition," 13, for a discussion of how the same argument is used to justify the work of the *mufassirun* (producers of tafsir) and, implicitly, its authoritative status.

5. The term for Islamic law, in the sense of God's binding will for humanity, revealed through the prophets, is Shari'a. *Fiqh* refers to the actual codes of law established by human beings trying to determine from sources of revelation the nature of divine will, and how to implement it in various times and places. Although Shari'a is often used to refer to both phenomena, this discussion will abide by the technical distintion between the two terms.

6. N. J. Coulson, *A History of Islamic Law* (Edinburgh: The University Press, 1964), 75.

7. See M. M. Bravman, *The Spiritual Background of Early Islam* (Leiden, 1972), 189. Fazlur Raman describes ijtihad as "the effort to understand the meaning of a relevant text or precedent . . . containing a rule, and to alter that rule by extending or restricting or otherwise modifying it in such a manner that a new situation can be subsumed under it by a new solution." Fazlur Rahman, *Islam and Modernity* (Chicago: University of Chicago Press, 1982), 8.

8. Wael B. Hallaq, "Was the Gate of Ijtihad Closed?" *International Journal of Middle Eastern Studies* 16 (1984): 5.

9. Ibid.

10. Ibid.

11. Joseph Schacht, *An Introduction to Islamic Law* (Oxford: Clarendon, 1982), 70.

12. See N. J. Coulson, *A History of Islamic Law* (Edinburgh: The University Press, 1964), ch. 2–3, upon which this account is based.

13. As Coulson puts it, "The legal scholars were publicly recognized as the architects of an Islamic scheme of state and society which the ʿAbbasids had pledged themselves to build, and under this political sponsorship the schools of law developed rapidly." Ibid., 37.

14. See Majid Khadduri, trans., *Al-Imam Muhammad ibn Idris al-Shafiʿi's al-Risalah fi Usul al-Fiqh*, 2nd ed. (Cambridge: Harvard University Press, 1987). Wael Hallaq has argued that Shafiʿi's systematization of the sources of Islamic law (*usul*) was not immediately accepted. Nevertheless, it eventually became standard. Wael B. Hallaq, "Was al-Shafiʿi the Master Architect of Islamic Jurisprudence?" *International Journal of Middle East Studies* 25 (1993): 587–605.

15. Coulson says, "[H]is fundamental thesis—that the terms of the divine will were more precisely indicated than had hitherto been recognized, that the supreme manifestation of God's will lay in the sunna or practice of Muhammad, and that the function of human reason in law was subsidiary and complementary—was never after him seriously challenged." *History of Islamic Law*, 61. Cf. Hallaq's discussion of the gradual acceptance of Shafiʿi's formulation in Wael B. Hallaq, "Was al-Shafiʿi the Master Architect of Islamic Jurisprudence?" *International Journal of Middle Eastern Studies* 25(4): 587–605.

16. See e.g., eleventh-century legist Muhammad b. ʿAli al-Basri, *al-Muʿtamad fi Usul al-Fiqh*, ed. M. Hamidullah et al. (Damascus, 1964), 2:929–31. Thirteenth-century Shafiʿi legist al-Amidi adds knowledge of *nasikh* and *mansukh* (abrogating and abrogated verses of the Qurʾan) to the list of required qualifications for mujtahids. See Fazlur Rahman, *Islamic Methodology in History* (Karachi: Central Institute of Islamic Research, 1965), 169–70.

17. Hallaq argues in "Was the Gate of Ijtihad Closed?" (*International Journal of Middle East Studies* 16 [1984]: 7 that the requirements for the practice of ijtihad were not overly strenuous: "It would therefore be implausible to maintain that the qualifications for ijtihad as set forth in Muslim legal writings made it impossible for jurists to practice ijtihad." This conclusion was meant to refute (among other things) Fazlur Rahman's statement that the qualifications for the practice of ijtihad became "humanly impossible of fulfillment." Fazlur Rahman, *Islam* (Chicago: University of Chicago Press, 1979), 78. Though some scholars, as Hallaq points out, have indeed held that opinion, it is important to recognize that Fazlur Rahman's position on the matter was more subtle than it appears in Hallaq's presentation. He wrote in 1965, for example:

> The list of traditional disciplines given . . . is no doubt seemingly imposing and, at first glance, seems difficult to fulfill. But when one closely examines this list and its contents, it does not seem to us an over-requirement. . . . When, therefore, Iqbal says, "the theoretical possibility of this degree of ijtihad (i.e., *ijtihad mutlaq* [absolute ijtihad]) is admitted by the Sunnis, but in practice it has always been denied ever since the establishment of the schools, inasmuch as the idea of complete ijtihad is hedged round by conditions which are well-nigh impossible of realization in a single individual," he cannot be referring to any stated conditions by jurists but simply to their unwillingness to perform ijtihad or to allow it to be performed. Theoretically speaking, the

conditions of ijtihad are not, after all, too difficult of attainment. (*Islamic Methodology in History*, 171–72)

In fact, he does not fully accept the closing of the door of ijtihad. Again, in *Islamic Methodology in History*: "There is no doubt that even in later times Islam did assimilate new currents of spiritual and intellectual life—for, a living society can never stand quite still, but this Islam did not do so much as an active force, master of itself, but rather as a passive entity with whom these currents of life played. An important instance of this point is Sufism" (24). "Although the 'gate of ijtihad' was never formally closed . . . taqlid or acceptance of mere authority became so rampant that ijtihad became practically nonexistent. Taqlid was originally recommended for the common man, although for long it was conceded that even the common man has the power of discernment enough to decide between conflicting views. Later, however, taqlid enveloped almost all members of the Muslim society. Voices against this have been arising, particularly since the appearance of Ibn Taymiyya, and taqlid and closing of the door of ijtihad have been imputed to the immediately earlier generations ever since" (173). Elsewhere: "The World of Islam and Islamic scholarship are by now familiar with the proposition that 'the gate of ijtihad (fresh thinking) in Islam was closed.' Nobody quite knows when the 'gate of ijtihad' was closed or who exactly closed it. There is no statement to be found anywhere by anyone about the desirability or the necessity of such a closure, or of the fact of actually closing the gate, although one finds *judgments* by later writers that the 'gate of ijtihad has been closed' " (149, emphasis in the original). Similarly: "We shall find, among other things, that so far as jurisprudence is concerned, the gate of ijtihad was never formally closed but that a gradual contraction of thinking occurred over a period of several centuries through various causes" (150). And: "However, in the face of the evidence it is impossible to conclude that the 'gate of ijtihad was closed' " (157). Finally: "The denial of ijtihad in practice has been the result not of externally overstrenuous qualifications but because of a deep desire to give permanence to the legal structure, once it was formulated and elaborated, in order to bring about and ensure unity and cohesiveness of the Muslim Ummah. . . . But at the theoretical level the door of ijtihad has always remained open and no jurist has ever closed it" (172).

18. Joseph Schacht, *Introduction to Islamic Law*, 71.

19. See "The 'Closing of the Gate of Independent Reasoning' and the Further Development of Doctrine" in ibid., 69–75. See also Coulson, *History of Islamic Law*, 80; Rahman, *Islamic Methodology in History*, 24, 49–50, 157, 172–73.

20. Some proponents of ijtihad include in their arguments that even those who rejected ijtihad continued to employ it. For example, Dawud ibn Khalaf (d. 884 C.E.) rejected the notion of analogical reason eventually accepted by the Malikis, Hanafis, and Shafi'is. He and his followers believed that the literal (*zahir*) meaning of the Qur'an and hadiths should be accepted and followed. They rejected the idea of determining principles behind revealed statements and then extending them to fit cases similar to, but not exactly the same as, those in the revealed verse (or traditional report). Although Schacht, Coulson, and Hallaq note that this stance is a rejection of ijtihad (of which qiyas is but a variety), nevertheless, the rejection of qiyas led the Zahiris to rely on ijtihad whether they liked it or not. According to eleventh-century legist al-Mawardi,

one who follows the Zahiri approach "does reject analogy, but still uses independent judgment in legal deduction through reliance on the meaning (spirit) of the words and the sense of the address." See Schacht, *Introduction to Islamic Law,* 63; Coulson, *History of Islamic Law,* 71. Hallaq points out that the Zahiris' failure to accept the qiyas-based approach to legal reasoning embraced by the dominant schools resulted in their being drummed out of the corps of jurisprudents: "[Dawud's] ijtihad was rejected by the Sunnis since he avoided the procedure of qiyas. Nevertheless, until the first half of the fourth century, Dawud's school remained as Sunni as any other major school. But when the legal theory was finally established and promulgated as the only Sunni doctrine, the Zahiri school gradually slipped outside the orb of Sunnism." Hallaq, "Was the Door of Ijtihad Closed?" 8.

21. Hallaq calls attention to the well-known hadith claiming that the further one lived from the time of the Prophet, the more degenerate one's age would be; he claims it gained popularity as the practice of ijtihad diminished. Hallaq, "Was the Door of Ijtihad Closed?" 37, n. 102, where he cites Abu al-Fida Ibn Kathir.

22. Sayyid Abuʾl Aʿla Maududi, *A Short History of the Revivalist Movement in Islam,* 3rd ed. (Lahore: Mohammad Yusuf Khan, 1976), 32–33.

23. Al-Ghazali accepted the extinction of absolute ijtihad (the degree of ijtihad needed to establish a new school of law), but he called for a revival of limited ijtihad—within the confines of an established school, at least—and criticized those who "believe they are bound to a blind . . . submission to . . . human authority and to the literal meaing of the revealed books." Quoted by Hallaq, "Was the Door of Ijtihad Closed?" 9.

24. Quoted by Fazlur Rahman in *Islam,* 112, from Ibn Taymiyya, *Al-Ihtijaj biʾl-Qadar* in his *Rasaʿil* (Cairo, 1323), 2:96–97.

25. Contrary to what Coulson said was the ahistoricity of the orthodox position, Ibn Taymiyya, in Fazlur Rahman's words, "seeks to go behind all historic formulations of Islam by all Muslim groups, to the Qurʾan itself and to the teaching of the Prophet." Fazlur Rahman, "Revival and Reform in Islam," *The Cambridge History of Islam,* ed. P. M. Holt, Ann K. S. Lambton, and Bernard Lewis (Cambridge: Cambridge University Press, 1970), 635. Fazlur Rahman criticizes limitations in Ibn Taymiyya's work, including "the fact that rationalism is condemned on principle, and the fact that "the Sunna was taken in a literalist sense." Ibid., 636. Ibn Taymiyya's critique of rationalism, however, was in the context of Greek philosophers who rationalized without regard for revelation. In contrast, his view on rationality in general was very positive: "[T]raditional authority can never be divorced from reason. But the fact that something is a Shariʿa value cannot be validly opposed to something being rational," as Fazlur Rahman quoted Ibn Taymiyya in *Islam,* p. 111.

26. See his *Rafʿ al-Malam ʿan al-Aʾimmah al-Aʿlam* [In Defense of the Learned Imams] (Beirut: Al-Maktab al-Islami, 1970).

27. See his *Fatwa fiʾl-Ijtihad* in the appendix of *Rafʿ al-Malam ʿan al-Aʾimmah al-Aʿlam.*

28. Translated by Victor E. Makari in *Ibn Taymiyyah's Ethics: The Social Factor* (Chico, Calif.: Scholars Press, 1983), 98, from Ibn Taymiyya's *Al-Fatawa al-Kubra* (Cairo: Dar al-Kutub al-Haditha, 1966) I:484.

29. See Makari, 106.

30. Fazlur Rahman, "Revival and Reform in Islam," *The Cambridge History of Islam* (Cambridge: Cambridge University Press, 1970) 2B:639.

31. For a discussion of Shah Wali Allah's thought, see J. M. S. Baljon, *Religions and Thought of Shah Wali Allah Dihlawi* (Leiden: E. J. Brill, 1986).

32. See his discussion in Muhammad b. ʿAli al-Shawkani, *Al-Qawl al-Mufid fi Adillat al-Ijtihad waʾl-Taqlid* (Cairo: Matbaʿat al-Maʾahid, 1970). See also discussion in Rudolph Peters, "Ijtihad and Taqlid in 18th and 19th Century Islam," *Die Welt Des Islams* 20 (1980): 131–45.

33. Coulson, 150. For a description of these developments, the "capitulations" in particular, see Marshall G. S. Hodgson, *The Venture of Islam* (Chicago: University of Chicago Press, 1974) 3:142–44.

34. See Tamara Sonn, "Tawhid," *Oxford Encyclopedia of the Modern Islamic World* (New York: Oxford University Press, 1995) 4:190–98.

35. Muhammad ʿAbduh, *The Theology of Unity,* trans. Ishaq Musaʿad and Kenneth Cragg (London: Allen & Unwin, 1966), 39–40.

36. The passage continues:

Its very custodians themselves began to rival kings for their authority and to vie in wealth with the idle rich. The great mass of people declined sadly from its noble quality through "reinterpretation" and their vain fancies imported all kinds of false accretions. . . . As for dogmas, these were compromised by schism and heresy. The custodians abandoned all its principles, except one they mistakenly supposed to be its strongest pillar and chief ground, namely the veto on intellectual enquiry into faith, or indeed into the details of the universe and on the pursuit of the secret things of the mind. They promulgated the principle that reason and religion had nothing in common, but that rather religion was the inveterate enemy of science. It was not simply that this view could be taken by anyone for himself: rather they strenuously imposed it as the proper thing for all. They pressed the doctrine with such force as to provoke the most shameful of all conflicts in human history, namely civil war within the household of religion for the imposition of religious decrees. And thus the foundations were broken up and communal relationships destroyed. (Ibid.)

37. Ibid., 127.

38. Ibid. Elsewhere ʿAbduh speaks of Islam's "respect for evidence" and "the utmost possible devotion and endeavor through all the worlds of knowledge." Ibid., 103–4.

39. Ibid., 101. Cf. 145, 151.

40. Ibid., 66.

41. Ibid., 126.

42. Ibid.

43. Ibid., 156.

44. Ibid.

45. Some scholars, such as Albert Hourani, have characterized ʿAbduh's insistence on Islamic rationality as resulting from the influence of European culture. Aziz al-Azmeh finds him guilty of "epistemological *legerdemain,* which operates by assuming the scriptures do not mean what they say," and his liberal ideas "heavily impregnated with Western notions." See Aziz al-Azmeh, *Islams and Modernities* (London: Verso, 1993), 33, 79; cf. 52, 53, 56, 80. But as the

foregoing discussion reveals, his ideas concerning ijtihadist hermeneutics, at least, share far more in common with those of his Muslim forebears than with anything else. Al-Azmeh also believes ʿAbduh marginalizes history in an essentialist glorification of some pristine "true" Islam. But again, as demonstrated in his emphasis on ijtihad, the need for reassessment of traditional knowledge in recognition of the impact of historical circumstances on specific institutional and ideological developments, ʿAbduh seems to display a distinct historical sense. Interestingly, in fact, Hourani recently reconsidered his evaluation of these so-called "early modernists." He says the analysis he presented in *Arabic Thought in the Liberal Age* "now seems to me to have been wrong in laying too much emphasis upon ideas which were taken from Europe, and not enough upon what was retained, even if in a changed form, from an older tradition." Albert Hourani, "Writing the History of the Middle East," *International Journal of Middle East Studies* 23 (1991): 128–29. Perhaps his estimation of ʿAbduh is a case in point; as the foregoing discussion has demonstrated, ʿAbduh's orientation toward Islam's rationality is not essentially different from that of thinkers as far back as Ibn Taymiyya. There were and are no doubt Muslim thinkers affected by "foreign" cultures, attempting to refashion Islamic ideas in accordance with models found outside Islamic tradition. But the mere effort to reform Islamic institutions in accordance with changing circumstances does not, except for the most conservative observers, require going outside Islamic tradition.

46. See Albert Hourani, *Arabic Thought in the Liberal Age: 1789–1939* (London: Oxford University Press, 1970).

47. Ibid., 6.

48. Ibid., 12.

49. "[T]he early doctors of law . . . evolved a number of legal systems. . . . But with all their comprehensiveness, these systems are, after all, individual interpretations and as such cannot claim finality." Muhammad Iqbal, *The Reconstruction of Religious Thought in Islam* (Lahore: Institute of Islamic Culture, 1986), 168.

50. Ibid., 117.

51. Ibid.

52. "For Islamic law is supposed to be based on the Qurʾan, "which embodies an essentially dynamic outlook on life." Ibid., 11.

53. Ibid., 118.

54. Ibid., 119–20.

55. Ibid., 121.

56. Ibid.

57. Ibid. Cf. 128–34 where he criticizes "liberalism" and describes the positive elements in "conservativism." The latter, for Iqbal, is preservation of the Islamic heritage. He does on occasion, however, use the term "liberal" with a positive connotation, when contrasting it as an attitude with the traditionalism of the jurisprudents, and the term "conservative" with a negative connotation, when discussing the idea that Islamic law is not adaptable to changing circumstances.

58. Ibid., 133–34. Iqbal gives an example of the kind of interpretation he means in a discussion of calls by certain reformers of his day for the equality of women. Iqbal claims that this requires no reinterpretation of the Qurʾan at all, for the equality of women is clearly there. But the implications of the

Qur'anic teaching seem to have been lost on some of the 'ulama': "The truth is that the principles underlying the Qur'anic law of inheritance . . . have not yet received from Muslim lawyers the attention they deserve." And, "[I]f we study our laws in reference to the impending revolution in modern economic life, we are likely to discover, in the foundational principles, hitherto unrevealed aspects which we can work out with a renewed faith in the wisdom of these principles." Ibid., 135.

59. Ibid., 141.

60. In a brief discussion of early controversies between Iraqi and Hijazi (Arabian) legists, Iqbal concludes that the former tended to privilege ideals or principles in their judgments, whereas the latter tended to privilege "the concrete" or actual precedent. The upshot of the controversy was that Abu Hanifa's school "emancipated the concrete as it were, and brought out the necessity of observing the actual movements and variety of life in the interpretation of juristic principles." Accordingly, Hanafi law became much more open to "creative adaptation" than any of the other schools, although, unfortunately, Abu Hanifa's followers then elevated his interpretations to the level of exemplary precedent, thus falling into the same pattern of imitation as the others. Ibid., 140–41.

61. Ibid., 141.

62. Ibid., 138.

63. Ibid. Iqbal does recognize that the inclination toward taqlid is at least partly due to a desire to avoid misinterpretations. He therefore addresses the question of how to avoid erroneous judgments. Iqbal cites the effort of the Persian constitution of 1906, and determines that inclusion of the 'ulama' in the *majlis* (parliament) is no greater guarantee of rectitude than blind imitation of precedent. (Indeed, he believes granting the 'ulama' power over the majlis is a "dangerous arrangement." Ibid., 139.) Rather, he sees the need for renewed vigor in Islamic education: "The only effective remedy for the possibilities of erroneous interpretations is to reform the present system of legal education in [Muslim] countries, to extend its sphere, and to combine it with an intelligent study of modern jurisprudence." Ibid., 140.

Chapter 3

1. See E. A. Belyaev, *Arabs, Islam and the Arab Caliphate in the Early Middle Ages,* trans. A. Govritch (Jerusalem: Israel Universities Press, 1969), 239.

2. Nizam al-Mulk, *Siyasat Name,* ed. and trans. C. Schefer (Paris: E. Leroux, 1891–97), 268.

3. Ikhwan al-Safa', *Rasa'il Ikhwan al-Safa',* trans. Seyyed Hossein Nasr in *Isma'ili Contributions to Islamic Culture* (Tehran: Imperial Institute of Philosophy, 1977), 33ff.

4. Ibid., 300.

5. The Epistles themselves claim: "We do not seek assistance from any of our brothers in religious matters before we assist them in worldly affairs. If a brother were needless of us, that is what we want for him. If he needed us, that is what we want for him, until we have provided for him all that is essential for him in worldly matters, so that he can be free from care and unify his thoughts for us, thereby becoming independent by the strength of his soul, discernment of his reason and purity of his nature." Ibid., 40.

Chapter 4

1. Abu'l-A'la Mawdudi, *Islamic Law and Constitution,* ed. and trans. Khurshid Ahmad (Lahore: Islamic Publications, 1967), 172. See also Seyyed Vali Reza Nasr, *Mawdudi and the Making of Islamic Revivalism* (New York: Oxford University Press, 1996).

2. Mawdudi, *Islamic Law and Constitution,* 158.

3. Ibid., 148.

4. Quoted from Sayyid Qutb, *Maarakat al-Islam wa'l-Rasmaliyya* (Beirut: Dar al-Shuruq, 1975), 66, by Yvonne Y. Haddad, "Sayyid Qutb: Ideologue of Islamic Revival," *Voices of Resurgent Islam* (London: Oxford University Press, 1983), 71.

5. This theme runs throughout his Qur'anic commentary, *Fi Zilal al-Qur'an* (Beirut: Dar al-Shuruq, 1973–74), e.g. in his commentary on Surahs 32 and 59.

6. For an interesting discussion on Sayyid Qutb's apparently ambivalent attitude toward historical studies as they concern religion in general and the Qur'an in particular, see Olivier Carré, *Mystique et Politique: Lecture révolutionnaire du Coran par Sayyid Qutb, Frere musulman radical* (Paris: Les Éditions du Cerf, 1984), 67–73.

7. Haddad, "Sayyid Qutb: Ideologue of Islamic Revival," 81.

8. Sayyid Qutb, *Milestones,* trans. Ahmad Zaki Hammad (Indianapolis, Ind.: American Trust Publications, 1990), 30.

9. Quoted from the Qur'an 29:69 in Syed Qutb Shaheed, *Islam, The True Religion,* trans. Rafi Ahmad Fidai (Karachi: International Islamic Publishers, 1981), 3.

10. Sayyid Qutb claims that the Qur'an gives standards that people must continually determine how to realize in their own circumstances: "The ideal Islamic age of glory has granted man some principles, thoughts, values and standards of testing and examining." Ibid., 42–43.

11. Abdulaziz Sachedina, "Ali Shariati: Ideologue of the Iranian Revolution," *Voices of Resurgent Islam,* John L. Esposito, ed., 193.

12. Paraphrased by Sachedina from a lecture Shari'ati gave on ijtihad. Ibid., 203.

13. See Ferdinand de Saussure, *Course in General Linguistics,* trans. W. Baskin (London: Fontana/Collins, 1974). Good secondary sources include Jonathan Culler, *Ferdinand de Saussure* (New York: Penguin, 1979), and *Structuralist Poetics: Structuralism, Linguistics, and the Study of Literature* (Ithaca: Cornell University Press, 1975).

14. Peter Steiner, *Russian Formalism: A Metapoetics* (Ithaca: Cornell University Press, 1984), discusses the variety of expressions of Russian Formalism.

15. *The Formal Method in Literary Scholarship: A Critical Introduction to Sociological Poetics,* generally attributed to Mikhail Bakhtin, but published under both his name and Pavel Medvedev. That was followed in 1929 by *Marxism and the Philosophy of Language,* published under the name of Bakhtin's colleague Valentin Voloshinov.

16. The following discussion excludes extremely controversial critical reinterpretations of Islamic heritage, such as the work of Nasr Hamid Abu Zayd of Cairo University. See his *Mafhum al-Nass: Dirasah fi 'ulum al-Qur'an* (Beirut: al-Markaz al-Thaqafi al-'arabi, 1990) and *Naqd al-Khitab al-Dini* (Cairo: Sina

li'l-Nashr, 1994), where he applies contemporary literary criticism methods to the Qur'an.

17. See 'Abd al-Kabir al-Khatibi, *al-Naqd al-Muzdawij* [Double Criticism] (Beirut: Dar al-'Awda, 1980) and Abdelkebir Khatibi, "Double Criticism: The Decolonization of Arab Sociology," *Contemporary North Africa: Issues of Development and Integration,* ed. Halim Barakat (Washington, D.C.: Georgetown University Center for Contemporary Arab Studies, 1985).

18. Abdelkebir Khatibi, "Double Criticism: The Decolonization of Arab Sociology," *Contemporary North Africa: Issues of Development and Integration,* 12.

19. Derrida believes logocentrism, effectively the effort to fix meanings, results from the elusiveness of the "other." We can never really capture the "other," yet we continually strain after its "presence." He finds an example of logocentrism in the structuralist assumption that texts (whether they purport to be literary, historical, sociological, or other) have a stable and identifiable structure. Like the assumption that there is a transcendent ego at the "center" of an individual life, he claims, the assumption of a stable, identifiable structure of meaning in texts is based on the human propensity to organize what could just as well be fragmentary and probably even contradictory elements into some kind of unit. The structuralist approach to literary analysis, like modernist thought in general, operates by organizing things into a binary and hierarchical system of opposites: good/evil, strong/weak, mind/body, cause/effect, single/ multiple, speech/writing, and so on. Meaning is expressed (in the literal sense of being forced out) by privileging one element of the pair as positive or prior or paradigmatic. This tendency to center things in this way is what Derrida calls logocentrism. He discusses the irrepressibility of logocentrism in *Of Grammatology,* trans. Gayatri Chakravorty Spivak (Baltimore: Johns Hopkins University Press, 1976), 49ff.

20. Ibid.

21. Ibid., 13.

22. See Muhammad 'Abid al-Jabiri, *Nahnu wa'l-Turath: Qira'at Mu'asira fi Turathina al-Falsafi* [We and the Heritage: Contemporary Readings in our Philosophical Heritage] (Beirut: Dar al-Tali'a, 1980).

23. See Muhammad 'Abid al-Jabiri, *Naqd al-'Aql al-'Arabi* [Critique of the Arab Intellect], vol. 1, *Takwin al-'Aql al-'Arabi* [Creation of the Arab Intellect] (Beirut: Dar al-Tali'a, 1984). See also his *al-Khitab al-'Arabi al-Mu'asir: Dirasa Tahliliyya Naqdiyya* [Contemporary Arab Discourse: A Critical Analytical Study] (Beirut: Dar al-Tali'a, 1982).

24. Abdallah Laroui, *The Crisis of the Arab Intellectual: Traditionalism or Historicism?"* trans. Diarmid Cammell (Berkeley: University of California Press, 1976), 26.

25. Ibid., 69–70.

26. Ibid., 73.

27. Ibid., 72.

28. See Mohammed Arkoun and Louis Gardet, *L'Islam: Hier-Demain* (Paris: Editions Buchet/Chastel, 1978).

29. Mohammed Arkoun, "Logocentrisme et verite religieuse dans la pensee Islamique," *Essais sur la pensee islamique,* 3rd ed. (Paris: Editions Maisonneuve et Larose, 1984), 185–232.

30. Mohammed Arkoun, *Ouvertures sur l'Islam* (Paris: Jacques Grancher, 1989), 22: "When one recognizes that space and time are for all people the coordinates of every perception of an object of knowledge, one can measure the impact of theological systems on all modes of intelligibility in force in the societies of the Book, where the revealed, Holy Book has engendered all the books containing the knowledge constitutive of each cultural 'tradition.' " [Translations of Arkoun's work from the French are my own, unless otherwise noted.]

31. Ibid., 125. Cf. Muhammad Arkun and Louis Gardet, *Al-Islam: al-Ams wa'l-Ghad* [Islam: Yesterday and Tomorrow], trans. ʿAli al-Muqallid (Beirut: Dar al-Tanwir, 1983), 246.

32. Arkoun, *Ouvertures sur l'Islam*, 46–47. Cf. Muhammad Arkun, *Tarikhiyyat al-Fikr al-ʿArabi al-Islami* [The Historicism of Arab Islamic Thought], trans. Hashim Salih (Beirut: Markaz al-Inmaʾ al-Qawmi, 1986).

33. Arkoun, "Logocentrisme et verite religieuse dan la pense Islamique," *Essais sur la pensee islamique*, 216–18.

34. Arkoun, *Ouvertures sur l'Islam*, 38. See also ibid, p. 39: "One can say that since the death of the Prophet Islam has never recovered the privileged conditions of a double expression, symbolic and political: Muhammad put in place a political order by articulating immediately and adequately a process of symbolization wherein each juridical-political decision received justification and finality in an authentic relationship with God."

35. Ibid., 58: "The substitution of texts for oral discourse . . . placed the peoples of the Book in a hermeneutic situation; that is to say, in need of *reading* the holy texts in order to derive a law, prescriptions, systems of belief and nonbelief which have commanded the moral, juridical, and political order until the triumph of secularization" (emphasis in the original). He continues with a highly nuanced analysis of forms of discourse utilized in the Qurʾan, distinguishing five—"prophetic, legislative, narrative, wisdom, and hymnal"—and concludes that they all "proclaim an intention to reveal." Ibid., 68. This, in order to be rid of "the dualist framework of knowledge that places reason in opposition to imagination, history to myth, true to false, good to evil, and reason to faith. One assumes a plural, changing, receptive rationality, the solidarity of all the psychological operations that the Qurʾan situatés in the heart and that contemporary anthropology tries to reintroduce under the name of the imaginary." Ibid., 65.

36. Ibid., 85–86.

37. Fazlur Rahman, *Islamic Methodology in History* (Karachi: Central Institute of Islamic Research, 1965), 17–18, 27, 78.

38. Ibid., 11.

39. Ibid., 12.

40. Ibid., 27.

41. As previously noted, Fazlur Rahman does not claim that ijtihad ceased altogether, only that it was so limited as to lose its responsive and creative impact.

42. Ibid., 87.

43. Ibid., 75.

44. Ibid., 77–78.

45. Fazlur Rahman, born in what is now Pakistan in 1919, received his M.A. in Arabic from Punjab University in Lahore in 1942. He received his Ph.D. from Oxford University (1949), where his subject was Islamic philosophy. Neither in

his publications prior to the late 1970s nor in personal discussions or public lectures did he give any indication of awareness of postmodern discourse on the subject of hermeneutics. See Tamara Sonn, "Fazlur Rahman," in *Oxford Encyclopedia of the Modern Islamic World* (New York: Oxford University Press, 1995), 3:88.

46. Fazlur Rahman, *Islam and Modernity: Transformation of an Intellectual Tradition* (Chicago: University of Chicago Press, 1982), 8.

47. Ibid., 9.

48. Ibid., 165.

49. Ibid., 86.

50. Ibid., 143.

51. Regarding postmodernity and uncertainty, Raman Selden writes, "If there is a summarizing idea, it is the theme of the absent center. The postmodern experience is widely held to stem from a profound sense of *ontological uncertainty.*" See Raman Selden, *A Reader's Guide to Contemporary Literary Theory* (Lexington, Ky.: University of Kentucky Press, 1989), 72 (emphasis in the original). Elsewhere: "Poststructuralist thought has discovered the essentially *unstable* nature of signification." Ibid., 71 (emphasis in the original). When discussing Derrida, Selden says he "hesitates before the yawning abyss of indeterminacy, which threatens it with chaos." Ibid., 98.

52. From Jacques Derrida, *L'Ecriture et la difference* (Paris: Editions du Seuil, 1967), 414; quoted by Abdelkebir Khatibi in "The Decolonization of Arab Sociology," in *Contemporary North Africa* (Washington D.C.: Georgetown University Center for Contemporary Arab Studies, 1985), 15.

53. Mohammed Arkoun articulated as much when he said it is necessary for Muslims

> to *think* the historical situation created by the evolution of Muslim societies during the past thirty years . . . to linger over all those problems rendered *unthinkable* by the ideology of struggle with the hope of opening a new historic stage in this process of evolution: a stage where critical thought anchored in modernity, but criticizing this modernity itself, making it more profound with the Islamic example, will accompany, or even precede, for the first time, political action, economic decisions, and great social movements. (Arkoun, *Ouvertures sur l'islam,* 28 [emphasis in the original])

PART II

Owing to the incomplete bibliographic information and the inaccessibility of Jawzi's sources, Jawzi's notes are presented here as he cited them, except where noted. Notes in brackets are translator's notes, suggesting editions to which Jawzi had access, when possible.

Introduction

[1. The quotation marks indicated by Jawzi have been left in place, although the quote is not identified. It is similar in spirit to Schlosser's statement: "One can easily comprehend that, insofar as the ancient institutions of these peoples can be represented by their existing organizations, they do not have, properly speaking, a history." *Histoire Universelle de l'Antiquité,* trans. M. P. A. DeGoldbery (Paris: F. G. Levrault, 1928), I:85. However, Schlosser's reference is to "Mongols," whom he considers "orientals"; he refers to "the Semitic and Aramaean peoples" as Caucasians (ibid., 75).]

[2. The quotation marks are again left as Jawzi set them, although he did not identify the quote. His reference is probably to Renan, whom he quotes in a similar vein in note [7]. Throughout this translation I leave the author's quotation marks in place, identifying the quote where possible.]

[3. Jawzi does not cite a reference for this statement. It seems to correspond with the general tone of Schlosser's arguments as expressed in note [1]. *Histoire Universelle*, 72–91.]

[4. The beginning point of this quote is not indicated by Jawzi, nor is its source cited. It seems to be, however, a paraphrase of the previous quote.]

[5. The beginning point of this quote was not indicated by the author. Nor, as in note [4], did Jawzi identify its source. It is likely, however, that his reference is to the ideas of Gustave LeBon, as expressed in his *La Civilisation des Arabes* (Paris: Firmin-Didot et cie, 1884), or Hugo Winckler, in *The History of Babylonia and Assyria* (New York: Scribner, 1907).]

[6. Ibid.]

[7. "De la part des peuples semitiques dans l'histoire de la civilisation" (The Part of the Semitic People in the History of Civilization) in Renan's *Studies of Religious History and Criticism,* trans. D. B. Frothingham (New York: Carleton, 1864), 149–68.]

[8. Ibid., 164–65.]

[9. Ibid., 152.]

[10. Ibid., 153–54.]

1. Second edition, p. 31. [St. Petersburg, 1925; *La decouverte de l'Asie; histoire de l'orientalisme en Europe et en Russie,* French trans. B. Nikitine (Paris: Payot, 1947).]

2. *Journal of the Eastern Sector,* from the Imperial Russian Society of Antiquities, 17:7.

Chapter One

1. *Annali del'Islam,* 1:2. [There is no part 2 to vol. 1. Caetani does, however, express the sentiment conveyed in the quote in vol. 1, sections 2–5 of the introduction (Milano e Roma: U. Hoepli, 1905–26), especially p. 11.]

2. *The New Russian Journal of the East,* vol. 4.

3. On these markets, see *Encyclopedia of Islam* 21:209–14.

4. H. Lammens, "The Commercial Republic of Mecca" (4th part of the periodical *Institut Egyptien*), 37.

5. H. Lammens, *La Mecque a la veille de l'hegire* [(Beirut: Imprimeire Catholique, 1924),] 125.

6. Ibid., 306–32.

7. On usury and usurers in the Qur'an, see Emil Cohn, *Der Wucher im Quran* (Berlin[: n.p.], 1903).

8. The pronoun in "write it down" could refer to the fixed period or the debt.

9. That was known as *al-musaʿat.*

10. See the following chapters: 11:29, 24:111.

11. His name before the call was probably [Abu'l-Qasim] b. ʿAbd al-Lat.

12. M. Grimme, *Muhammed,* part 1 (Munster[: W. Aschendorff], 1892).

13. See chapters 28:7, 81:22, etc.

14. See chapters 55:7–9; 6:152; 21:20; 7:82; 11:86; etc.

[1. R. A. Nicholson quotes: "Paradise and Hell had no traditional associations, and the Arabic language furnished no religious terminology for the expression of such ideas; if they were to be made comprehensible at all, it could only be done by means of precise descriptions, of imagery borrowed from earthly affairs." See his *A Literary History of the Arabs* (New York: Scribner, 1907), 168.]

15. Except for 'Uthman b. 'Affan, one of the wealthy and educated Umayyads, and perhaps Abu Bakr al-Siddiq.

16. These are the Satanic verses. (See the commentaries on Surat al-Najm, verses 19–21.)

17. On slavery in Islam, see the book of B. Roberts under the title *Das Familien—Sklaven und Erbrecht im Qoran* (Leipzig[: n.p.], 1908).

18. See Lammens, *La Mecque,* 233–51.

19. On this vast question, see the writing of Baron (Tornau) under the title "Das Eigentumsrecht nach Moslem" (ZDMG [*Zeitschrift der Deutschen morgenlandischen Gesellschaft*] 35:285), and the book of M. M. Berchem, *La propriété territoriale [et l'impôt foncier, étude sur l'impôt du kharag* (Geneva: n.p., 1996)]; H. Lammens, *Études sur la règne du Calife Moawia* [1st ed. (Beirut: Imprimeire Catholique, 1930)], 1:225.

Chapter Two

1. See Lammens, *Études,* 233.

2. See A. Muller, *History of Islam* 1:311. [Probably F. A. Muller, *Der Islam im Morgen- und Abendland* (Berlin: G. Grote, 1885–87).]

3. Ibid., 1:354 (of the Russian translation) [see note 2 above]; C. Becker, *Islamstudien* [(Leipzig: Quelle and Meyer, 1924–32), vol. unknown], 256.

4. This group appeared in the beginning of the reign of the Umayyads. It was the position of the Kurds against the views of the Qadiris. (See *Kitab al-Milal wa-l'Nihal* of al-Shahristani, Ibn Hazm, and the article in the periodical *Assyriologie,* 169.)

5. Read on the Shu'ubiyya movement: J. Goldziher, *Muhamm[edianische] Studien* [(Halle: S. M. Niemeyar, 1890)], 1:147–77.

6. Sinariya was a strong nation beyond the Caucasus which attacked the borders of the republic of Azerbaijan (formerly in the states of Baku and Ganj) and part of the Persian Azerbaijan. Its people were probably from Armenia.

7. Read the history of al-Ya'qubi on these people.

Chapter Three

1. Mas'udi said in *[Kitab] Tanbih wa'l-Ishraf* ([ed. M. deGoeje (Leiden: E. J. Brill, 1893–94)], 378): "Matters were, in his time (the days of al-Muqtadir), unlike any in Islam before. For example, the women dominated in power and administration, to the extent that a slavegirl of his mother's, known as Tamil al-Qahrimana, held sessions of the Council of Grievances of the Upper Classes and Common People; and the ministers, clerks, judges and learned people attended them." Ibn al-Athir ([*Al-Kamil fi'l-Ta'rikh.*, ed. C. J. Tornberg

(Leiden: E. J. Brill, 1867–74),] 8:159) said, "The cause of that was that, when they returned al-Muqtadir to the caliphate, their arrogance and his indebtedness to them increased. They began to say things caliphs could not bear, i.e., God gives the power of tyranny to whomever aids tyrants, and whoever can take a donkey to the roof can take him down again." See also al-Fakhri, *Al-Adab al-Sultaniyyah*. [I am grateful to Professor Farhat J. Ziadeh for his suggested reading of *himar* for the text's *khimar*, in this rather obscure passage.]

2. See *Mulhaq al-Mu'arrikh* (Theophanis), Pt. 5, 21, p. 112; Michel le Syrien, 3:52; and the work of the Russian professor of philosophy [V. Vasiliev], "Byzantium and the Arabs," 37.

3. See *Mulhaq*, Theophanis, 112; [F. W.] Gesenius, 54; and Aba al-Faraj Ibn al-ʿArabi; and others.

4. See [F. W. Gesenius], Part M, 119.

5. See his *Ta'rikh*, 2:577.

6. Abu Mansur al-Baghdadi, in *[Kitab] al-Farq bain al-Firaq*, 266.

7. [Ibid.], 331–34.

8. See *Fragm[enta] Hist[oricorum] Arab[icorum]*, ed. G. deGoeje (Leiden: E. J. Brill, 1869–71)], 1:406.

9. See the Al-Yaʿqubi's work *Ta'irkh*, ed. Th. Houtsma (Leiden: E. J. Brill, 1883)], 2:583.

10. Armenia and Azerbaijan were one region or emirate before Babak's attack. See al-Yaʿqubi, 2:565 (from the Leiden edition). [See note 9.]

11. Al-Dinawari, *Kitab al-Akhbar al-Tawal*, 360 (from the Petersburg edition).

12. See [G.] Weil, *Geschichte der Caliphen* [(Mannheim: F. Rosserman, 1846–62], 3:237.

13. [J. Laurent,] *L'Armenie entre Byzance et l'Islam [depuis le compuete arage jusque'en 886* (Paris: Fontemoing, 1919)], 318.

14. [G. Weil,] *Geschichte der Chalifen*, 2:237. [See note 12.]

15. The Khurrami flag was actually red. (ZDMG [*Zeitschrift der Deutschen morgenlandischen Gesellschaft*], 23:534.)

16. [Abu Mansur al-Baghdadi, *Kitab]al-Farq [bain al-Firaq]*, 268.

17. [Al-Tabari, *Ta'rikh al-Rusul wa'l-Muluk*,] 10:305 (Cairo edition).

18. The history of al-Tabari, 10:279. [See note 17.]

19. Ibid., 338.

20. [Abu Mansur al-Baghdadi, *Kitab] al-Farq*, 252, in our article "Babak and the Babakis," Baku, 1921.

21. We find numerous tales and lies about the Khurramis in the book *Al-Bad' wa'l-Ta'rikh* of al-Maqdisi.

22. [Abu Mansur al-Baghdadi, *Kitab] al-Farq [bain al-Firaq]*, 268.

23. See *Grundriss d[er] iranische Philologie [unter Mitwirkungs von Chr. Bartholomee*, ed. W. Geiger (Strassburg: n.p., 1895–1904)], B. KK., 558.

24. [Ibn ʿAbd Allah al-Hamawi Yaqut, *Kitab al-]Muʿjam al-Buldan*, ed. Wustenfeld (Leipzig: F. A. Brockhaus, 1866–73)], 2:569.

25. On the situation of the peasants in the days of the Sasanids, see the book of Professor A. [E.] Christensen, *L'Empire des Sasanides*.

26. See *The History of Islam*, by A. Müller, I:306. [Probably F. A. Muller, *Der Islam im Morgen- und Abendland* (Berlin: G. Grote, 1885–87).]

27. On the Sasanid system, see [A. E.] Christensen, *L'Empire*. [See note 25.]

28. See *Muʿjam al-Buldan*, under "Ahwaz" and "Fars." [See note 24.]

29. [A. E.] Christensen, *Le règne du roi Kawadh*, 73.

30. [Abu Mansur al-Baghdadi, *Kitab] al-Farq [bain al-Firaq]*, 252.

31. [Abu al-Fath Muhammad al-Shahristani,] *Kitab al-Milal wa'l-Nihal*, I:291.

32. [Aba al-Faraj 'Ibri,] *Ta'rikh Mukhtasar al-Duwal*, 241; [al-Maqdisi,] *Kitab al-Bad' wa'l-Ta'rikh*, 6:117.

33. The journal *Flugel* on the Khurramis in *ZDMG*, 23:523–33. [See note 15.]

34. Among them: Michel le Syrien, 7:50, and [al-Maqdisi,] *Al-Bad' wa'l-Ta'rikh*, 6:117.

35. Among their names mentioned by the Arab historians: Ashab al-Ftan, al-Qita', al-Kharrab al-Di'ar, etc.

36. [A. E. Christensen,] *Le règne*, 103.

37. Ibid., 103–4.

38. [Mutahhar b. Tahir al-Maqdisi, *Kitab al-Bad' wa'l-Ta'rikh*], 4:24.

39. Ibid. He said regarding the differences among peoples in the Khurrami sects: "Everyone describes of his school what the other denies of this group, as those we mentioned describe, denying what they know of it." 4:391.

40. [Mutahhar b. Tahir al-Maqdisi, *Kitab] al-Bad' wa'l-Ta'rikh*, 6:116–17.

41. Al-Hamawi Yaqut said, "In it (i.e., in Baddin) gathered the leading figures known to the Khurramis." [*Kitab al-Mu'jam al-Buldan*, ed. Wustenfeld (Leipzig: F. A. Brockhaus, 1866–73)], 2:528.

42. As we can gather from the words of al-Mas'udi, *Kitab al-Tanbih wa'l-Ishraf* [ed. M. deGoeje (Leiden: E. J. Brill, 1893–94)], 453.

43. [Abu Mansur al-Baghdadi,] *Kitab al-Farq bain al-Firaq*, 268.

44. [Al-Tabari,] *Ta'rikh [al-Rusul wa'l-Muluk*, ed. M. deGoeje et al. (Leiden: E. J. Brill, 1879–1901)], 10:255, 269.

45. [Ibid.], 10:294–95.

46. Ibid., 205.

47. Abu Tamam said about it:

Oh Day of Arshaq, on which was affixed the day of death
Of the Khurramis, a suitable destiny!

48. See [al-Maqdisi,] *Kitab al-Bad' wa'l-Ta'rikh*, 6:117, and [Mas'udi,] *Muruj al-Dhahab [wa Ma'adin al-Jawhar*] [ed. and trans. de Meynard and de Courteilli (Paris: Imprimarie Imperiale, 1861–66)].

49. It was Friday, 14 Ramadan 223 (838).

50. See the work by Prof. Bartol'd, member of the Petersburg Scientific Academy, *Historical and Geographic Insights on Iran*, 149.

51. [Abu Mansur al-Baghdadi, *Kitab] al-Farq [bain al-Firaq]*, 252.

Chapter Four

1. See his letters on the merits of the Turks. (Van Vloten edition, Leiden.)

2. See [R. P. A.] Dozy, *Histoire des musulmans d'Espagne* [(Leiden: E. J. Brill, 1861)], 3:8.

3. "The Batinis did not reveal their religion except to those who were sworn not to reveal their secrets to others." See [Abu Mansur al-Baghdadi, *Kitab] al-Farq [bain al-Firaq]*, 278.

4. The number of steps at the beginning was seven. Then it became six, and every degree had a name appropriate to the knowledge which was given the initiate in this stage. These names were: *al-tafarrus, al-taʾanis, al-tashkik, al-taʿliq, al-rabt, al-tadlis,* and *al-taʾsis.* [Abu Mansur al-Baghdadi, *Kitab*] *al-Farq* [*bain al-Firaq*], 282. These names were taken, it seems to me, from the book of the Ismaʿilis, and did not vary. The rendering of the oath before the missionary was really in it, no doubt, since it appears in books other than al-Baghdadi's. See, e.g., M. deGoeje, *Mémoire sur les Carmathes du Bahrain* [(Leiden: E. J. Brill, 1886)], 172.

[1. The paragraph that follows here in the Jerusalem edition has been omitted, since it is repeated below and was, therefore, probably mistakenly inserted here.]

5. Among the indications of the similarities between the Ismaʿilis and Masons is that the Ismaʿilis had lodges (*mahwil, mahawil*) similar to the Masons' *mahfil* (lodge of initiation). (See al-Maqrizi, in *Encyc[lopedia] Musulmane,* 32:812.)

6. "They also told their missionaries not to drop their seeds on saline ground. They meant by that not to spread their innovation among those upon whom it had no effect, as seeds on saline soil have no effect." [Abu Mansur al-Baghdadi, *Kitab*] *al-Farq* [*bain al-Firaq*], 283.

7. See [Louis] Massignon's article in *Encycl[opedia of] Islam,* 30:816.

8. [Abu Mansur al-Baghdadi, *Kitab*] *al-Farq* [*bain al-Firaq*], 290.

9. See [M.] deGoeje, [*Memoir sur les Carmathes* (Leiden: E. J. Brill, 1886)], 117.

10. Ibid., 226–28. The verse mentioned is taken from the *qasida* mentioned by [ʿAli b. al-Hasan] al-Khazradji, in *Taʾrikh al-Yaman:*

Take your tambourine and beat it;
Sing your merry songs;
The prophet of the Bani Hashem has taken control.
This is the prophet of the Arabs.
Every past prophet has his law; this is the law of this prophet.
He took off our backs the duty of the salat,
He removed also the fast, effortlessly: Should people rise to pray, you
    remain seated.
When they fast, you eat and drink.
Do not set out to run the course of Safa,
And do not visit the tombs of Yathrib.
Do not refrain from marrying
Whether relatives or foreigners.
For why are you allowed one relationship
And forbidden the other?
Does not the crop belong to whomever plants it,
And waters it in the dry seasons?

11. Abu Mansur [al-Baghdadi] said that among the things required of the missionaries was that they be familiar with the various methods by which parties can be swayed, for the call was not for groups of one sort only but to all kinds of people. Those the missionary considered inclined toward devotional services, he urged to asceticism and devotional service. Then he asked them about the meaning of those devotions and to explain religious duty, and filled

them with doubt about them. To those he considered shameless and morally depraved, he said religious devotion is stupidity and foolishness, and advocated cleverness in the attainment of pleasure, quoting as an example:

Those who treat people well for fear of God die grieving;
The bold win pleasures.

To those he considered doubtful of their religion or the afterlife and rewards for pious deeds and punishments he urged the denial of those ideas and urged them to approve of the forbidden acts and rely with him on the words of the poet al-Lajin:

Shall I renounce the pure pleasure of wines
When they promise me meat and wine?
Life then death then resurrection.
Fiction and superstition, O mother of ʿAmr.

Those he considered among the Ghulat (Rawafids [fanatics, extremists]), such as the Sabbabiyya, and so on, he did not argue with over interpretation of verses and messages, because they interpreted them in accordance with their ideas. To those he considered among the Zaidi or Imami dissenters, inclined to challenge the traditions of the Companions of the Prophet, he expounded abuse of the Companions and suggested hatred of the Bani Taim because Abu Bakr was among them, and hatred of the Umayyads because ʿUthman and Muʿawiyya were among them. Perhaps the Batinis in our age find support for that in the comment of Ismaʿil b. ʿAbad:

Entering hell for love of the legal heir
In preference to the sons of the Prophet
Is more appealing to me than the gardens of Eden
Staying there forever with Taim or ʿAdi.

Then he mentioned to him gradually the classifications of some of the inter-pretations. If he accepted them, he revealed to him the rest but if he did not accept the first interpretation, he concealed the rest from him and filled the initiate with doubts about the pillars of the law. . . . So this is the explanation of their degree of *al-tafarrus.*" [Abu Mansur al-Baghdadi, *Kitab*] *al-Farq* [*bain al-Firaq*], 283.

12. ʿImad al-Din al-Isfahani, author of *Mukhtasar taʾrikh al-Saljuq:* "Khura-san was the home of the Batinis and their shelter" (88).

13. M. deGoeje, *Mémoire sur les Carmathes du Bahrain* [(Leiden: E. J. Brill, 1886)], 170.

14. Ibid., 171.

15. Ibid.

16. *Encycl*[*opedia*] *Musulmane*, 30:815.

17. As a result, they were called *al-taʿlimis* ["the inducationals" or "educa-bles"], according to what al-Shahristani, al-Ghazali and others say.

18. It is strange that the Druze, who were one of the branches of the Is-maʿilis, do not advocate equality of men and women (see *Encycl*[*opedia*] *Musul-m*[*ane*], 30:817).

19. There is no need to mention the errors that occurred in the Egyptian edition of Abu Mansur al-Baghdadi's book [*Kitab al-Farq bain al-Firaq*]. We have corrected some of them in what we have cited from it, although it is

unfortunate that printing this valuable book was undertaken by a man who had studied neither the history of religions nor history in general. [For discrepancies in Abu Saʿid's name, see Philip K. Hitti, *History of the Arabs* (New York: St. Martin's 1970), 10th ed., 445.]

20. See [Louis] Massignon's article on the Qaramati in *Encycl[opedia] Musulm[ane]*.

[2. For a listing of al-Maʿarri's quatrains, with translations into English, see R. A. Nicholson, *Studies in Islamic Mysticism* (Cambridge: Cambridge University Press, 1921), 43–289.]

21. Ibn Battuta (Pt. 1, 166–67) mentioned that the Ismaʿilis of Syria were in the service of the Mamluks of Egypt as secret murderers. If that is true, the Ismaʿilis are not to blame, because in the days of Ibn Battuta they had dispersed and did not comprise a group.

22. See [al-Hamadhani,] *Taʾrikh Daulat al-Seljuq*, 174.

Chapter Five

1. M. deGoeje thought the Qaramatis were not apprised of the greatest of the Ismaʿili secrets, i.e., of the philosophic interpretation of the return of Muhammad b. Ismaʿil (*Mémoire sur les Carmathes du Bahrain*, [Leiden: E. J. Brill, 1886], 165).

2. He was Akhou Muhsan and his story is in the book of al-Nuwairi. See [A. I. Silvestre] deSacy, *Chrestomathie arabe* [(Paris: Imprimeire royale, 1826–27)], I:182.

3. Abu Saʿid was probably a laborer, for it was mentioned that he worked mending flour sacks for very small fees.

4. The reader knows that the residents of Bahrain were apostates and outside Islam after the death of the Prophet. (See Prof. [V. V.] Bartol'd's article on Musailima al-Katab which will appear shortly in *al-Rabita al-Sharqiyya*, in Egypt.)

5. It was he who was on Abu ʿAlaʾ al-Maʿarri's mind in his verse: "Man wisely rejected his lord. The hijra will pass judgment on him and he will be elevated."

6. See Ibn al-Athir, [*Al-Kamil fiʾl-Taʾrikh*], 5:182–89, Egyptian edition.

7. See Ibn Miskawayh, *Tajarib al-Umam*, 7:5 (E. J. W. Gibb memorial edition) [ed. Leone Caetani (Leiden: 1913)].

8. "For example, in the years 314, 315 and 316 [A.H.], no pilgrimage was made to Mecca from Iraq, accordingly to what al-ʿAqiqi said . . . out of fear of the Qaramati." See [*Die Gesammelt und auf Kosten der Deutschen Morgenlandischen Gesellschaft (Akhbar Mekka)*, ed. H. F. Wustenfeld (Beirut: Maktabah Khyat, n.d.)], 2:345.

9. It was known as the Baratha mosque, "where the dissenters would gather and vilify the companions of the Prophet."

10. He was the chief of the dissenters advocating the Qaramati sect.

11. See M. deGoeje, *Mémoire sur les Carmathes du Bahrain* (Leiden: E. J. Brill, 1886)], 216.

12. Ibid., p. 91.

13. See *Taʾrikh al-Saljuq*, 23.

14. [Ibn al-Athir, *Al-Kamil fiʾl-Taʾrikh*, ed. C.J. Tornberg (Leiden: E. J. Brill, 1867–74)], 7:362.

15. See M. deGoeje, *Mémoire sur les Carmathes du Bahrain* (Leiden: E. J. Brill, 1886)], Appendix, 215.

16. "When al-Muqtadir learned the number of his army and the army of the Qaramati, he said: God curse the 80,000 some; they lack the strength of 2,700." Ibn al-Athir, [*Al-Kamil fi'l-Ta'rikh*, ed. C. J. Tornberg (Leiden: E. J. Brill, 1867–74)], 8:127.

17. "The news reached Baghdad and it shook with fear of the highest and lowest of the Qaramatis. They decided to flee to Hilwan and Hamdan. The defeated entered Baghdad, most of them on foot, barefoot and naked." On another subject: "When the Qaramatis overtook the caliph's army, a large part of them fled to Baghdad instead of facing them." Ibn al-Athir, [*Al-Kamil fi'l-Ta'rikh*, ed. C. J. Tornberg (Leiden: E. J. Brill, 1867–74)], 8:125.

18. He was Muhammad b. Isma'il, known as Ibn Mukhallib (or Muhlib or Muharib).

19. "Abu Tahir approached the door of Mecca and broke it down and began to say: I am of God; of God I am. He forms the creatures and I destroy them."

20. *Al-na'ira* means hostility and hatred.

21. See *Chroniken d[er] Stadt Mekka* [*Die gesammelt und auf Kosten der Deutschen Morgenlandischen Gesellschaft (Akhbar Mekka)*, ed. H. F. Wustenfeld (Beirut: Maktabah Khiyat, n.d.)], 3:162.

22. M. deGoeje, *Mémoire sur les Carmathes du Bahrain*, [(Leiden: E. J. Brill, 1886)], 230.

23. Ibid. (Because of the absence of sources available to us, we translated into Arabic the words cited from the French translation.)

24. "This disaster was unprecedented in Islam." See the Collection, *Chron. d. Stadt Mekka*, 3:17. [See note 21.]

25. Al-Mas'udi said about the governors, "We are not concerned with describing the morals of al-Muttaqi, al-Mustakfi and al-Muti', since they were like clients to them; no power passed through to them. . . . They carried out the orders of others and became the fearful subdued, pacified with a nominal caliphate and satisfied with security" (396). It was the same with most caliphs of that age (see Ibn Tabataba's *Kitab Ta'rikh al-Wuzara'*). [Ibn Tabtaba is Muhammad b. 'Ali b. al-Tiqtaqa, *Kitab al-Khilafat wa'l-Wuzara'*, ed. H. Derenbourg (Paris: E. Bouillon, 1895).]

26. See "Tuhfat al-Umara' " in Hallal al-Sabi's *Ta'rikh al-Wuzara'* (Beirut, 1904), 315. [See note 25.]

27. See 'Abd al-Razzaq al-Ras'ani, *Mukhtasir Kitab al-Farq bain al-Firaq* [ed. P. K. Hitti (Cairo: Al-Hilal Printing, 1924)], 177.

28. The Qaramatis apparently had concluded from observation of the stars that the 'Abbasid state would fall in the year 320/932.

29. Abu Tahir was probably murdered by order of the Fatimid caliph in Egypt out of envy and fear of his power in Syria.

30. This type of government was not familiar to the Arabs, so you see their writers were very careless in writing about it.

31. See [Nasr Khusrow,] *Safar Name*, [trans. and ed. C. Schefer (Paris: E. Leroux, 1891–97)], 226–28.

32. "They were massacred and then left, out of fear that the Sawad would be laid waste; they were its farmers," [Ibn al-Athir, *Al-Kamil fi'l-Ta'rikh*], 7:178 (Egyptian edition).

33. See [Khusrow,] *Safar Name*, 227–28.

34. Ibid.

35. Ibid.

36. Ibid.

37. Ibid.

38. Khusrow lived among the Bedouins six months. We do not know how much time he spent with the Qaramatis. See [ibid.,] 233.

39. [Ibid.,] 277.

40. From the Latin *fossatum*, meaning "excavated" or "ditch" (from the Persian *khandah*, "dug").

41. M. deGoeje, *Mémoire sur les Carmathes du Bahrain* [(Leiden: E. J. Brill)], 162.

42. [Ibn al-Athir, *Al-Kamil fi'l-Ta'rikh*, ed. C. J. Tornberg (Leiden: E. J. Brill, 1867–74)], 8:127.

43. [Abu Mansur al-Baghdadi,] *Kitab al-Farq bain al-Firaq*, [280].

44. Ibid., 278.

45. [Khusrow,] *Safar Name*, 288.

46. Ibid.

47. Ibid., 229.

48. [M. d]eGoeje, *Mémoire sur les Carmathes du Bahrain*, 175.

49. [Ibn al-Nadim, *Fihrist*, ed. G. Flugel (Leipzig: F. C. W. Vogel, 1871)], 189.

50. It is known that, in his days, the Druze faction appeared, which was an extremist branch of the Isma'ilis in religious matters.

51. [Khusrow,] *Safar Name*, 233. Bahrain was known, and especially her capital, Hajar, for dates to the extent that it gave rise to the well-known proverb, "like importing fruit to Hajar."

52. See M. deGoeje's article on the Qaramatis of Bahrain in the later centuries in *Journ[al] Asiatique*, 1895.

53. [Ibid.], 198.

Conclusion

1. On the roots of this nomenclature, see the German journal *Der Islam*, 1:22–26, 3:324.

2. These epistles (52 of them) were first published in Bombay; then a part of them was republished in Cairo. We are now in need of a third publication—scientific, not commercial.

3. *Encycl[opedia Musulmane]* 25: 287.

4. On the history of the asnaf in the East, see H. Thorning, *Beiträge zur Kenntniss d. islamischen Vereinwesens* (Berlin[: Mayer and Muller], 1913).

5. On "akhilar" in Asia Minor, see the diary of Ibn Battuta (2:260–360, Paris edition) and the book of the head of the literature department at University of Istanbul, Prof. [Zade Mehmed Fu'ad] Köprülü, [*Turk Edebiyyat inde Ilk Mutesawwifler* (Istanbul: Matbai Amire, 1918)].

6. It is probable that many Isma'ili groups moved from Persia—because of the entrance of Hulagu Khan—into Asia Minor, and that a large part of them joined the Naqshbandi order.

7. See on this movement the Turkish chronicles and the above-mentioned work by Prof. Köprülü, p. 234. [See note 5.]

8. See *Encycl[opedia] Musulm[ane]*, 7:555.

9. It pleases us to point out here that the late Professor Goldziher also saw that the Babi movement echoed that of the Isma'ilis (see his article in *Islam*, p. 41).

10. We remind the reader that 'Ali was "patron" of the guilds in the Islamic East.

11. From an article on the guilds, published in the Russian encyclopedia, by [F. A. Brockhaus?] and Afrun.

12. We refer the more demanding reader to the German book mentioned [in note 4].

13. The derivation of this word is from the Arabic word *sinf*.

14. It is known, for example, that Ibn Burajah instituted a Sufi Qaramati school in Spain. (See *Adab Name*, which some orientalists presented to Professor Browne in honor of his work, p. 333.)

15. Of them we mention: H. Mullet, *Les origines de la compagnie de Jésus*, 1896; Charbonnel, *L'origine musulmane des Jésuites*; and articles that appeared in the journals *Quarterly Report on Semitic Studies* and *Revuredes Revues*, and others.

Index

Sultan Galiev, 16–22. *See also* sultan-
　galievism
sultangalievism, 16, 180 nn. 15, 19
Sunbat, Sahl b. *See* Sahl b. Sunbat

Tabari, Abu Ja'far Muhammad b.
　Jarir al-, 24, 48, 97, 102, 108,
　112, 116, 119
tafsir, 24
taqlid, 29–30, 32–34
Taymiyya, Taqiyy al-Din Ibn, 30–32,
　36

'Ubaidullah, 146, 160
Umayyads, 26, 37–38, 91–100, 107,
　133

Voll, John O., 23, 181 n. 2
von Ranke, Leopold, 40, 71

Wahhab, Muhammad b. 'Abd al-.
　See Ibn 'Abd al-Wahhab, Mu-
　hammad
Wahhabis, 32, 36, 159
Wajdi, Farid, 35
Wali Allah, Shah, of Delhi, 32
Weber, Max, 19, 43
Winckler, Hugo, 41–72

Ya'qubi, Ibn Wadih, 97, 102, 105–6,
　111
Yusuf, Abu, 27

Zamakshari, Mahmud al-, 24
Zarkashi, 37
Zikrawaih al-Dindani, 142–43, 146
Zurayk, Constantine, 4